THE PELICAN CLASSICS

WINSTANLEY: THE LAW OF FREEDOM AND OTHER WRITINGS

Very little is known about Gerrard Winstanley. He was probably born in Wigan in 1609. His father was a mercer, and the family had several Puritan connections. Gerrard went to London in 1630 as an apprentice in the cloth trade and became a freeman of the Merchant Taylors' Company seven years later. In September 1640 he married Susan King but found it very difficult to make a living in the City. In 1643 they moved to Surrey and settled at Walton-on-Thames near Cobham where Gerrard herded cows as a hired labourer. These years were full of hardship, but in them his ideas developed rapidly from religious mysticism to materialistic pantheism. In April 1649 a group of 'Diggers' led by Winstanley took over a patch of waste land near Cobham and established a communist colony there. Despite local opposition the colony survived until 1650, winning much support in southern and central England. Winstanley published a number of pamphlets on its behalf; in 1652 he summarized his ideas in *The Law of Freedom in a Platform*, dedicated to Oliver Cromwell. Winstanley was living in Cobham in 1660, but then disappears into obscurity.

Christopher Hill is Master of Balliol College, Oxford, and a Fellow of the British Academy. From 1934 to 1938 he was a Fellow of All Souls College, Oxford, and from 1936 to 1938 Assistant Lecturer in Modern History, University College, Cardiff. He was Fellow and Tutor in Modern History at Balliol College, Oxford, from 1938 to 1965, and Special Lecturer in sixteenth- and seventeenth-century English History at Oxford University from 1958 to 1965. He is the author of many books, including *Antichrist in Seventeenth-century England*, *Lenin and the Russian Revolution*, *Reformation to Industrial Revolution* and *God's Englishman* (a biography of Oliver Cromwell). (The last three are published by Penguins and *The World Turned Upside Down* will be appearing in Penguin shortly.)

WINSTANLEY

THE LAW
OF
FREEDOM

and other Writings

Edited with an Introduction
by Christopher Hill

PENGUIN BOOKS

Penguin Books Ltd, Harmondsworth Middlesex, England
Penguin Books Inc., 7110 Ambassador Road, Baltimore, Maryland 21207, U.S.A.
Penguin Books Australia Ltd, Ringwood, Victoria, Australia

—

Published in Pelican Books 1973

—

Introduction Copyright © Christopher Hill, 1973

—

Made and printed in Great Britain
by Hazell Watson & Viney Ltd
Aylesbury, Bucks
Set in Linotype Georgian

CONTENTS

To Leonard,
Trudie, and the other Diggers
of 1939–40

PREFACE

THE present selection contains about one third of the published works of Gerrard Winstanley. In my Introduction I have quoted extensively from pamphlets not here reprinted. Most of them were included by G. H. Sabine in *The Writings of Gerrard Winstanley* (Cornell University Press, 1941): I refer to this edition as 'S.' followed by a page number. Any biographical details for which no reference is given in the Introduction will be found in D. W. Petegorsky's excellent *Left-Wing Democracy in the English Civil War*, referred to as Petegorsky. The reader must remember that all of these pamphlets except *The Law of Freedom* were issued for immediate propaganda purposes: Winstanley therefore sometimes repeats himself when addressing different audiences. But his thought was developing all the time, and so it seemed better to reprint complete pamphlets rather than snippets. Spelling, punctuation and capitalization have been modernized, including even (reluctantly) Winstanley's own name, which he usually wrote 'Jerrard'.

My main debt of gratitude is to Dr L. D. Hamilton and other members of the Oxford University History Society of 1939–40, who made a complete and most accurate transcript of all Winstanley's writings before they learnt that Sabine had forestalled them. I have drawn on their transcript of *The Saints Paradice*, which was kindly lent to me by Dr Hamilton, who edited the only selection from Winstanley's works hitherto published in this country. I am grateful to Professor G. E. Aylmer and to *Past and Present* for permission to reprint verses from *Englands Spirit Unfoulded*; to Mr Alan Simpson for help with legal terminology; and to Mr R. Palmer for advice about the Diggers' Song. I have written about Winstanley and the Diggers at greater length in *The World Turned Upside Down* (Temple Smith, 1972).

CHRISTOPHER HILL

INTRODUCTION

He takes upon him to tell you the meaning of other men's words and writing by his studying or imagining what another man's knowledge might be, and by thus doing darkens knowledge and wrongs the spirit of the authors who did write and speak those things which he takes upon him to interpret.

> G. Winstanley, *The Law of Freedom* (1652), p. 351 below.

Winstanley's Place in History

MODERN political thought begins in the English Revolution of the seventeenth century. Thomas Hobbes's *Leviathan* (1651) is the classic statement of the 'possessive individualism' which underlies traditional English Whig and Utilitarian theories.[1] Ideas later developed by radicals and democrats were expressed in the Putney Debates of 1647 and in Leveller pamphlets of the late sixteen-forties. James Harrington's *Oceana* (1656) was the first systematic statement of the thesis that political change is determined by economic change. In exactly these years Gerrard Winstanley was working out a collectivist theory which looks forward to nineteenth- and twentieth-century socialism and communism as well as glancing backwards to a vanishing village community.

Winstanley had grasped a crucial point in modern political thinking: that state power is related to the property system and to the body of ideas which supports that system. He is modern too in wanting a revolution which would replace competition by concern for the community, in insisting that political freedom is impossible without economic equality, and that this means abolishing private property and wage labour. Experience during the English Revolution

1. C. B. Macpherson, *The Political Theory of Possessive Individualism*, Oxford University Press, 1962, *passim*.

taught him some of the dangers of substituting an arbitrary revolutionary régime for an arbitrary traditional one. He insisted that all state officials should be elected, and that a people's militia should be the only armed force. At a time when the clergy were society's ideologists and educators, Winstanley wanted church and state to be separated, leaving each congregation free to elect its own minister. Education should be taken out of clerical hands, and made scientific, equal and universal. He rejected élitism and professionalism in all spheres. Previous radical thinkers had postulated a past golden age; Winstanley believed in the possibility of human progress, and looked to a future in which reason and international brotherhood would prevail, in which science should be applied to improving not only economic conditions but also the quality of human life.

Sir Thomas More's *Utopia* (1516) had sketched a communist society, but this was a *jeu d'esprit*, written in Latin, the language of the intellectual élite. More as Lord Chancellor had a short way with the radical revolutionaries of his own day. But Winstanley's pamphlets were published in the vernacular, at the height of a great revolution, and they aimed at rousing the poorer classes to political action. Winstanley himself took the lead in establishing a communist colony, which he hoped would be widely imitated. So neither Russia nor Germany nor France but England gave the world its first communist political programme; and England can also claim to have produced, within ten years of one another, the starting texts of modern political thought – conservative-individualist and liberal-democratic as well as socialist-communist. But Winstanley is not merely the ultimate ancestor of the English labour and cooperative movements. He wrote before the Industrial Revolution, and some of his insights may be of interest to those in the Third World today who face the transition from an agrarian to an industrial society. There are many reasons for his being better known and more seriously studied in our century than in his own.

Early Life

We know very little about the life of Gerrard Winstanley except what he tells us himself. He was a Lancashire man, and has plausibly been identified with the Gerrard Winstanley who was baptized in Wigan on 10 October 1609.[2] If this identification is correct, his father Edward was a mercer, a man of some standing in Wigan, burgess at least by 1627; he died in 1639. He and his wife were presented to the church courts in 1605 for holding conventicles.[3] An Ellen Winstanley, not Gerrard's sister, who was baptized in Wigan in 1604, married the Puritan divine John Angier in 1628. There seem to have been many Puritan connections in the family, for Ellen was a niece of Mrs John Cotton, and another eminent Puritan, Oliver Heywood, married Ellen's daughter.[4] Angier was the son of a clothier of Dedham, Essex: it looks as though it was through the clothing industry that Edward Winstanley came into contact with the outside world. It was as a clothing apprentice that Gerrard went to London.

'I was never brought up to beg or work for day wages,' Winstanley tells us later. He probably went to a grammar school, for he quotes Latin (p. 184 below). But he did not follow the career traditionally marked out for the clever son of middle-class parents, going to a university and becoming a clergyman. His parents were presumably unfriendly to the church: certainly Gerrard himself at a later date had no use at all for universities. On 10 April 1630 he was apprenticed to Sarah Gater of Cornhill, widow of William Gater, Merchant Taylor. Seven years later he became a freeman of the Merchant Taylors' Company. In September

2. Not 10 July, as Sabine has it.

3. I owe this information to the Manchester Ph.D. thesis of Dr R. C. Richardson, 'Puritanism in the Diocese of Chester to 1642', p. 276.

4. Oliver Heywood, *Life of John Angier of Denton*, ed. W. Axon, Chetham Soc., New Series, Vol. 97, 1937, pp. 54–5; R. Halley, *Puritanism and Nonconformity in Lancashire*, 1869, Vol. II, pp. 148–9.

1640 he married Susan King: he was then living in the parish of St Olave's in Old Jewry.

It was a bad time to set up in trade, a period of great political uncertainty just before the outbreak of civil war. Communications with the north and west of England, including Lancashire, were soon disrupted by fighting. By 1643 Winstanley had been 'beaten out of both estate and trade' (p. 127 below). 'Though I was bred a tradesman', he wrote later, 'yet it is so hard a thing to pick out a poor living that a man shall sooner be cheated of his bread than get bread by trading among men, if by plain dealing he put trust in any' (S., p. 188). As late as 1660 Winstanley was still being sued by the executors of Richard Aldsworth, citizen of London, for a debt of £114, which Winstanley admitted having incurred 'for fustian, dimities and linen-cloth and such like commodities'. By 1643 he had 'left off his trading with the said Richard Aldsworth and with all other persons, by reason of the badness of the times'.[5] Winstanley had to raise money from friends, and moved to Surrey, somewhere in or near Cobham: he mentions being in Kingston, seven or eight miles from Cobham, in 1643; in 1649 he was described as of Walton-on-Thames, five miles from Cobham; in 1660 he was still living in Cobham. Here in the forties he herded cows, apparently as a hired labourer (pp. 127, 136, 139, 206). Among economic disasters to which man is liable Winstanley listed 'losses of his estate by fire, water, being cheated by false-spirited men, death of his cattle, or many such like casualties, whereby he becomes poor ... and meets with hard language, hungry belly, to be despised, imprisoned'.[6] One suspects that he had experienced many of these himself. 'Men that are guided by principles of fair dealing, void of deceit, know not this day how to live, but they will be cheated and cozened' (S., p. 137). One object of Winstanley's career was to create a society in which such men would know how to live.

5. Petegorsky, pp. 123–4.
6. Winstanley, *The Saints Paradice*, n.d. ?1648, p. 60; cf. pp. 33–4.

Introduction

Winstanley's World

If we are to understand the development of Winstanley's ideas, we must remind ourselves of the world in which he was living. In the civil war of 1642–6 Parliament had defeated Charles I and his supporters, but only after a long-drawn-out struggle. The conflict between Parliament and King had been complemented by a conflict between those whom we call 'Presbyterians' and 'Independents' on the Parliamentary side. The latter were those who thought, like Oliver Cromwell, that there was no point in fighting unless you were determined to win. The 'Presbyterian' grandees, strong in the House of Lords and among the gentry and ruling oligarchies of London and other big trading towns, were anxious for a compromise peace if only the King would accept their terms. Charles was most unaccommodating, and slowly military necessity strengthened the hands of the win-the-war party. Their support came from 'the middling sort', lesser gentry, yeomen and artisans. Oliver Cromwell's policy of promoting by merit among the troops under his command was designed to make use of those who, though not gentlemen, had 'the root of the matter in them'. The Self-Denying Ordinance of 1645 cleared peers out of the higher command, and allowed the New Model Army to be officered by men good at their jobs and anxious to win.

Religious toleration was the natural accompaniment of this approach to men outside the ruling class. Before 1640 all Englishmen had perforce been members of the Church of England, liable to punishment in its spiritual courts for a wide variety of 'sins', including working for one's living on one of the innumerable saints' days which divided up the agricultural calendar. All Englishmen had to pay tithes, ten per cent of their income, to maintain the parson of their parish, in whose selection the parishioners normally had no say. It was a punishable offence until 1650 to absent oneself from Sunday service in one's own parish church, even in order to hear a more congenial sermon in a neighbouring parish. The clergy were appointed by bishops, by deans and chapters, by Oxford and Cambridge colleges, by the King or (most often) by the local squire. Only in a very few town parishes did the congregation choose its own minister. Such patrons naturally tended to be conservative in outlook; and the clergy themselves were linked to the social order (or so the radicals claimed) by their education at Oxford or Cambridge, a degree from either of which automatically made a poor man's son a gentleman. This was important since the Church was the greatest opinion-forming machine in the days before newspapers, radio, television and cinema. The clergy were expected to read government hand-outs from the pulpit. They were told what subjects not to preach on, and were punished if they disobeyed. Control over the Church was a question of power, which seemed to Charles I more important even than control of the armed forces.

Many men and women bitterly resented this apparatus of coercion, persuasion and exploitation. But if they stayed away from church, and met in their own houses for worship and discussion, this too was an offence punishable in the church courts, as Edward Winstanley and his wife had found. In the sixteen-thirties, when no parliament was called, William Laud, Archbishop of Canterbury, was virtual Prime Minister. The hierarchy of the Church reached a pinnacle of power. Many thousands of English men and women emigrated to the Netherlands or New England in order to be free to worship as they wished. Others, not so rich or so fortunate, formed underground separatist organizations, which inevitably, as the political crisis deepened, became revolutionary cells. Religion and politics were inextricably mixed.

Then in 1640 the Long Parliament met, and the church hierarchy collapsed. Separatist congregations came up from underground and met openly, electing their own ministers, rejecting the state church and its parochial clergy. Religious toleration was therefore a social and political as well as a

religious question. Were men and women, chiefly of the
'meaner sort', to be permitted to meet togther in their own
self-selected congregations, unsupervised by a university-
educated clergyman, for religious discussions which would
inevitably cover politics as well? Were laymen to be allowed
to preach? If so, why should men go on paying tithes to
maintain parish ministers whom they did not want to hear?
If tithes were unpaid, there would be no state church to tell
ordinary people what to think – and no livings for the clergy.
Worse still, Oxford and Cambridge colleges were largely
financed by tithes, and many gentlemen up and down the
kingdom collected 'impropriated' tithes, which before the
Reformation had been paid to monasteries. So behind the
demand for religious toleration lurked abolition of the state
church, the traditional means of social control over the
lower orders, and an attack on property. No wonder the
respectable and the timid opposed it.

Yet Oliver Cromwell and the 'Independents' supported it,
Cromwell at least on genuinely conscientious grounds. The
need for a wide mass basis of support and enthusiasm in
order to beat the King enabled their views to triumph. By
the end of the civil war religious toleration existed in fact if
not in theory, and was guaranteed by the existence of the
New Model Army, which had won the war and was in no
mood to stand any nonsense from the worried 'Presbyterian'
majority in the House of Commons. Puritan preachers had
called on soldiers to fight against Antichrist, a vague symbol
of all that was oppressive and tyrannical in the old order.
Millennarian hopes for a reconstruction of society to benefit
the poor and lowly were in the air. 'What do you know',
rank-and-file Parliamentarian soldiers were asking a horri-
fied royalist divine in 1644, 'but that this is the time of her
ruin [the Whore of Babylon], and that we are the men that
must help to pull her down?'[7] By Antichrist or the Whore
of Babylon Parliamentarian divines referred to the Pope or

7. E. Symmons, *Scripture Vindicated*, 1644, Preface.

bishops; others were to apply the name to the royalist party, to the 'Presbyterians', to Oliver Cromwell himself; Winstanley was to apply it to the rule of the landed class.[8] It was a widely extensible term. Winstanley shared the widespread view that he was living in the last days, though he was to give a special meaning to this phrase (p. 55 below).

In 1647 Parliament ordered the Army to disband, without even providing for full payment of arrears of wages due, and without producing any of the social and political reforms which the troops had expected. The rank and file revolted. After a period of hesitation, most of the officers supported them, and an Army Council was set up in which officers and elected representatives of the rank and file ('Agitators') sat side by side. This was a unique demonstration of the popular and national nature of the force which proudly claimed to be 'no mere mercenary Army'. It advanced on London, and Parliament submitted.

This was a beginning, not an end. The Army itself was divided, as we can see in the debates in Putney church at the end of October and the beginning of November 1647. The subject for discussion was *The Agreement of the People*, the democratic constitution put forward by the Leveller party which had recently come into being in London. The Secretary of the Army Council took down verbatim the conflicting views of all ranks, from Lieutenant-General Cromwell and other officers to Agitators, and of civilian Levellers. History knows no similar record before the Russian Revolution. Agitators, Levellers and some officers called for a wide extension of the franchise, for abolition of monarchy and House of Lords, for equality before the law and for an end to coercion in religion. The generals and most of the officers rallied behind Commissary-General Ireton's defence of the existing constitution, modified by the sovereignty of Parliament which the civil war had established, and especially behind his defence of the existing property franchise. 'Liberty

8. See p. 56 below.

cannot be provided for in a general sense', Ireton declared, 'if property be preserved.' 'The main thing that I speak for, is because I would have an eye to property.'[9]

A lucky combination of circumstances saved the generals in November 1647. The King escaped from captivity and fled to the Isle of Wight, where he started to organize a second civil war. The Army had to reunite, and after a half-hearted attempt at mutiny at Ware it reunited around Generals Fairfax and Cromwell, who had led it to victory in the first civil war. There were royalist risings in Kent and South Wales, and a Scottish invasion of the north of England. As the troops marched and countermarched across England in that wet summer of 1648, their fury with the King mounted. The generals who had negotiated with him in 1647 now saw that he must be sacrificed. In December 1648 Colonel Pride purged the House of Commons of the leading 'Presbyterian' M.P.s, and in January Charles was brought to trial 'as a tyrant, traitor and murderer and public enemy to the Commonwealth'. The scene was unprecedented in the history of Europe: a king publicly tried, condemned and executed in the name of his people. It was followed by the abolition of monarchy (17 March 1649) and House of Lords (19 March); the Republic was proclaimed on 19 May. But that was all. The Army received arrears of pay, but the representative Army Council was replaced by a Council of Officers. The apocalyptic hopes of the radicals were not realized. Parliament refused to dissolve; there was no extension of the franchise, no social reform, no abolition of tithes.

Winstanley had supported Parliament in the first civil war, but in 1648 he rejected 'Presbyterians' and 'Independents' no less than royalists. God's 'sincere-hearted ones, scattered abroad in the kingdom', he thought, 'shall stand and look on whilst Royalists, Presbyterians and Independents sheathe their swords in one another's bowels'. Never-

9. A. S. P. Woodhouse (ed.), *Puritanism and Liberty*, 1938, pp. 73, 57.

theless, 'this wrath, bitterness and discontent that appears generally in men's spirits in England' seemed to Winstanley to suggest that 'liberty is not far off', and that the British Isles might be 'the tenth part of the city Babylon that shall fall off first'. Winstanley hoped to help God in this 'great work'.[10]

Winstanley in 1648

Winstanley, like Oliver Cromwell, was approaching forty years of age before he began to do the work for which he was to be remembered. We know little of his intellectual or political development in the years before 1648. He had learnt enough law to quote Coke's *Institutes, The Mirror of Justice* and fourteenth-century statutes (p. 132 below). He tells us that he was for long a good Puritan church-goer, believing as the learned clergy believed. But he came to see that such a life was one of 'confusion, ignorance and bondage'. He went through 'the ordinance of dipping', but he did not long remain a conventional Baptist (S., pp. 243, 141). In the early months of 1648 he published three theological tracts which wrestle with the subjects of poverty, evil and selfishness, foreseeing a glorious future in which God will reveal himself to 'the despised, the unlearned, the poor, the nothings of this world'. But already Winstanley had broken with the traditional theological framework which most of his contemporaries accepted: he suggested that in the end everyone will be saved. One of his main concerns was already to insist on freedom for the poor. It was wrong too that 'sharp punishing laws were made to prevent fishermen, shepherds, husbandmen and tradesmen from ever preaching of God any more', and that preaching was restricted to 'scholars bred up in human letters'.[11]

God is to be found inside every human being. 'He that looks for a God without himself and worships God at a

10. Winstanley, *The Saints Paradice*, pp. 22–3, 62–3.
11. Winstanley, *The Breaking of the Day of God*, 1648, *passim*; *The Mysterie of God*, 1648, esp. p. 115.

distance, he worships he knows not what, but is led away and deceived by the imaginations of his own heart.' But 'he that looks for a God within himself...is made subject to and hath community with the spirit that made all flesh, that dwells in all flesh and in every creature within the globe.' This God is Reason – a social Reason which says 'Do as thou wouldst be done unto ... For Reason tells him, Is thy neighbour hungry and naked to-day, do thou feed him and clothe him, it may be thy case to-morrow, and then he will be ready to help thee.'

So far Winstanley had got by July 1648, trying to understand the poverty and humiliation which had overtaken him and so many others 'in the midst of these national hurly-burlies'.[12] Dozens of other 'mechanick preachers'[13] were using the newly-won liberty of the press to grapple with the problems of the revolutionary epoch: most of them hoped that the national crisis marked the beginning of God's kingdom on earth. We have to read Winstanley's first three pamphlets carefully to appreciate how much more radical their author already was. We must make allowances for the Biblical idiom which Winstanley shared with almost all his contemporaries, and try to penetrate through to the thought beneath. Already we have some clues in his use of God to mean Reason, and of Babylon to stand for the old order which has to be overthrown.

A new note comes in with Winstanley's next pamphlet, *Truth Lifting up its Head above Scandals*, whose title-page says 1649 but whose introductory letter Winstanley dated 16 October 1648. This is a fiercely anti-clerical note. The pamphlet was written after a dispute with some clergymen at Kingston-on-Thames in which Winstanley had engaged together with William Everard. Everard was almost certainly a former trooper and Agitator in the New Model

12. Winstanley, *The Saints Paradice*, pp. 89–90, 122–4, 19.
13. The greatest of these was Bunyan; see W. Y. Tindall, *John Bunyan, Mechanick Preacher*, New York, 1964, *passim*. Cf. p. 43 below.

Army, who had been cashiered for taking part in the mutiny at Ware. Everard was arrested and imprisoned, and Winstanley 'was slandered as well as Everard, having been in his company'. The treatise deals, however, only with Winstanley's views, explaining his use of 'the word Reason instead of the word God in [his] writings'. It was dedicated, in a fierce counter-attack, 'to the scholars of Oxford and Cambridge and all that call themselves ministers of the gospel in city and country'. The clergy, Winstanley declares, have no special claims to respect as interpreters of the Scriptures, for the very text of the Bible depends on tradition. The clergy themselves are time-servers. 'First here in the Presbytery, then there in the Independency: and thus you lead the people like horses by the nose, and ride upon them at your pleasure.' A privileged state church must be abolished, and all men be given liberty to worship as they please (S., pp. 100, 103–4, 129–30, 391–2).

The Land

So much for the immediate political background against which Winstanley was working out his ideas. We must now glance briefly at longer-term economic developments. The sixteenth and early seventeenth centuries had seen a rapid increase in the population of England. Production of food had not kept pace with this expansion. The situation was aggravated by other factors – enclosure and consolidation of farms sometimes led to eviction, often to sheep replacing corn. Fewer people grew their own food; corn had to be imported. There was a large pauper, vagabond and squatter population, and the big towns (London especially) harboured an underworld of unemployed or casual labour. A series of bad harvests, such as occurred in the fifteen-nineties, or a slump in the clothing industry, such as occurred in the second and third decades of the century, could make life desperately hard for those dependent on money wages. The years from 1620 to 1650 have been described as among the most terrible in English history, bringing extreme hardship for the lower classes.[14]

If we look forward to the end of the seventeenth century, the gravest problems have been solved. New land has been brought under cultivation. New crops enable cattle to be kept alive through the winter; the increased supply of manure, together with diversified crop rotations and new techniques, have brought grain production to a point at which England no longer needs to import corn in a normal year, has indeed become a corn-exporting country. But this agricultural revolution was the consequence of decisions taken in the mid century. There were two problems. First, unproductive land must be brought under intensive cultivation – common and waste lands, royal forests, fens and marshes. This raised the second question – by whom? If economic efficiency and the maximization of food production were all that mattered, then enclosure of land by rich individuals who could invest large units of capital was clearly the answer. But this would cut across the interests of all those who enjoyed customary rights in commons, forests and fens. The Midlands rising of 1607, in which we first come across the names Levellers and Diggers, was caused by enclosure. Risings in western England in the late twenties and early thirties turned in large part on royal enclosure and rights of squatters in the forests. Oliver Cromwell first won a national reputation as the defender of commoners who opposed the draining of the Fens. Just as the breakdown of the authority of the state church in the sixteen-forties allowed underground sects to surface, so the breakdown of secular authority released a series of riots against enclosure all over the country. As a recent historian put it, 'the whole Digger movement can be plausibly regarded as the culmination of a century of unauthorized encroachment upon the forests and wastes by squatters and local

14. P. J. Bowden, in *The Agrarian History of England*, Vol. IV, *1500–1640*, ed. J. Thirsk, Cambridge University Press, 1967, p. 621.

commoners, pushed on by land shortage and pressure of population'.[15]

'Do not all strive to enjoy the land?' Winstanley was to ask. 'The gentry strive for land, the clergy strive for land, the common people strive for land; and buying and selling is an art whereby people endeavour to cheat one another of the land' (p. 185 below). The problems were exacerbated by the civil war, which simultaneously disrupted agriculture and increased the number of those who had to be fed whilst themselves producing nothing. A series of bad harvests after 1645 (that of 1648 being particularly disastrous) more than doubled the price of bread by 1649. Yet this was a period in which men were being demobilized and having to find jobs, and it came at the end of more than a century of falling real wages, in years when taxes on food were higher than ever before and free-quarter for soldiers was an added burden on the civilian population (p. 26 below). Then the land problem was forced on the attention of all by the confiscations of the Revolution. Episcopacy was abolished in 1646; bishops' lands were sold to private individuals to pay for the war. But dean and chapter lands were still in the possession of the state in 1649, as were crown lands and forests after the abolition of monarchy, and the lands of obdurate royalists which had been seized during the war. Here was a great land fund.

On 3 April 1649, two days after Winstanley and his comrades started digging on St George's Hill, Peter Chamberlen suggested using the confiscated lands of crown, church and royalists, together with common and waste lands, for a public bank. 'If you provide not for the poor', he declared, 'they will provide for themselves.'[16] Such thoughts had indeed already occurred. A continual anxiety during the civil war had been lest 'the necessitous people of the whole kingdom' should 'set up for themselves, to the utter ruin of

15. K. V. Thomas, 'Another Digger Broadside', *Past and Present*, No. 42, p. 58.

16. P. Chamberlen, *The Poore Mans Advocate*, 1649, Epistle and pp. 2–3.

all the nobility and gentry'.[17] A third party of the poor was a continual nightmare for the men of property, threatened by the Clubmen of the south-west in 1645 and by Levellers in London and the Army in the years which followed. Pamphlets and petitions in 1647 and 1648 demanded common lands for the poor.[18]

Winstanley guessed that from a half to two thirds of England was not properly cultivated, and that one third of the country was barren waste. But if the poor were allowed to manure and cultivate the wastes and commons, there was land enough to maintain ten times the existing population. Begging and poverty could be abolished (pp. 115, 165 below). This was the vision that he conceived some time between 16 October 1648 and 26 January 1649. Hitherto, living disconsolately in the country with the help of friends, he had indulged in escapist and compensatory dreams of a community of the spirit by which men should rise above mere temporal evils. But now he had a programme of action. Four days before the execution of Charles I he solemnly announced 'when the Lord doth show unto me the place and manner, how he will have us that are called common people to manure and work upon the common lands, I will go forth and declare it in my action, to eat my bread with the sweat of my brows, without either giving or taking hire, looking upon the land as freely mine as another's ... The spirit of the poor shall be drawn forth ere long, to act materially this law of righteousness' (S., p. 194).

Winstanley himself, when discussing the origin of his communist theories, insisted that he never read them in books, 'nor heard from the mouth of any flesh'; 'since the light was given me, I have met with divers to whom the same light of truth is revealed, but never heard any speak of it before I saw the light of it rise up within myself'. A voice

17. *Portland MSS.*, Historical Manuscripts Commission, Vol. I, p. 87.

18. D. M. Wolfe (ed.), *Leveller Manifestoes of the Puritan Revolution*, New York, 1944, pp. 194, 216, 270, 288.

within told him 'that the earth should be made a common treasury of livelihood to whole mankind, without respect of persons', and bade him declare this to all abroad, which he did by word of mouth and in writing (pp. 127, 155-7 below). Men in the seventeenth century spoke more freely than we do today of a vision or revelation to describe a sudden mental clarification. In this sense Lord Herbert of Cherbury, Descartes and Pascal all had visions, no less than Nicholas Culpeper, George Fox and John Bunyan. Winstanley's later dismissal of a personal God (p. 351 below) suggests that he can hardly have continued to rely on the promptings of an inner voice.

The months between October 1648 and January 1649 were crucial to the English Revolution. In them the Army seized power, purged Parliament, negotiated with the Levellers a modified Agreement of the People, and brought the King to trial. Charles was sentenced the day after Winstanley signed the dedication to *The New Law of Righteousness*. It was a time when almost anything seemed possible, a time at which ideas developed rapidly. The point was made by Winstanley's title. For most conservatives there could be no *new* law of righteousness: there was only an old-established and well-known one. Confidence in novelty was itself new, and the property of the radicals.

We can see why Winstanley's sudden insight struck him as a divine revelation. The generals' coup d'état had not solved England's economic problems. All over the country poor squatters and cottagers, the victims of enclosure and heavy taxation, were ready for drastic remedies. It was no accident that the Diggers' standard was first set up in north Surrey, which was not only close to the radical South Bank of London but was also an area in which there were large crown estates, parks and forests, and where there had been a great deal of enclosure and consequent hardship to the peasantry. Near by was Windsor Great Forest, which squatters were illegally cultivating.[19] Other areas from which we

19. B. Whitelocke, *Memorials of the English Affairs*, 1682, p. 381.

have evidence of Digger activity or sympathy for the Diggers include Buckinghamshire and Northamptonshire, counties in which there had been much enclosure and which had been the scene of considerable fighting and free-quarter in the civil war. In the parish of Wellingborough (Northamptonshire) 1,169 persons were receiving alms in 1650. The Justices had ordered a workhouse to be set up

but as yet we see nothing is done, nor any man that goeth about it; we have spent all we have, our trading is decayed, our wives and children cry for bread, our lives are a burden to us, divers of us having five, six, seven, eight, nine in family, and we cannot get bread for one of them by our labour. Rich men's hearts are hardened, they will not give us if we beg at their doors; if we steal, the law will end our lives. Divers of the poor are starved to death already, and it were better for us that are living to die by the sword than by the famine.[20]

Those were circumstances in which revolutionary solutions might be well received; they must have existed in many parts of the country.

Winstanley's previous religious interests may or may not have been rationalizations of his economic concerns; his present programme certainly seemed to him to accord with the will of God. 'True religion and undefiled', he wrote, 'is to let everyone quietly have earth to manure' (S., p. 428). But not all agreed. In 1646 a Presbyterian divine had told the House of Commons that 'if a man plead conscience in the point of community of goods', he put himself beyond the pale and should not be tolerated.[21]

20. [Anon.], *A Declaration of the Grounds and Reasons why we the Poor Inhabitants of the Town of Wellinborrow . . . have begun and give consent to Dig up, manure and Sow Corn upon the Common and Waste Ground, called Bareshanke . . .*, 1650, in S., p. 650.

21. Francis Cheynell, *A Plot for the Good of Posterity* (1646), p. 37.

Levellers and True Levellers

The economic and political situation in the early months of 1649 was particularly explosive. Many in London were starving. Levellers and Army radicals felt that they had been deceived in the negotiations which led to the trial and execution of the King: the republic which the Independent Grandees had set up fell far short of the reformed democratic society they had hoped to see. They demanded reappointment of Agitators and recall of the General Council of the Army. The title of a Leveller pamphlet of March 1649, *Englands New Chains,* conveys their point of view. At the end of the month four of the Leveller leaders were arrested. In April mutinies broke out when soldiers who refused to serve in Ireland were demobilized without payment of arrears. On 27 April Trooper Robert Lockier was shot; his funeral two days later was a vast demonstration of popular support for the Leveller movement in London. In May more serious revolts broke out among troops in Oxfordshire, Wiltshire and Buckinghamshire, with rumours of civilian support from the old Clubman areas in the southwest. Cromwell and Fairfax cornered and annihilated the mutinous regiments at Burford on 14 May. The military régime was henceforth secure, never to be seriously threatened so long as Cromwell lived.

Nevertheless, the opening months of 1649 had been a terrifying time for the men of property. The Digger movement appeared at the height of the panic, when it was by no means obvious that the radical threat had been overcome. On Sunday 1 April a group of poor men collected on St George's Hill in the parish of Walton-on-Thames and began to dig the waste land there, sowing it with corn, parsnips, carrots and beans. It was a symbolic assumption of ownership. The Diggers' numbers soon rose to twenty or thirty. 'They invite all to come in and help them', an observer noted, 'and promise them meat, drink and clothes ... They

give out, they will be four or five thousand within ten days
... It is feared they have some design in hand.'

Local property-owners called on the Council of State to
intervene with military assistance. Thinking that 'great con-
flux of people may be a beginning whence things of greater
and more dangerous consequence may grow', the Council
of State alerted the Surrey J.P.s and General Fairfax. The
latter sent a couple of troops down to see what was happen-
ing. From the report which Captain Gladman sent in to
Fairfax it is clear that he thought the Council was being
unduly alarmist.[22] On 20 April two of the principal Diggers,
Everard and Winstanley, were brought before the Com-
mander-in-Chief. They kept on their hats in Fairfax's presence, the traditional symbolic refusal to recognize social
superiority and political authority. Lilburne had made the
same gesture of protest when on trial before Star Chamber
in 1637; it was later made a point of principle by the Quakers.
Fairfax, the Digger leaders said, was 'but their fellow-
creature'.

Their intention, they told the general, was to cultivate
the waste lands as a communal group: they would 'meddle
only with what was common and untilled'. Any rights in the
commons claimed by lords of manors, Winstanley later
explained, had been 'cut off with the King's head' (p. 37, 168
below). They hoped that before long the poor everywhere
would follow their example, and that property-owners would
voluntarily surrender their estates and join in communal
production. On the same day a manifesto, *The True
Levellers Standard Advanced*, signed by Winstanley and
fourteen other Diggers, was sent to the printer. It appeared
on 26 April, the day on which Lockier was sentenced. 'The
old world ... is running up like parchment in the fire', Winstanley told 'the powers of England and all the powers of
the world' (pp. 78–9 below).

Fairfax thought Everard was mad, and refused to take the

22. *Clarke Papers*, Vol. II, Camden Soc., 1894, pp. 209–12; Whitelocke, *Memorials of the English Affairs*, p. 383.

incident seriously. He visited the colony at the end of May and had an amicable exchange with Winstanley, in which the latter repeated his assurance that the Diggers had no intention of using force. But local property-owners were not so tolerant. The colony at St George's Hill was raided more than once, crops and huts were destroyed, individuals beaten up, horses killed. On or before 1 June 1649 the Diggers published a second manifesto, with forty-five signatures this time: *A Declaration from the Poor oppressed People of England directed to all that call themselves, or are called Lords of Manors*. In this they claimed that the timber on the waste no less than the land belonged to the poor, and warned the local lord of the manor to stop carrying off wood from St George's Hill. The Diggers intended to cut and sell it in order to maintain themselves until their crops were ready for harvesting (pp. 99–101 below). An action for trespass was brought against the Diggers in the court at Kingston, where they were not allowed to plead unless they would hire an attorney. When they refused to do this – 'It is contrary to your own laws,' Winstanley exclaimed – they were condemned unheard. 'Their jury was made of rich freeholders,' who brought in damages of £10 a man against the Diggers, plus 29s. 1d. costs. There were no assets to meet these fines, so the Diggers' property was distrained. An exciting tussle ensued over Winstanley's cows, which changed hands many times and acquired a symbolic significance for him (pp. 130–35 below).

Some time in or before August 1649 the colony abandoned St George's Hill and transferred to Cobham Heath, a mile or two away. But they were not left in peace there either. After a meeting at the Red Lion in Cobham, at which a great deal of sack was consumed, a boycott of the Diggers was organized. Winstanley found that a landlord from whom he had contracted to purchase hay refused to fulfil the bargain 'but sold it to another before my face'. Then Francis Drake, lord of the manor of St George's Hill and an M.P. who had been purged by Colonel Pride, together with Parson Platt, lord of the manor of Cobham, proceeded to more direct measures. Winstanley was arrested and fined £4 for trespass. In November the troops were called in again. The rank and file were not unsympathetic to the Diggers; one trooper gave them a shilling. But their presence emboldened the local gentry and freeholders. The troops stood by whilst houses were pulled down, tools and implements destroyed, the corn trampled, men beaten and imprisoned. The landlords gave the soldiers 10s. to buy drinks. But Winstanley was convinced that the poorer tenants had been forced to act under threat of eviction and that 'in their hearts they are Diggers' (pp. 179, 209 below). Perhaps the landlords and officers thought he was right. That would account for the persistent brutality with which the Diggers were treated. By the winter of 1649–50, their summer's crop destroyed, the colony was in dire financial straits.

The Diggers called themselves True Levellers, though Leveller leaders like Lilburne fiercely denounced communism. The Leveller movement which grew up in London after 1646 was never a united, disciplined party, with an agreed programme. There may well have been a more radical wing in London and the Army which did not share Lilburne's attachment to private property. Communist views were attributed to William Walwyn, another of the Leveller leaders, and there seem to have been disagreements between those who wanted full manhood suffrage and those who wished to preserve some property qualification. There was certainly support for True Levelling in the countryside, more than historians have recognized until recently. A group of Buckinghamshire Levellers produced three or four pamphlets, of which the first (*Light Shining in Buckinghamshire*) appeared in December 1648, before Winstanley had announced his conversion to communism. Its sequel, *More Light Shining in Buckinghamshire*, was published on 30 March 1649, two days before digging started on St George's Hill. *Light Shining in Buckinghamshire* called for equality of property – on the same principle as the Agitators at Putney had called for equal electoral rights. 'All men being alike privileged by birth, so all men were to enjoy the creatures alike without property one more than the other' (S., p. 611). This was just what Ireton had foreseen and feared.

It is possible, though unlikely, that Winstanley had a hand in drafting the Buckinghamshire pamphlets, since Cobham is only a dozen miles from the border of the county. But he can hardly have been associated with *The Humble Representation of the Desires of the Soldiers and Officers in the Regiment of Horse for the County of Northumberland*, which made similar demands, also at the beginning of December 1648. More or less sophisticated versions of the same ideas were arising simultaneously in various parts of the country. Early newspaper accounts of the Diggers treated them as adherents of the Levellers. The aim of this could of course be to smear the Levellers with the accusation of communism. But the Leveller newspaper *The Moderate* itself printed the first Digger declaration with no hostile comment.[23] The connection was emphasized by the title of this manifesto, *The True Levellers Standard Advanced* (April 1649). St George's Hill may have been only the visible tip of the iceberg of True Levellerism, appealing to those whom the 'constitutional' Levellers at Putney would not have enfranchised – servants, labourers, paupers, the economically unfree.

By the beginning of 1650 other Digger colonies were beginning to appear, at Wellingborough in Northamptonshire, Cox Hall in Kent, Iver in Buckinghamshire, Barnet in Hertfordshire, Enfield in Middlesex, Dunstable in Bedfordshire, Bosworth in Leicestershire, and at unknown places in Gloucestershire and Nottinghamshire.[24] In the spring of 1650, as food and money ran short on Cobham Heath, two emissaries were sent out by the Digger colony with a letter signed by

23. *The Moderate*, No. 41, 17–24 April 1649, p. 433, quoted in J. Frank, *The Beginnings of the English Newspaper, 1620–1660*, Harvard University Press, 1961, p. 179.

24. K. V. Thomas, 'Another Digger Broadside', pp. 57–68.

Winstanley and twenty-one others asking for financial support. They went backwards and forwards through the Home Counties and the Midlands, visiting existing colonies and groups of sympathizers (S., pp. 440–41). But it was too late. In April 1650 the colony on Cobham Heath was finally dispersed, the huts and their furniture burned. Tenants were ordered not to take Diggers in as lodgers, and men were hired to keep a twenty-four hour watch on the Heath to prevent the Diggers returning (S., p. 435). At the beginning of April 1650 Windsor Great Park, confiscated from the King, was put up for public sale. The Diggers' presence might have discouraged purchasers.

Winstanley's Later Career

The little that is known of Winstanley's career after April 1650 can be briefly summarized. In the autumn of that year he and some of his 'poor brethren' hired themselves to Lady Eleanor Davies at Pirton, Hertfordshire – near which Digger agents had passed earlier in the year on their fund-raising tour. Lady Eleanor was an eccentric personality whose public prophecies had given her 'the reputation of a cunning woman amongst the ignorant common people'.[25] Winstanley wrote a letter to her in December 1650, with a fine disregard for her rank and her direct relation to God. He complained of her failure to pay what she owed him and his group for threshing tithe wheat, of her jealous accounting, her secret pride and her self-willed spirit.[26] This may be the incident to which Winstanley's fellow-Lancastrian the Ranter Lawrence Clarkson referred when he said that Winstanley conducted 'a most shameful retreat from George-Hill ... to become a real tithe-gatherer of property'. Clarkson decided,

25. P. Heylyn, *Cyprianus Anglicus*, quoted by T. Spencer, 'The History of an Unfortunate Lady', *Harvard Studies in Philology and Literature*, XX, p. 52.

26. P. Hardacre, 'Gerrard Winstanley in 1650', *Huntington Library Quarterly*, XXII, pp. 345–9.

after the event, that 'there was self-love and vain-glory' in Winstanley's heart, and that his object was 'by digging to have gained people to him, by which his name might become great among the poor commonalty of the nation'.[27]

Winstanley's last and most systematic work, *The Law of Freedom in a Platform*, was published early in 1652, with dedicatory epistle to Oliver Cromwell, dated 5 November 1651. This was a time when general discontent with the rule of the Rump of the Long Parliament caused schemes of 'healing government' to be put forward, and Winstanley offered his in that spirit. It is difficult to believe that he had great hopes of converting the Lord General to communism, or that Cromwell would carry out at one blow from above the revolution which the Diggers had failed to bring about from below. But, Winstanley told Cromwell, 'You have power in your hand ... I have no power.' He no doubt wished to present his maturer views to as wide an audience as possible. He says that he had intended the pamphlet for Cromwell's view 'above two years ago', but laid it aside because of 'the disorder of the times'. If we take this literally, *The Law of Freedom* must have been drafted not later than the winter of the Digger experiment. But Winstanley speaks of putting 'together as many of my scattered papers as I could find' and compiling them 'into this method' (p. 285 below). I suspect that *The Law of Freedom* took its present form only in 1651, the year which saw the publication of Hobbes's *Leviathan*.

We catch another glimpse of Winstanley at Cobham in 1660, when he was involved in a lawsuit.[28] Attempts have been made to identify the Digger Gerrard Winstanley with a man of the same name who in 1666 claimed that Ferdinando Gorges owed him £1,850 and had promised an annuity of £200 to his wife and two sisters. This Gerrard Winstanley

27. L. Clarkson, *The Lost Sheep Found*, 1660, p. 27. Clarkson was born in Preston in 1615, and seems to have known Winstanley personally. See p. 250 below.
28. See p. 12 above.

was a corn-chandler living in Bloomsbury, who died a Quaker in 1676, aged about sixty-two, leaving a widow named Elizabeth (*née* Stanley). The coincidence of name is striking, but Winstanley was not an uncommon surname. Our Gerrard Winstanley would have been sixty-seven, not sixty-two, in 1676 (if, that is, we accept the entry in the Wigan parish register as referring to him: the chances of there being two Gerrard Winstanleys were far smaller in Wigan than in London). There is no evidence that our Winstanley left Cobham, where he was still living in 1660, nor that he ever became a corn-chandler, nor that he experienced any such striking reversal of fortune as to be dealing in very large sums of money by 1666 – unless we take Lawrence Clarkson's sneer metaphorically rather than literally. There is no record of the death of Winstanley's wife Susan, *née* King, nor of his marrying again. There is no other evidence to suggest that he joined the Quakers. The language used in his Chancery petition of 1660 is not that of a Quaker. Attempts to link the Diggers generally with the Quakers have not been successful.[29] It is not impossible that the two Gerrard Winstanleys are one and the same man, but the case is unproven.

The Digger colony in Surrey lasted almost exactly a year. At their peak the Diggers were cultivating some eleven acres – land of which the agricultural writer Walter Blith said with an audible sniff that there were 'thousands of places more capable of improvement'.[30] We know the names of some seventy-three adherents, plus nine more at Wellingborough and ten at Iver. About Gerrard Winstanley we have the few facts I have indicated. On the face of it the whole episode seems a not very important footnote to history. Why

29. R. T. Vann, 'From Radicalism to Quakerism: Gerrard Winstanley and Friends', *Journal of the Friends Historical Soc.*, XLIX, pp. 42–4; 'Diggers and Quakers – A Further Note', ibid., L, pp. 66–8; 'The Later Life of Gerrard Winstanley', *Journal of the History of Ideas*, XXVI, pp. 133–6. See p. 70 below.

30. W. Blith, *The English Improver Improved,* 1652, Sig. C 2v–3.

should we bother about Gerrard Winstanley today? Why should he be treated in this edition for the first time as a classic?

I hope the contents of this book will speak for themselves. It is a selection from the pamphlets in which Winstanley defended and elaborated his theoretical position in the years from 1649 to 1652. In the first place Winstanley was a very acute and penetrating social critic, with a passionate sense of justice, who tells us a great deal about an England of which we all too rarely hear at this date – that of the underdog. But, secondly, his writings are much more than a cry of pain from an oppressed peasantry. Communist theories appear on the fringe of all the great middle-class revolutions – Münzer, John of Leyden and the Anabaptists in the German Reformation, Winstanley and the Diggers in the English Revolution, Baboeuf and the Conspiracy of the Equals in the French Revolution, Marxist communism in 1848, the Bolsheviks in 1905. Each of these groups helps us to understand the revolutions through which they lived precisely because they felt that their own revolution had not gone far enough. We should not see a continuous communist tradition: Marx and Engels were aware of the German Anabaptists and of Baboeuf but not of Winstanley. He was rediscovered in the late nineteenth century, and popularized by followers of the American radical Henry George and by the German Marxist Eduard Bernstein. But ideas are not passed on in writing only. Winstanley has a place in the transition from the backward-looking agrarian communism of the Middle Ages to modern socialism.

At this great turning-point of English history Winstanley outlined, firmly and consistently, an alternative programme. Instead of a society based on private property, competition and the protestant ethic, a society which would challenge world empire, he sketched a communist society based on co-operation and a secular humanist ethic, with no aspirations to dominate other peoples. There had been communist theories before Winstanley's, but he was the first to insist

34

that 'there cannot be a universal liberty till this universal community be established' (S., p. 199). He was perhaps not the first to suggest the reconstruction of the whole social order on rational principles, but he was the first to put forward such a political programme ('in a platform') in the vernacular and to call on a particular social class to translate it into action – the poor squatters and cottagers who were soon to be dispossessed of their commons. Winstanley's writings are limited by their propagandist purpose, but their scope is remarkable; they deal with God and matter, heaven and hell, education and science, marriage and the family, as well as politics and economics. His philosophy is coherent, and on almost every subject he covered Winstanley had pioneering things to say.

Thirdly, the way he said it is almost as important as what Winstanley said. He wrote some of the finest prose that even seventeenth-century England produced, and has a place in that evolution of popular prose which extends from the Marprelate Tracts in the reign of Elizabeth to Bunyan, Defoe and the novel.

These claims I shall now try to substantiate.

Politics and Economics

Winstanley shared many of the views of the Levellers. He thought of the civil war in political rather than religious terms, though he hoped that religious liberty would be one of its by-products. But he saw it in class terms, a struggle in which the gentry and merchants whom Parliament represented had defeated the King and the church hierarchy with the help of the common people, who joined Parliament relying on their promises of freedom.

> When great men disagree
> About supremacy
> Then do they warn poor men
> To aid and assist them,

sang Robert Coster, the Digger poet. But the help was required only

> In setting up their self-will power,
> And thus they do the poor devour (S., p. 667).

The Parliamentary leaders, Winstanley told the Council of State in 1649, said in effect 'give us your taxes, free-quarter, excise, and adventure your lives with us; cast out the oppressor Charles, and we will make you a free people'. But England cannot be free unless the commoners have the use of the land: the Diggers claimed freedom to enjoy the common lands, 'bought by our money and blood',[31] just as the gentry in Parliament by abolishing the Court of Wards had set themselves free from the arbitrary death-duties and interference with long-term planning which wardship represented (pp. 119–20 below).

Winstanley postulated a primitive libertarian communism. 'In the beginning of time the great creator Reason made the earth to be a common treasury.' But covetousness overcame reason and equality together. A ruling class began violently to appropriate what had hitherto been common property. The earth was bought and sold. The establishment of private property led to the setting up of state power: 'the sword brought in property and holds it up, which is no other but the power of angry covetousness'. So the earth ceased to be a common treasury and became 'a place wherein one torments another'. Private appropriation was 'the cause of all wars, bloodshed, theft and enslaving laws that hold people under misery'. Only the abolition of private property can end 'this enmity in all lands'. The structure of society creates hatred between man and man: 'it is a pitched battle between the Lamb and the Dragon', Winstanley told Fairfax, 'and these two powers strive in the heart of every single man, and make single men to strive in opposition one against the other' (pp. 77–80, 99–101 below; S., pp. 281–2, 290).

31. *Calendar of State Papers, Domestic*, 1653–4, p. 338 (wrongly dated: should be 1649).

The Diggers, Winstanley claimed, were not against government as such, but against the government which 'gives freedom to the gentry to have abundance' and locks up 'the treasures of the earth from the poor'. 'If they beg, they whip them by their law for vagrants; if they steal they hang them; and if they set themselves to plant the commons for a livelihood, that they may neither beg nor steal, and whereby England is enriched, yet will they not suffer them to do this neither' (p. 170 below; S., pp. 188, 435). This class rule is symbolized as 'kingly power'. Winstanley took over from the Levellers the traditional English revolutionary myth of the Norman Yoke. But he pushed this a great deal further than most exponents of the theory, to attack the whole structure of existing society and the state. He asked:

Whether lords of manors have not lost their royalty to the common land since the common people of England, as well as some of the gentry, have conquered King Charles, and recovered themselves from under the Norman conquest? . . . Everyone upon recovery of the conquest ought to return into freedom again without respecting persons, or else what benefit shall the common people have (that have suffered most in these wars) by the victory that is got over the King? . . . Seeing they have paid taxes and given free-quarter according to their estates, as much as the gentry to theirs, . . . surely all sorts, both gentry in their enclosures, commonalty in their commons, ought to have their freedom, not compelling one to work for wages for another?

The questions go on remorselessly:

Whether all laws that are not grounded upon equity and reason, not giving a universal freedom to all but respecting persons, ought not to be cut off with the King's head? We affirm they ought . . . Whether the laws that were made in the days of the kings does give freedom to any other people but to the gentry and clergy, all the rest are left servants and bondsmen to those task-masters? . . . And surely if the common people have no more freedom in England but only to live among their elder brothers and work for them for hire, what freedom then have they in England more than we can have in Turkey or France? (S., pp. 286–9; cf. p. 168 below).

The war, Winstanley thought, had not been finally won yet. Only the top branch of kingly power had been cut off by the execution of Charles I: its roots remained. The Levellers' argument was familiar. 'I would fain know', Rainborough had asked at Putney, 'what the soldier hath fought for all this while. He hath fought to enslave himself, to give power to men of riches, men of estates, to make him a perpetual slave.'[32] Winstanley extended this argument from the Army as a professional unit to all the common people of England whom it represented, as Parliament represented the rich. Winstanley wanted a far more complete break with the old order than had been achieved by the merely political changes of 1648–9. 'The King's blood was not our burden, it was those oppressing Norman laws whereof he enslaved us that we groaned under.' 'True religion and undefiled is ... to make restitution of the earth, which hath been taken and held from the common people by the power of conquests' (pp. 85–6, 117–20, 128–9, 185, 372–3 below).

In 1650 Winstanley came to argue that the social revolution he was advocating was not only desirable but actually legal. Crown lands had reverted to the common people by conquest. By the laws abolishing the monarchy and establishing a Commonwealth, he insinuated, and by the Engagement of 1650 which 'all sort of people' had taken to be faithful to the Commonwealth,

the tenants of copyholds are freed from obedience to their lords of manors, and all poor people may build upon and plant the commons, and the lords of manors break the laws of the land and the Engagement and still uphold the kingly and lordly Norman power if they hinder them ... If the tenants stand up to maintain their freedom against their lords' oppressing power, the tenants forfeit nothing, but are protected by the laws and Engagement of the land ... And if any say that the old laws and customs of the land are against the tenant and the poor,

32. Woodhouse, op. cit., p. 71.

and entitle the land only to lords of manors, still I answer, all the old laws are of no force, for they are abolished when the King and House of Lords were cast out (S., pp. 411–13).

It is in the light of this attitude that we must see Winstanley's defence of the English republic in the spring of 1650. He had already pointed out to Fairfax in December 1649 that some of the 'gentlemen that set the soldiers on' against the Diggers were always Cavaliers, and had been involved in the Kentish rising of 1648 against Parliament (S., pp. 344, 346; cf. p. 177 below). In a recently discovered pamphlet, not reprinted here, Winstanley called on all Englishmen to accept the Engagement to be true and faithful to the Commonwealth. As Professor Aylmer argues, this was tactically sound. Winstanley can hardly have expected to convince many of his compatriots, certainly not those in positions of power, that the Engagement *did* give the common lands to the poor: but he was right to regard the Commonwealth as a lesser evil than a restoration of monarchy, for which some of the Levellers were working.[33]

Winstanley shared to the full both the patriotism and the utopian hopes to which the civil war had given rise, that England would set the world an example of a more just society, and at the same time become 'the most flourishing and strongest land in the world' (pp. 111, 198 below). Again fusing religion with his economic and political theories, Winstanley declared that 'the reformation that England now is to endeavour is not to remove the Norman yoke only and to bring us back to be governed by those laws that were before William the Conqueror came in ... but ... according to the Word of God, and that is the pure law of righteousness before the Fall' (S., p. 292).

The Diggers insisted that they wished to proceed by persuasion, by peaceful means, not by coercion. 'We shall not strive with sword and spear', Winstanley told Fairfax,

33. G. E. Aylmer (ed.), *Englands Spirit Unfoulded, Past and Present*, No. 40, p. 6. Cf. pp. 289, 304, 344 below, and S., pp. 411–12, 431.

'but with spade and plough.' He seems really to have hoped, initially, that the Diggers would be allowed to take over the waste land peacefully, and cultivate it in common, since 'they take no man's proper goods from them'. Non-violence was a matter of principle. 'Freedom gotten by the sword', Winstanley said, 'is an established bondage to some part or other of the creation.' But non-violence was also political common sense. The Diggers were a tiny band, who wanted to inspire others to follow their example. They must have known how nervous the propertied class was in 1649, and how overwhelming was the force at the Army's disposal. To advocate violence would have been foolish. 'To conquer them by love, come in now, come in now', ran the Digger song (pp. 190, 197, 393–5 below, S., p. 286).

Moreover, Winstanley was aware of the enormous in-fluence of the Church on the illiterate mass of the popula-tion, and regarded the clergy as propagandists in the ser-vice of the existing property system. He saw therefore the danger of appealing to an uneducated democracy, and could not find in contemporary conditions of society the social force which would put through the changes necessary even to make the common people aware of what might be done. Initially God seemed the only answer. 'The whole earth we see is corrupt, and it cannot be purged by the hand of crea-tures, for all creatures lies [34] under the curse and groans to be delivered, and the more they strive, the more they entangle themselves in the mud, because it must be the hand of the Lord alone that must do it.' And so he wrote, 'I do not speak that any particular man shall go and take their neighbour's goods by violence or robbery (I abhor it) as the condition of the men of the nations are ready to do in this fleshly settled government of the world. But everyone is to wait till the Lord Christ do spread himself in multiplicities of bodies.' Later he seems to have had more confidence in this change of heart, as a result of which men 'will easily cast off their burden' (S., pp. 182–7; p. 242 below).

34. For this grammatical usage see p. 64 below.

Winstanley was no absolute pacifist. Although he abjured violence for the Diggers, he had supported Parliament in the civil war, of which he approved (pp. 283, 357–8 below); in 1648 he looked to the civil power for defence against what he then regarded as the greatest enemy, ecclesiastical tyranny.[35] In 1650 he urged men to take the Engagement to support the Commonwealth. He believed that Biblical threatenings against the rich 'shall be materially fulfilled, for they shall be turned out of all'. He advocated extreme forms of non-violent resistance. In January 1649 he called on 'you dust of the earth, that are trod underfoot, you poor people that makes both scholars and rich men your oppressors by your labours, ... if you labour the earth and work for others that lives at ease ... the hand of the Lord shall break out upon every such hireling labourers and you shall perish with the covetous rich men'. This was an attack on the whole developing system of wage labour. In April he repeated the call to refuse to work for landlords for wages: he advocated, that is to say, something like a general strike (S., pp. 181, 194; p. 90 below). His paean in praise of the new society which he envisaged was anything but pacifist. Liberty is secured in Winstanley's commonwealth by a right of popular resistance (S., p. 414; p. 318 below).

In his early pamphlets attacking the existing social and political order Winstanley seems to be advocating an anarchist form of communist society, without state, army or law. He expected the state, in Marx's phrase, to wither away as soon as communal cultivation was established. To put even a murderer to death would itself be murder; only covetousness regarded theft as a sin (S., p. 197; p. 192 below). But by the time he came to draft *The Law of Freedom* the heyday of the Revolution was over, and with it Winstanley's optimistic confidence. His bitter experience at St George's Hill made him realize that laws would be needed against 'the spirit of unreasonable ignorance', and that a citizen army might have to defend the commonwealth against

35. *The Breaking of the Day of God*, pp. 119–23.

domestic and foreign enemies (pp. 333–4, 356–8 below). There are therefore laws in his ideal commonwealth, and by modern standards some of the punishments envisaged seem very severe. We should remember that pain and suffering of all kinds were more familiar in an age when anaesthetics were still unknown, and Bunyan regarded whipping or burning in the hand as minor penalties.[36] Imprisonment in the fever-ridden gaols of the time was little better than a death-sentence. Winstanley thought of whipping and forced labour as corrective punishments.

Religion and the Church

When Winstanley asked himself why 'most people are so ignorant of their freedom, and so few fit to be chosen commonwealth's officers', his answer was that 'the old kingly clergy ... are continually distilling their blind principles into the people, and do thereby nurse up ignorance in them' (p. 324 below). One of the most powerful of his passions is hatred of parsons and the state church – a virulent anti-clericalism which he shares with John Milton. Their reasons are similar: parsons are paid to do a job that no one should be paid for; and they use their privileged position to impose standards of conduct on others.

Anti-clericalism has a long history in the English radical movement. The Lollards rejected a separate clerical caste. William Tyndale attacked priests who act 'not for the love of your souls (which they care for as the fox doth for the geese)'.[37] In the sixteen-forties the Leveller William Walwyn was one of the most forceful exponents of anti-clericalism. The clergy, he wrote, pray, preach and do all for money. Ministers should have no power of jurisdiction, but should be limited to preaching; and no one should be compelled to come and hear them. Heresy-hunting was due to the clergy's

36. J. Bunyan, *Works*, ed. G. Offor, 1860, II, p. 127.
37. W. Tyndale, *Doctrinal Treatises*, Parker Soc., 1848, p. 161. For an echo of this phrase in Winstanley, see pp. 63, 239 below.

fear for their power and emoluments. Their concern for learning was self-interested too: if it was not kept up 'their trade will go down'.[38] Similarly the anonymous author of *Tyranipocrit Discovered* (1649) denounced scholarly parsons who 'have no experience in that honest simple life of tilling the land, nor keeping of sheep'.[39] Such critics wanted to get rid of a trained university clergy, appointed from above and paid by tithes, and to leave the field open to 'mechanick preachers', craftsmen who would maintain themselves by labouring six days a week and so would not need tithes.

For Winstanley the English state church was antichristian, a cheat by means of which vested interests and the covetous sought to defend themselves against the searching light of truth (S., p. 211; pp. 353–4 below). Against it he appealed confidently to the poor and humble, to the oppressed: and to the power of human reason, of education, of science. For Winstanley kingly power, clergy, lawyers, buying and selling, were all linked. William the Conqueror, so Winstanley's myth ran, had appointed two national officers to see that the laws were obeyed: the lawyers to look after property, and the clergy to keep the people quiet by telling them 'of a heaven and hell after death, which neither they nor we know what will be'. In return they got 'tithes for their pains'. 'A man must not take a wife but the priest must give her him', and the same is true of christenings, burials, education. 'And what is the end of all this but to get money? If a man labour the earth to get his bread, the priests must have the tenths of his increase, or else some oppressing impropriator' (pp. 193, 297–9 below; S., p. 187).

Tithes were crucial to the existence of a state church, and linked the clergy to the propertied class. 'The sheep of

38. Walwyn, in W. Haller and G. Davies, *The Leveller Tracts 1647–1653*, Columbia University Press, 1944, p. 257; Haller, *Tracts on Liberty in the Puritan Revolution*, Columbia University Press, 1933, III, pp. 74–8, 83, 327, 332.

39. op. cit., in *British Pamphleteers*, I, ed. G. Orwell and R. Reynolds, 1948, p. 97.

Christ', as Winstanley put it, 'shall never fare well so long as the wolf or red dragon pays the shepherd their wages.' He saw a professional clergy as at best superfluous, at worst the paid propagandists of a wicked social order. Ploughmen, he thought, may do better 'than they that take tithes to tell a story' (p. 200 below; S., p. 233). Priests 'lay claim to heaven after they are dead, and yet they require their heaven in this world too, and grumble mightily against the people that will not give them a large temporal maintenance. And yet they tell the poor people that they must be content with their poverty, and they shall have their heaven hereafter. But why may not we have our heaven here (that is, a comfortable livelihood in the earth) and heaven hereafter too, as well as you?' Winstanley's moral indignation flashes out against the whole profession in words similar to those of Voltaire or Marx (S., p. 409; pp. 353-4 below).

Winstanley held what was then the highly unorthodox view that all mankind shall be saved at last, since it does not make sense to believe in an omnipotent and beneficent God who will torment his creatures to all eternity. He denied the existence of a local hell or heaven, a personal devil or a bodily resurrection. Heaven he equated with mankind – an idea of which Blake might have approved (pp. 193, 222-3 below; S., p. 290). God – that is to say Reason within men – will ultimately redeem them from the only true hell, the hell they have created for each other on earth. Winstanley leaves open the question of the existence of any other hell: he merely says that nobody knows or can know anything about it, least of all the preachers who emphasize it so much. Hell exists in men because of the evil organization of society; and the conception is then used to perpetuate that society by those who benefit from it (pp. 299, 350-3 below).

In certain areas Winstanley's scepticism was explicit – e.g. his reference to people like 'wise-hearted Thomas', who believe 'nothing but what they see reason for'. He frontally attacked the Law of Moses. 'Aaron and the priests were ... the first that deceived the people' (pp. 81, 299 below). He re-

jected the God of the traditional churches – the 'God of this
world' from whom landlords claim title to the land and
priests a right to tithes (p. 310 below). The Trinity seems
to have had for Winstanley only a metaphorical existence,
since the spirit within man is both Jesus Christ and the Holy
Ghost.[40] Prayer is 'the reasonings of the heart' by which men
distinguish between covetousness and reason: 'words or
utterance . . . is the remotest part of prayer'. Holy communion is not a sacrament but eating and drinking in any
house 'in love and sweet communion with one another' –
as the Diggers did on St George's Hill (S., pp. 136–43).

One of Winstanley's main complaints against the clergy
was that they claimed a monopoly of interpreting the Bible,
and suppressed the free spirit in the uneducated. The spirit
in men today is above the Gospel, he asserted. 'The Scriptures were not appointed for a rule to the world to walk by
without the spirit . . . For this is to walk by the eyes of other
men.' The Bible, Winstanley argued, should be used to
illustrate truths of which one is already convinced. He
advocated complete religious toleration for anyone to worship his own God, to read and teach what he wished. This
would presumably include Jews and papists. In his state
there was to be no religious test for office-holders. Although
he wrote a pamphlet to dissociate the Diggers from the
Ranters' 'excessive community of women', he was careful to
say: 'Let no one go about to suppress that ranting power by
their punishing hand, for it is the work of the righteous and
rational spirit within, not thy hand without, that must suppress it. But if thou wilt needs be punishing, then see thou
be without sin thyself.' Winstanley firmly believed that the
cure for intolerance and ignorance alike was social (S., pp.
99–102, 126–7, 165, 402; pp. 296, 323, 379 below).

Winstanley's Reason, which is synonymous with God,
pervades the whole universe and 'dwells in every creature,
but supremely in man'. 'If you subject your flesh to this
mighty governor, the spirit of rightousness within yourselves,

40. *The Saints Paradice*, p. 21.

he will bring you into community with the whole globe.'
'O ye hearsay preachers, deceive not the people any longer',
Winstanley cried, 'by telling them that this glory shall not
be known and seen till the body is laid in the dust. I tell you,
this great mystery is begun to appear and it must be seen by
the material eye of the flesh. And those five senses that is in
man shall partake of this glory'. The conclusion of the
Diggers' Song called for 'glory *here*'.[41] In *The Law of Freedom* Winstanley has one of the most magnificent panegyrics
of rational science, with its feet on the earth, to be found in
the whole of seventeenth-century English literature (S., pp.
164–71, pp. 348–9 below). Yet this passage – 'to know the
secrets of nature is to know the works of God' – is almost a
paraphrase of Calvin: 'This most beautiful order of nature
silently proclaims [God's] admirable wisdom ... As for those
who proudly soar above the world to seek God in his un-
veiled essence, it is impossible but that at length they should
entangle themselves in a multitude of absurd figments. For
God ... clothes himself, so to speak, with the image of the
world, in which he would present himself to our contemplation ... Let the world become our school if we desire
rightly to know God'.[42]

Winstanley may also draw here on the Hermetic tradition,
still inadequately studied by historians of seventeenth-
century England. The works attributed to Hermes Tris-
megistus were probably written in the late second or early
third centuries A.D. They were popularized in Europe in the
late fifteenth and sixteenth centuries. Among many other
Hermetic doctrines the following are of interest: God is
reason; all things are God and come from him; the universe
is God; at death the body returns to its four elements; some
men may become sons of God, attaining to perfection on

---

41. Cf. Milton: man on earth may reach 'a far more excellent state
of grace and glory than that from which he had fallen' (*Works*,
Columbia ed., 1931–41, XV, p. 251).

42. J. Calvin, *A Commentary on Genesis* (trans. J. King, 1965),
I, p. 60.

earth: then communion or fellowship drives out cupidity.[43] Some such ideas may have been floating around the radical underground in Winstanley's day, though we can believe him when he claimed not to have got his main ideas from anybody else. His system was his own.

Anyone acquainted with the history of education in England will appreciate how very advanced are Winstanley's ideas on the subject (pp. 361–5 below). Education was to be universal in his commonwealth, regardless of sex or class; book-learning was to be combined with manual dexterity and vocational training, so that there should be no specialized scholarly class. His views are coloured by his sense of the innate goodness of man, if not corrupted by the institutions of society, and of the worthlessness of thought without action. He wanted universities to cease to turn out clergymen – their main function in seventeenth-century England. Why, he asked, do university men and scholars try to suppress free preaching by laymen? It is, he replied, 'because the light of truth that springs up out of the earth, which the scholars tread under feet, will shine so clear, as it will put out the candle of those wicked learned deceivers'. 'Those that are called preachers ... seeks for knowledge abroad in universities and buys it for money, and then delivers it out again for money, for £100 or £200 a year.' These 'hearsay preachers' use their knowledge of the writings of the Apostles (themselves mechanics) to 'slight, despise and trample' under their feet 'lay people, tradesmen, and such as are not bred in schools', forbidding them to speak or write as the spirit moves them. 'The upshot of all your universities and public preachers ... is only to hinder Christ from

43. F. A. Yates, *Giordano Bruno and the Hermetic Tradition* (1964), *passim*; *The Rosicrucian Enlightenment* (1972), *passim*; W. Shumaker, *The Occult Sciences in the Renaissance* (California University Press, 1972), chapter 5. Winstanley's rejection of any attempt 'to reach God beyond the creation' (p. 348 below) also looks forward to Herder (cf. Roy Pascal, *The German Sturm und Drang*, Manchester University Press, 1953, p. 185).

rising'; university divinity is 'a cloak of policy' to cheat the poor of 'the freedom of the earth'. Before reformation will be possible the clergy's 'mouths must be stopped', though not, Winstanley is careful to add, 'by the hand of tyrannical human power', as they themselves have stopped the mouths of others. Only then will each of us be free to 'read in your own book, your heart' (S., pp. 213–14, 237–42; cf. pp. 351–4 below).

So through his theology Winstanley reached conclusions that scientists were arriving at by other means in the seventeenth century: that new ideas drawn from experience were better than traditional untested truths. John Wilkins, future secretary of the Royal Society, said it was the devil who persuaded mankind that novelty was a sign of error.[44] Winstanley echoed this, saying that the devil tells a man 'he must believe what others have writ or spoke, and must not trust his own experience' (p. 349 below).

Political Theory

The mid-seventeenth century in England was a period of great achievement in political thinking. The Levellers, Thomas Hobbes, James Harrington and Gerrard Winstanley produced political systems of permanent importance. Lesser lights like Henry Parker, John Milton, Marchamont Nedham, Sir Robert Filmer, Anthony Ascham, George Lawson and Richard Baxter would seem more important in any other age. The fantastic thing is that all these thinkers are so different from one another. It was an age of great fecundity.

The only student of political theory who seems to me to have done justice to Winstanley's stature is Perez Zagorin, who described him as 'one of the pre-eminent thinkers of his time'. He was the 'first to give a reasoned elaboration to

44. J. Wilkins, *A Discovery of a World in the Moon* (1640), p. 2. First published 1638.

the doctrine which upholds the eternal inseparability of political liberty and economic equality', and he had 'astonishing views on education and enlightenment'. He 'reproduced, even if on a far less sophisticated plane and in other terms, one of the great movements of thought that culminated in Spinoza, in which God and nature were made one'. He 'rejected the social order in favour of one which reason was to shape'.[45]

There are obvious parallels between the Levellers and Winstanley, and between Winstanley and Harrington. The Levellers sought to establish *political* democracy, a state in which the poorest would be as free as the richest. They based this on a system of inalienable natural rights, one of which was a right to property. This at once gave rise to contradictions: in order to safeguard the property rights of small men against the rich and powerful, some Levellers would have withheld the vote from those who were economically dependent, servants and paupers. Winstanley, like the Levellers' shrewdest critic, Commissary-General Ireton, saw that a natural right to accumulate property was incompatible with liberty. For Ireton this was a decisive argument against extending the vote to those who were not landowners or freemen of corporations: for Winstanley it was an argument for complementing political freedom by economic freedom. 'There cannot be a universal liberty till this universal community be established' (S., p. 199). Where Lilburne said 'the poorest that lives hath as true a right to give a vote as well as the richest and greatest',[46] Winstanley wrote that 'the poorest man hath as true a title and just right to the land as the richest man'. 'Pleading for property and single interest divides the people of a land and the whole world into parties, and is the cause of all wars and bloodshed and contention everywhere' (pp. 128–9, 90 below; S., p. 199).

45. P. Zagorin, *A History of Political Thought in the English Revolution*, 1954, pp. 47, 56–7.
46. J. Lilburne, *The Charters of London*, 1646, p. 4.

Introduction

With Harrington Winstanley shares the belief that property in land is the basis of all political power – so much so that some have thought Harrington got the idea from Winstanley. There is no evidence for this, and the proposition was an obvious enough one in the seventeenth century, though Winstanley and Harrington formulated it more clearly than anyone else. Harrington wanted by means of an agrarian law to establish a balance of property which would prevent excessive competition and excessive accumulation: but he accepted with equanimity the idea that men of property like himself must have a preponderance of political power. Winstanley, from a similar starting point, concluded that private property in land must be abolished if true liberty and equality were to be established. It is sometimes suggested that Winstanley's emphasis on land-ownership as the crucial issue led him to ignore other aspects of economic life. This would be odd in a man born in a clothing town, in an area where coal-mining was developing, who himself followed his father's trade of clothier. But in fact *The Law of Freedom* does discuss industry (in the seventeenth century almost always concerned with collecting or processing natural products) as well as the organization of labour, trade, commercial secrets and inventions. Winstanley foresaw the necessity for a state monopoly of foreign trade, like that which the Bolsheviks established immediately on taking power in 1917 (p. 384 below).

Parallels between Winstanley and Hobbes are less immediately obvious, but both lived in the same brutally competitive world of early capitalist relations. Hobbes, looking around him, was convinced that a strong sovereign authority was required to curb the competitive drives of individualistic men all roughly equal in physical strength and enjoying equal natural rights. Winstanley too thought that the sovereign state was necessary in the world of possessive individualism – 'the government of highwaymen' – but for him this seemed a reason for getting rid of property and competition. This, he thought, would reduce to a minimum the functions of the state and its officials (pp. 306–9 below). Hobbes's view of humanity is basically that of Calvin: for Calvinist theologians the evil in competitive human nature is explained by the Fall of Man; for Hobbes it is something given, not to be moralized over. As Professor Macpherson has shown, the Levellers and Locke both accept Hobbes's assumptions about the competitive individualism which is basic to man's nature. They too ignore the Fall, accept competition (and consequent inequality) in the name of freedom.[47]

For Hobbes the principal problem was to establish safeguards against the dangers which arise from competing individualist atoms with equal rights. The Levellers tried to evade this problem: they had nothing to say when the Hobbist Ireton told them that absolute liberty and property were ultimately incompatible. Winstanley was the only one of Hobbes's contemporaries who faced what was for the sage of Malmesbury the supreme problem: equality plus individualism equals anarchy, unless there is a sovereign umpire with absolute overriding powers. Winstanley may even refer to Hobbes's state of nature, the only way to escape from which is 'to make one man king over you all, and let him make laws, and let everyone be obedient thereunto' (pp. 268, 309 below). For Winstanley equality must be communal, non-competitive, if real liberty is to be established for all and the Hobbist state is to become unnecessary. Equality alone makes possible the rule of Winstanley's Reason, its triumph over Imagination. This latter personifies something very like the passions which rule men in the Hobbist state of nature. 'Imagination fears where no fear is; he rises up to destroy others, for fear lest others destroy him: he will oppress others, lest others oppress him'; he takes by violence that which others have laboured for, for fear lest he shall be in want hereafter. Imagination 'makes

47. C. B. Macpherson, *The Political Theory of Possessive Individualism*, esp. pp. 154–60; cf. my *The World Turned Upside Down*, Appendix 1.

you lust after everything you see or hear of'.[48] Reason is the law of the universe. When Reason rules in man he lives 'in community with the globe and ... in community with the spirit of the globe'. Then 'he dares not trespass against his fellow creature, but will do as he would be done unto. For Reason tells him, is thy neighbour hungry and naked to-day, do thou feed him and clothe him; it may be thy case to-morrow, and then he will be ready to help thee.' [49] Only then can the function of the state be reduced to protecting the community against any resurgence of individual selfishness (pp. 221, 225–6 below).

We must pay attention here to Winstanley's use of words whose meaning has changed since his time. 'Imagination' since Coleridge suggests something of which we approve. But Winstanley's usage is that of the Authorized Version, of the early Quakers and of Milton: we do not approve of 'vain imaginings' or of 'the imagination of their hearts'. Winstanley's Imagination is opposed to Reason, which is also Love. Imagination distorts reality by looking at it through the eyes of covetousness or self-love. 'Imagination is that God which generally everyone worships and owns.' It 'fills you with fears, doubts, troubles, evil surmisings and grudges, ... stirs up wars and divisions'. Not until true knowledge overcomes imaginary thoughts, and 'all imaginary coverings shall be taken off everywhere', will Reason rule and peace prevail (pp. 19 above, 221–6 below; S., p. 203).

Winstanley's Reason sometimes sounds like an anticipation of Rousseau's General Will, though it is not confined to one community. The light of Reason is in all men, but does not completely dominate the thinking of any single individual all the time: some may calculate that it is to their advantage to compete and destroy one another. But this will

48. Cf. Hobbes's 'perpetual and restless desire of power after power that ceaseth only in death' (*Leviathan*, ed. C. B. Macpherson, Penguin, 1968, p. 161).

49. Sabine, pp. 109–12; *The Saints Paradice*, p. 123; cf. H. Marcuse, *An Essay on Liberation*, Penguin, 1972, p. 19.

change as Reason itself 'knits every creature together into a oneness, making every creature to be an upholder of his fellow, and so everyone is an assistant to preserve the whole'. The less selfish men are, the more closely will they approximate to this Reason, which 'guides all men's reasoning in right order and to a right end'. For all humanity is one (p. 89 below; S., pp. 105, 222).

Winstanley's relation to traditional theology is like Karl Marx's relation to Hegelianism: he found it standing on its head and set it the right way up. Winstanley saw an intimate connection between a class-divided society and the Eternal Decrees which condemned the mass of humanity to an eternity of suffering (p. 307 below). For Calvinists and other Anglican theologians the Fall of Man led to covetousness, to private property, to the division of society into classes, and to the state which protects property. Laws are necessary safeguards against the sinfulness of fallen nature. The Thirty-Nine Articles of the Church of England rely heavily on original sin to justify property and the authority of magistrates against Anabaptist heresies. Laws, said the judicious Hooker, 'are never framed as they should be ... unless presuming man to be in regard of his depraved mind little better than a wild beast'.[50] 'In the depraved condition of human nature', John Pym agreed in 1641, laws are necessary to put 'a different betwixt good and evil'.[51] Winstanley reversed the order: covetousness and private property are the causes, not the consequences, of the Fall. 'When self-love began to arise in the earth, then man began to fall.' 'When mankind began to quarrel about the earth, and some would have all and shut out others, forcing them to be servants: this was man's fall.' Exploitation, not labour, is the curse. Buying and selling, and the laws regulating the market, are part of the Fall (pp. 192–3, 266 below; S., pp. 423–4). Property,

50. R. Hooker, *Of the Laws of Ecclesiastical Polity*, Everyman ed., I, p. 188.

51. J. Rushworth, *The Trial of Strafford*, 1680, p. 662.

as Robert Coster put it, originated in murder and theft (S., p. 655).

So for Winstanley and the Diggers covetousness – individualism – caused (or was) the Fall, and necessitated the state. It can therefore be overcome on earth. Winstanley did not *forget* the Fall, as some contemporaries alleged; he approached the story of the Fall of Man rather as a modern anthropologist would, as a myth which conceals a profound social truth. Like the myth of the Golden Age, or of the free Anglo-Saxons, the backward look to the Garden of Eden is the memory of an earlier equality still retained by the inhabitants of an unequal, class-divided society. That is why Winstanley could fuse the myths of the Fall and the Norman Yoke: he took neither of them too seriously as history.

Myths

We should read Winstanley as we read a poet, as we read William Blake, and as Winstanley himself read the Bible: concerned not too pedantically with the letter, but with the spiritual content which the myths have, or can be given. For Winstanley, Cain and Esau the elder brothers become symbols for great landlords, the propertied class; the younger brother, Abel or Jacob, 'hated, persecuted and despised, ... will rise up in you that you are trod underfoot like dust of the earth ... His time is now come.' The Fall too is a legend. 'We may see Adam every day before our eyes walking up and down the street.' All the prophecies in the Old and New Testaments relating to the calling of the Jews and the restoration of Israel refer to 'this work of making the earth a common treasury' (S., pp. 120, 149; p. 88 below). Even more remarkable is Winstanley's attitude towards the prophecies of *Daniel* and *Revelation*. These were generally thought to describe the battles which would precede the setting up of Christ's kingdom. Many radicals believed – with Milton – that this kingdom would come on earth in the near future. Winstanley coolly treated these prophecies as referring to conflicts within the minds of individuals as Christ rose in sons and daughters, overcoming Antichrist, the Beast, selfishness, and convinced men and women of the necessity of a communist society. So Christ's kingdom ceased to be otherworldly; its coming meant the destruction of private property, of selfishness, and the setting up of true community: not the end of history, but its beginning.

It is worth taking a little trouble to break down the barriers of Winstanley's Biblical language, just as it is worth penetrating through the mists of Hegelian jargon to understand the writings of the early Marx. Winstanley drew on Bible stories largely because he thought they would help his contemporaries to understand him: he used them as poetic imagery. He did not take Cain and Abel, Esau and Jacob, much more seriously than those moderns who will dismiss him as unreadable. Winstanley was less interested in Christ as a historical character than as a symbol of human potentiality: when universal love possesses us, we cast out covetousness and grow up to the perfection of a man anointed (p. 186 below). Human beings, that is to say, can attain to the perfection of Christ on earth. Winstanley was in a sense a precursor of Vico as an anthropological interpreter of myth. We shall make little of, for instance, *Fire in the Bush*, unless we approach it as we would approach one of Blake's prophetic books. Its high-flown metaphorical style is very different from the matter-of-fact *Law of Freedom*, in which Winstanley's object is to persuade by rational argument. Its insights are poetic insights.

Everything Winstanley touched he radicalized. He developed and fused into his own synthesis innumerable popular traditions, transforming them in the process. If we analyse one or two of his key concepts we may get some idea of the complexity of his inheritance, of the depths of his intellectual roots, as well as of the brilliance with which he transvalued. I can give only a few examples: readers will find more for themselves.

Sir Edward Coke and John Pym had believed that the

common law embodied Anglo-Saxon liberties: all that was needed was to abolish royal encroachments. Some Levellers carried this further, to suggest that the law itself legitimized inequality, that Magna Carta was but a beggarly thing. Radical reform was needed if pre-Conquest liberty was to be restored.[52] Winstanley extended this still further, from economics to politics, to suggest that the Norman yoke was the power of landlords: thus the Revolution could be justified only if it led to the abolition of private property in land.[53] The Puritan preachers had seen first the Pope, then bishops and cavaliers, as the antichristian enemy: Winstanley interpreted Antichrist as covetousness, the power which protects property. He similarly transformed the popular rhyme, often repeated in the sixteen-forties,

> When Adam delved and Eve span,
> Who was then the gentleman?

and transmuted it into something like a labour theory of value (pp. 85, 287 below). Sabbath observance had been heavily emphasized by Puritan preachers in the early seventeenth century. Winstanley extracted the social content from sabbatarianism, whilst rejecting its religious basis. He thought it rational to retain one day in seven as a day of rest for men and beasts, for parish fellowship and for education. But his clergy, elected annually, were more like unpaid W.E.A. tutors than priests (pp. 345–8 below).

Finally Winstanley carried his secularism into the heart of Puritan political theory. The Parliamentary leaders, notably Oliver Cromwell, argued from the fact of victory that God favoured their cause. Even Milton at times used this argument, though he lived to regret it. Winstanley no doubt found it easier to resist this temptation, since his cause never was victorious. But his rejection of it was complete

52. See my essay on 'The Norman Yoke' in *Puritanism and Revolution*, chapter 3. See also E. Dell, 'Gerrard Winstanley', *The Modern Quarterly*, IV, 1949, pp. 135–6.

53. See pp. 37–9 above.

and had far-reaching implications. 'Everyone that seems to prevail over another says God gave him the victory, though his conquest be tyranny over his brother, making the King of righteousness the author of his sorrows ... Victories that are got by the sword are but victories of the murderer' (S., p. 297).

Light and Darkness

For Winstanley there are two powers, 'day and night, the light and darkness, winter and summer, heat and cold, moon and sun, that is typed out by the fabric of the great world'. Christ is the son and the sun (S., pp. 166, 177, 236–7). These two powers extending throughout the universe may derive from the Paracelsan/Hermetic tradition: the theme has alchemical overtones, which Winstanley transmutes. The symbolism ran through the writings of the Ranters (cf. Jacob Bauthumley's *The Light and Dark Sides of God*, Clarkson's *A Single Eye: All Light, No Darkness; or Light and Darkness One*). The Quakers called themselves the Children of Light; we recall Milton's emphasis on light. The theme was taken up in the more general sense of contrast, of conflict, which pervades so much of seventeenth-century metaphysical poetry. Take for instance Marvell's

> conjunction of the mind
> And opposition of the stars.

The same sense of contrast is in Herbert's

> Oh that thou shouldst give dust a tongue
>   To cry to thee
> And then not hear it crying.

It is in Traherne's

> Corn for our food springs out of very mire,

or when Crashawe tells us how Christ came

> Lightly as a lambent flame,
> Leaping upon the hills to be
> The humble king of you and me.

The poets saw this first as a problem of the relation of man to the physical universe, to God or his fellows or himself. The title of Roger Brearley's *Self civil war* makes the point, and he expresses well the contrast between individual self-confidence and isolation:

> Myself agrees not with myself a jot ...
> I trust myself, and I myself distrust ...
> I cannot live, with nor without myself.[54]

The poets saw the conflict in social terms only in so far as social organization cut across and impeded the relation of man to the outside world, to God. We may compare Traherne's communism of the imagination:

> Hedges, ditches, limits, bounds,
>   I dreamed not ought of those,
> But wandered over all men's grounds,
>   And found repose.
> Properties themselves were mine ...[55]

Sin was one way of explaining this sense of frustration, of barriers to union with God, and so to satisfactory relations between man and man. Fulke Greville wrote that man is 'created sick, commanded to be sound'; Donne told God he never could be 'chaste, unless thou ravish me'. The extreme paradox is common to all the metaphysicals: the heavy emphasis on original sin is wholly conventional and commonplace. Metaphysical paradox is an expression of the awareness brought home to every sensitive soul that the times are out of joint. Most of the poets stopped there, as Winstanley did in his earlier theological pamphlets, or escaped into nature or childhood.

There is nothing in the poems of Vaughan or Traherne to suggest that they were fond of children as children: they look back to their own childhood as a period of angelic

54. In Theodor Sippell, *Zur Vorgeschichte des Quäkertums*, Giessen, 1920, p. 48.
55. T. Traherne, *Poems, Centuries and Three Thanksgivings*, ed. A. Ridler, Oxford University Press, 1966, p. 8.

innocence, a period in which they were unaware of the conflicts between idea and reality, the problems of social and economic adjustment which began to close about the growing boy. Wordsworth in a later revolutionary age looked back to an idealized version of his own childhood when he wanted to escape from the irreconcilable contradictions into which his attitude to the French Revolution had tied him.

Winstanley too saw childhood as innocent; the Fall is something which takes place within each child as he grows up in the world of greed and covetousness. Idealization of childhood as a state of innocence was rank heresy from the point of view of orthodox Calvinism. But the poets did not carry through to Winstanley's theological universalism, which was ultimately to break the bonds of eternal hell. So they stayed within the limits of theological respectability: they were 'quaint'. Nature for Winstanley was never an escape; knowing the world was the way to know God. The importance of his theory of communism for Winstanley was the vision it gave him of a society in which the conditions of man's life would no longer make for conflict but on the contrary community of property and community of spirit would open men's minds to true reason and science. A rational psychiatry might well ponder his dictum that 'if it be rightly searched into, the inward bondages of the mind, as covetousness, pride, hypocrisy, envy, sorrow, fears, desperation and madness, are all occasioned by the outward bondage that one sort of people lay upon another'. Winstanley elaborated this in the most impressive analysis of the psychology of religion to emerge before the nineteenth century (pp. 296, 350–4 below); cf. S., p. 218).

Prose

The English Revolution is a landmark in the history of English prose, in the transition from 'literary' to colloquial prose. Many streams converge here. First is the Puritan plain style in preaching. The Puritan preachers consciously set themselves against the baroque elaborations of court preachers like Lancelot Andrewes and Donne, learned, allusive, witty. The Puritan aim was to convince as many of their auditors as possible, the simple as well as the learned; countless treatises praised the plain direct style of Perkins, Preston, Sibbes and others. It was not primarily intended to appeal to the lowest groups of the population, the utterly illiterate: it was aimed at the middling sort, merchants, artisans, yeomen.

Preaching became an important political weapon in the revolutionary decades, which effectively killed the ornate style of the court preachers. (Quite apart from anything else, there was no court.) Preachers had a direct message to convey to as many of their congregation as possible. Sermon styles, journalism and pamphleteering styles move together towards a greater simplicity. There had long been a 'popular' pamphleteering style – racy, vulgar, knockabout – at least since the days of the illegal Marprelate Tracts in the late fifteen-eighties. But the censorship had been too effective: apart from pamphlets smuggled over from the Netherlands, like those of Thomas Scott, John Bastwick and John Lilburne, popular journalism languished. The dominant 'literary' prose was heavy, learned, ornate, allusive: the prose of Hooker, Burton, Sir Thomas Browne was admirable for its purposes but of no use as a weapon in pamphleteering warfare.

But the lower-class tradition was not dead, and it reappeared when the ecclesiastical censorship collapsed in the early sixteen-forties. Even royalist journalists had to adopt the new technique – John Berkenhead with conspicuous success.[56] But on the whole it was the radicals and especially the Levellers who perfected the popular approach. Lilburne's wordy style at least conducts a dialogue with the reader. Other Levellers, notably Walwyn and Overton, the latter consciously looking back to the Marprelate Tracts as

56. P. W. Thomas, *Sir John Berkenhead, 1617–1679*, Oxford University Press, 1969, *passim*.

a model, evolved a highly sophisticated simplicity in which art concealed art and wit was disciplined to effect. Take this passage of Walwyn's: 'If anything be displeasing or judged dangerous or thought worthy of punishment, then Walwyn's the author; and no matter, says one, if Walwyn had been destroyed long ago. Says another, let's get a law to have power ourselves to hang all such: and this openly and yet unreproved; affronted in open court, aspersed in every corner, threatened wherever I pass; and within this last month of March was twice advertised by letters of secret contrivances and resolutions to imprison me.' [57] That is good prose because it is doing a job.

Simultaneously the radical sects, the mechanick preachers, emphasizing personal experience as against tradition, developing the spiritual autobiography as a literary form, evolved a prose of comparable directness and conversationality. At its worst this could be garrulous and banal: at its best, in Fox and Bunyan, it perfected a direct spoken democratic eloquence, its narrative and dialogue drawing on popular dramatic traditions. Pepys's *Diary* is hardly a spiritual autobiography in the Quaker sense. But it is a form of spiritual book-keeping, and its style is that of uninhibited conversation. (I have said nothing about another strand of which Pepys reminds us – what we might call 'civil-servant prose', the prose of Marvell, Dryden, Pepys, all of whom were government officials during the Revolution.)

A third tradition is what we may call 'craftsman's prose', the simple direct narratives of Hakluyt's mariners, the clear expositions of the scientific popularizers from Robert Recorde through John Dee to Nicholas Culpeper. Bacon called on scientists to emulate craftsmen: the Royal Society urged scientists to write craftsman's prose, 'the language of artisans, countrymen and merchants'.[58] An important link

57. W. Walwyn, *The Fountain of Slaunder*, 1649, in Haller and Davies, op. cit., p. 247.

58. T. Sprat, *The History of the Royal Society of London*, 1667, p. 113.

figure was John Wilkins, who wrote a treatise on the plain style in preaching for a Puritan audience, and who undoubtedly influenced the Royal Society's insistence on clarity and directness in prose.

Historians of literature record the 'purification' of English prose style which took place after the Restoration, and speak of 'French influences'. It is possible that the gentry of the royalist emigration may have learnt in France how to write their own language with the affected convention of simplicity that we meet with in Restoration comedy, but they could have done equally well if they had stayed at home with Berkenhead and participated in the incursion of ordinary speech into written prose.

Winstanley, who published before either Fox or Bunyan, has his place in this evolution, linking mechanick preachers with political pamphleteers and scientific popularizers. No one can read him without being impressed by the colloquial immediacy of his words, their direct and earthy correspondence to the ideas he wishes to convey. His narrative prose, like that of the Levellers Walwyn and Overton, slips into dialogue and back again effortlessly. (This is less true of *The Law of Freedom*, his attempt at systematic presentation, than of the earlier occasional pamphlets.) His philosophy helps to give Winstanley's style its freshness and vigour. Oneness with nature is not an escape from the man-made conflicts of society, but the way to know God, reason, truth, through knowledge of the real world.

Like Walwyn and Overton, Fox and Bunyan, Winstanley has a pressing moral message to communicate. It is a rational message. He wants people to look and understand and *see* his simple logic. So his style is vivid and direct, though symbols loom up behind all he describes: the cows which the bailiffs beat come to stand for all those who suffer unjustly (p. 139–41 below). That is why metaphors spring so naturally and abundantly to Winstanley's mind. He thinks of the spiritual and the physical as closely interconnected: his abstract ideas grow out of the English landscape. Here

is a piece of simple description, from one of his earlier
books:

> The windows of heaven are opening, and the light of the son
> of righteousness sends forth of himself delightful beams and
> sweet discoveries of truth that will quite put out the covetous
> traditional blear-eyes ... The warm sun will thaw the frost and
> make the sap to bud out of every tender plant that hath been
> hid within, and lain like dead trees all the dark cold cloudy
> days of the Beast that are past ... Now the tender grass will
> cover the earth, the Spirit will cover all places with the abund-
> ance of fruit ... (S., p. 207; cf. p. 209 below).

Winstanley's metaphors illuminate the English rural
scene like lightning flashes: their total unexpectedness
enables us to see the familiar with unfamiliar clarity – which
is exactly what Winstanley is trying to do in the realm of
ideas. Take a few examples:

'All your particular churches are like the enclosers of
land, which hedges in some to be the heirs of life, and hedges
out others.' 'Kingly power is like a great spread tree; if you
lop off the head or top bough, and let the other branches and
root stand, it will grow again and recover fresher strength.'
'England is a prison: the variety of subtleties in the laws preserved by the sword are bolts, bars and doors of the prison;
the lawyers are the jailors, and poor men are the prisoners.'
'The law is the fox, poor men are the geese; he pulls off their
feathers and feeds upon them.' 'These great ones are too
stately houses for Christ to dwell in; he takes up his abode in
a manger.' 'These men make themselves ministers as a man
teaches birds to speak.' 'The sight of yourself is your hell'
(pp. 214, 162–3, 170, 239, 245 below; S., p. 211).

Even where Winstanley jars on our taste, we must see him
historically. Puns, for instance. I have just quoted Winstanley making effective play with the idea that the Son
(Christ) rises in each of us just as the sun rises on the
material universe (cf. S., pp. 181–7). But it must strike us
today as rather childish to base an argument on the false
etymology which derives Adam from 'a' and 'dam' (S., p.

131; p. 134 below). We must however recall not only Shakespeare's puns but also the fashionable etymologizing logic of the Ramists, especially popular among Puritan intellectuals. Abraham Fraunce in *Lawiers Logike* has a precisely similar argument deriving 'woman' from 'woe' and 'man'.[59] This is perhaps the place to remind readers that Winstanley's occasional use of a plural noun with what we should regard as a singular verb was then common colloquial usage, especially in the North – 'All landlords lives in the breach of the seventh and eighth commandments, *Thou shalt not steal nor kill*' (p. 85 below). Winstanley also sometimes uses the double comparative – 'more truer' – and 'rise' – probably pronounced 'riz' – as a past tense. There is an example of this in the first poem from *Englands Spirit Unfoulded* (p. 392 below).

The boldness of Winstanley's imagery continually reminds us that he is a contemporary of the metaphysical poets. Consider the phrase 'stoop unto our God' in the poem which concludes *Truth Lifting up its Head* (p. 391 below). This is not – as it might have been for some of the poets – deliberate cleverness, straining for effect. 'Stoop' is exactly what Winstanley wants 'proud priests' to do, to come down to earth both literally and metaphorically. The phrase concisely and vividly catches up and summarizes his main theme of the importance of the earth. As in Traherne's prose, this 'metaphysical' fusion of concrete and abstract, the here-and-nowness of his illustrations, gives life to passages whose content may be unexciting.

Winstanley obviously wrote very fast, under pressure of burning emotion, and his words pour out breathlessly, intimately. Key ideas and phrases recur too often, since his pamphlets were written for immediate effect, with no intention of their being read consecutively. At Winstanley's best, the extremely personal style of, say, *The New Law of Righteousness* continually reminds us of Bunyan. One at least of his readers found Winstanley's style a little too

59. op. cit., 1588, I, xii, p. 57.

homely. Where he wrote, 'But truly Gaffer Dragon, you had better yield at first', the original owner of the copy now in Jesus College Library, Oxford, sympathetic though he was to Winstanley, deleted the word 'Gaffer', presumably feeling it below the dignity of the treatise (S., p. 206).

With Walwyn, Overton, Winstanley, we are a long way from the prose of Donne, Browne, even Milton. The rhythms of ordinary speech are becoming literature. Yet the transition from the elevated to the popular style need involve no loss of dignity, as Walwyn had demonstrated. Nor is Winstanley just a writer of the occasional splendid phrase. He is also capable of sustained eloquence in many keys. One example of straightforward narrative whose fierce simplicity gives it symbolic overtones is that on p. 139 below about Winstanley's cows. It is closely followed by a superb warning passage about the re-assembly of William the Conqueror's Norman army, and another assuring even his enemies that he wants them to live in peace (pp. 141–2 below; cf. p. 358). Or take the passage written in March 1650, when the colony was collapsing, which defiantly proclaims Winstanley's continuing faith in his cause.

This commonwealth's freedom will unite the hearts of Englishmen together in love, so that if a foreign enemy endeavour to come in we shall all with joint consent rise up to defend our inheritance, and shall be true to one another. Whereas now the poor see, if they fight and should conquer the enemy, yet either they or their children are like to be slaves still, for the gentry will have all. And this is the cause why many run away and fail our armies in the time of need. And so through the gentry's hardness of heart against the poor the land may be left to a foreign enemy, for want of the poorer's love sticking to them. For, say they, we can as well live under a foreign enemy working for day wages as under our brethren (S., p. 414).

Two other passages of equal power but in quite different vein are the conclusion of *Fire in the Bush* and the oft-quoted glorification of science in *The Law of Freedom* (pp. 272, 348–9 below).

Introduction

Once men had begun to write like Walwyn, Winstanley and Bunyan, with a direct urgency and a personal appeal to the ordinary reader, when vivid and detailed description serves a moral and indeed structural purpose, the new prose has reached maturity. The gap between ornate, scholarly fine writing and utilitarian lower-class prose has been bridged. The prose of everyday speech has spread beyond the stage and the pulpit, and we are on the high road to Swift, Defoe and the novel.

Retrospect

The Diggers disappeared without trace, and Winstanley was left weary and bitterly disappointed, as the poem at the end of *The Law of Freedom* makes clear (p. 389 below). His revolution failed. The property system, the state church, priests, lawyers, all remained. Bunyan's Pilgrim, the common man, still carries a burden on his back, of which his own efforts cannot rid him on earth. The defeat of the radicals and of their agrarian programme led to the destruction of the English peasantry, the creation of a land fit for capitalist farmers to live in. From the point of view of the national economy this was splendid: farmers produced food enough to feed even the rapidly expanding population of the eighteenth century, and so laid the base for the Industrial Revolution. But Winstanley was not interested only in economics, but in how human beings lived. He would not have thought the way they lived during the Industrial Revolution was fit for free men: he might have had his doubts even about the very desirable residences which to-day cover St George's Hill. When he advocated abolishing trade secrets, and so stirring men up 'to employ their reason and industry', he saw this not merely (as a modern economist would) as a way of increasing the gross national product, but also of adding to 'the beauty of our commonwealth' (pp. 355–6 below).

Winstanley suggested an alternative approach to the

economic problems of seventeenth-century England which perhaps means more today than it did to most people in his own time. A recent historian saw him as one of the harbingers of welfare economics.[60] Winstanley had grasped that distribution was as important as production, justice and equality more important than wealth. The idea of economic equality, based on a communal organization of society, which Winstanley was the first to put forward as a programme for political action, has never lost its hold over working-class movements. Today much of the Third World faces economic problems similar to those of seventeenth-century England, and is understandably anxious to avoid the brutalities of the English path of capitalist development no less than the brutalities of the Soviet path of enforced collectivization. To this world the message of Winstanley and the Diggers may acquire a new actuality and relevance.

> Freedom is not won
> Neither by sword nor gun

sang Robert Coster (S., p. 672). Winstanley had no hesitation in supporting the Revolution against Charles I. But he knew from bitter experience that kingly power was very difficult to uproot, and that the wielders of power must be kept under continuous democratic surveillance.

Winstanley saw the whole universe as the clothing of God, the globe with its human, animal, vegetable and mineral inhabitants. It was designed by the great creator Reason as a harmonious whole for the use of mankind.[61] But man, by covetousness, by property-grabbing, by setting up hedges, by cut-throat competition, has as it were upset the balance of nature, poisoned the universe. Neither society nor the world of nature will be restored to harmony and beauty until

60. J. K. Fuz, *Welfare Economics in English Utopias* (The Hague, 1952), pp. 43–52.

61. Cf. Marx: 'Nature is [man's] body, with which he must maintain a constant interchange so as not to die' (*Economic and Philosophical Manuscripts*, in *Karl Marx: Early Texts*, ed. D. McLellan, Oxford 1971, p. 139).

it becomes a common treasury once more.[62] We may perhaps think Winstanley was too simple in believing that all human sinfulness and natural disorder can be righted merely by restoring community of property. But in our world of plastic litter and hoardings, of nuclear bombs, atomic waste and supersonic bangs, we may think this belief in the unity of man and nature not the least interesting of Winstanley's insights. As our rulers solemnly discuss pollution and conservation, we may indeed ask ourselves whether 'the beauty of the commonwealth' can ever be given priority until we have abolished competitive private property and competing nation states. We might, in short, listen to Winstanley a little more carefully than the rulers of seventeenth-century England did. 'Well, here is life and death set before you, take whether [i.e. which] you will' (p. 372 below).

There were times when Winstanley seemed to know that he was acting and writing for posterity at least as much as for his contemporaries, for other countries as well as for England. The *Declaration from the Poor oppressed People* was signed by him and forty-four other Diggers 'for and in behalf of all the poor oppressed people of England and the whole world' (p. 108 below). There is great sadness in the last lines Winstanley published, calling on death to make him one with nature (p. 389 below). But though he did not expect a life beyond the grave, Winstanley recognized the possibility of living on in the minds of men. His best epitaph is contained in the introductory poem to *A Watchword to the City of London* (p. 125 below):

When these clay bodies are in grave, and children stand in place,
This shows we stood for truth and peace and freedom in our
    days;
And true-born sons we shall appear of England that's our
    Mother.

62. Cf. Thomas Münzer: 'All creation has been made into property: the fish in the water, the bird in the air, the offspring of the earth. Creation too must become free' (quoted by Karl Marx, *On the Jewish Question*, 1844, in McLellan, op. cit., p. 112).

BIBLIOGRAPHICAL NOTE

THE two essential books for the student of Gerrard Winstanley are D. W. Petegorsky's *Left-Wing Democracy in the English Civil War* (Gollancz, 1940) and G. H. Sabine's edition of *The Works of Gerrard Winstanley* (Cornell University Press, 1941). Petegorsky's is a first-class biographical study, which has been added to and corrected only very slightly by later work. Sabine's is a complete reprint of Winstanley's political tracts, as they were known in 1941, with brief summaries of his first three religious tracts. It also contains additional matter relating to the Diggers (see p. 74 below). Sabine's only serious (and unmentioned) omission is of some of Winstanley's introductory and concluding poems, which is one reason for reprinting them in this book. Sabine also omits the Introduction to the 1649 collected edition of Winstanley's religious works.

The rediscovery of Winstanley dates from C. H. Firth's edition of Volume II of the *Clarke Papers* in 1894. He was introduced to a wider audience by G. P. Gooch's *History of English Democratic Ideas in the Seventeenth Century* (Cambridge University Press, 1898) and by G. M. Trevelyan's *England in the Seventeenth Century* (1904). Winstanley was written up by disciples of the American radical Henry George, J. M. Davidson, *Concerning Four Precursors of Henry George* (1902) and *The Wisdom of Winstanley the 'Digger'* (1904) and L. H. Berens, *The Digger Movement in the Days of the Commonwealth* (1906), the best study before Petegorsky's.

There was a brief reference to Winstanley in Karl Kautsky and Eduard Bernstein's *Die Geschichte des Sozialismus*, Band I (Stuttgart, 1895). But in Bernstein's *Sozialismus und Demokratie in der grossen Englischen Revolution* (Stuttgart, 1908), Winstanley receives full treatment. This work was not translated into English (under the curious title *Cromwell and Communism*) until 1930. Since then there have been valuable studies by Margaret James ('Contemporary Materialist Interpretations of Society in the English Revolution', in *The English Revolution, 1640*, ed. C. Hill, 1940) and E. Dell, 'Gerrard Winstanley the Digger', in *The Modern Quarterly*, IV, 1949; an edition of selections from Winstanley edited by L. D. Hamilton (Cresset Press, 1944); and a full-length study in Russian by M. A. Barg (*Lower-class Democracy in the English Bourgeois Revolution*, Moscow, 1967). Professor Barg is especially interesting on Levellers and True Levellers: see my review in *Agricultural History*, XVI, pp. 75–7. I have considered Winstanley against a rather wider background in *The World Turned Upside Down* (Temple Smith, 1972). There has been a novel, *Comrade Jacob*, by David Caute. There are useful chapters on Winstanley in J. K. Fuz, *Welfare Economics in English Utopias from Francis Bacon to Adam Smith* (The Hague, 1952), P. Zagorin, *A History of Political Thought in the English Revolution* (1954) and H. N. Brailsford, *The Levellers and the English Revolution* (1961). Three articles by R. T. Vann attempt to link Winstanley to the Quakers: much of the factual information in them had been published by Petegorsky, and I am not yet convinced ('From Radicalism to Quakerism: Gerrard Winstanley and Friends', *Journal of the Friends' History Soc.*, XLIX, 1959; 'Diggers and Quakers: A Further Note', ibid., L, 1962 'The Later Life of Gerrard Winstanley', *Journal of the History of Ideas*, XXVI, 1965).

Most exciting of all have been additions to the canon of Winstanley and Digger works by P. H. Hardacre, G. E. Aylmer and K. V. Thomas (see pp. 73–4 below). Mr Thomas has also established the correct date of publication of *Fire in the Bush* (*Past and Present*, No. 42, 1969). There are articles by W. S. Hudson: 'Gerrard Winstanley and the Early Quakers', *Church History*, XII, 1943, and 'Economic and Social Thought of Gerrard Winstanley', *Journal of Modern History*, XVII, 1946; and P. Elmen: 'The Theological Basis of Digger Communism', *Church History*, XXIII, 1954.

A LIST OF GERRARD WINSTANLEY'S WRITINGS

'DEDICATION' may refer to any introductory matter which is dated. 'Thomason' means the date which George Thomason wrote on his copy, the date at which he purchased it. The year is always given in the new style. 'S' indicates printed in Sabine's edition.

The Mysterie of God concerning the whole Creation, Mankind (1648).

The Breaking of the Day of God. Dedication 20 May 1648.

The Saints Paradice. No date. ?1648.

Truth Lifting up its Head above Scandals (1649). Dedication 16 October 1648 (S).

The New Law of Righteousness. Dedication 26 January 1649 (S).

The True Levellers Standard Advanced. Dedication 20 April 1649 (S).

A Declaration from the Poor oppressed People of England. Thomason 1 June 1649 (S).

A Letter to the Lord Fairfax, and his Councell of War. Delivered 9 June 1649 (S).

A Declaration of The bloudie and unchristian acting of William Star and John Taylor of Walton. Thomason 22 June 1649, the date of the 'acting' (S).

An Appeal To the House of Commons. Thomason 11 July 1649 (S).

A Watch-Word to The City of London, and the Armie. Dedication 26 August 1649 (S).

To His Excellency the Lord Fairfax and the Counsell of Warre. December 1649 (S).

To My Lord Generall and his Councell of Warr. Dated 8 December 1649 (S).

Several Pieces gathered into one volume (1650). Preface 20

December 1649. Reprint of the first five pamphlets listed above, in Manchester Central Reference Library.

A New-yeers Gift for the Parliament and Armie. Thomason 1 January 1650 (S).

Englands Spirit Unfoulded (1650). Date uncertain – ? February or March 1650. Published by G. E. Aylmer in *Past and Present*, No. 40, July 1968.

A Vindication of those ... called Diggers. Postscript dated 4 March 1650 (S).

Fire in the Bush. Thomason 19 March 1650 (S).

An Appeale to all Englishmen. Dated 26 March 1650 (S).

A Letter taken at Wellingborough. March 1650 (S).

An Humble Request, to the Ministers of both Universities, and to all Lawyers in every Inns-a-court. Dedication 9 April 1650 (S).

Letter to Lady Eleanor Davies, 4 December 1650. First published by P. H. Hardacre in *Huntington Library Quarterly*, XXII (1959).

The Law of Freedom in a Platform (1652). Dedication 5 November 1651 (S).

OTHER DIGGER OR NEAR-DIGGER WRITINGS

Light Shining in Buckingham-shire. Thomason 5 December 1648 (S).

More Light Shining in Buckingham-shire. Thomason 30 March 1649 (S).

A Declaration of the Wel-affected in the County of Buckinghamshire. Thomason 10 May 1649 (S).

Robert Coster, *A Mite Cast into the Common Treasury*. Thomason 18 December 1649 (S).

A Declaration ... [from] *Wellinborow*. Thomason 12 March 1650 (S).

The Diggers Mirth. Thomason 4 April 1650 (S).

A Declaration ... [from] *Iver*. Dated 1 May 1650. Published by K. V. Thomas in *Past and Present*, No. 42, February 1969 (S).

The Diggers Song. Undated. Published in *The Clarke Papers*, II, ed. C. H. Firth for the Camden Soc., 1894, pp. 221–4 (S).

The texts used in the present edition are those of the British Museum copies of the pamphlets, except for the Preface to *Several Pieces gathered into one volume*, the Diggers' Song and the two poems from *Englands Spirit Unfoulded*.

The True
Levellers' Standard
ADVANCED:

OR,

The State of Community opened, and
Presented to the Sons of Men.

By

William Everard,	*Gerrard Winstanley,*
John Palmer,	*Richard Goodgroome,*
John South,	*Thomas Starre,*
John Courton,	*William Hoggrill,*
William Taylor,	*Robert Sawyer,*
Christopher Clifford	*Thomas Eder,*
John Barker.	*Henry Bickerstaffe,*
	John Taylor, &c.

Beginning to Plant and Manure the
Waste land upon George Hill, in the
Parish of Walton, in the County of
Surrey.*

* A three-page introductory letter, signed by John
Taylor and dated 20 April 1649, is omitted. 'George
Hill' (for 'St George's Hill') conforms to the radical
protestant tradition of refusing to recognize the
saints of the old Church.

A declaration to the powers of England and to all the powers of the world, shewing the cause why the common people of England have begun and gives consent to dig up, manure and sow corn upon George Hill in Surrey; by those that have subscribed, and thousands more that gives consent.

In the beginning of time, the great creator Reason made the earth to be a common treasury, to preserve beasts, birds, fishes and man, the lord that was to govern this creation; for man had domination given to him, over the beasts, birds and fishes; but not one word was spoken in the beginning, that one branch of mankind should rule over another.

And the reason is this, every single man, male and female, is a perfect creature of himself; and the same spirit that made the globe dwells in man to govern the globe; so that the flesh of man being subject to reason, his maker, hath him to be his teacher and ruler within himself, therefore needs not run abroad after any teacher and ruler without him; for he needs not that any man should teach him, for the same anointing that ruled in the Son of Man teacheth him all things.

But since human flesh (that king of beasts) began to delight himself in the objects of the creation, more than in the spirit reason and righteousness, who manifests himself to be the indweller in the five senses of hearing, seeing, tasting, smelling, feeling; then he fell into blindness of mind and weakness of heart, and runs abroad for a teacher and ruler. And so selfish imagination, taking possession of the five senses and ruling as king in the room of reason therein, and working with covetousness, did set up one man to teach and rule over another; and thereby the spirit was killed and man was brought into bondage, and became a greater slave to such of his own kind, than the beasts of the field were to him.

And hereupon the earth (which was made to be a common treasury of relief for all, both beasts and men) was hedged into enclosures by the teachers and rulers, and the others were made servants and slaves: and that earth, that is within this creation made a common storehouse for all, is bought and sold and kept in the hands of a few, whereby the great creator is mightily dishonoured, as if he were a respecter of persons, delighting in the comfortable livelihood of some, and rejoicing in the miserable poverty and straits of others. From the beginning it was not so.

But this coming in of bondage is called A-dam, because this ruling and teaching power without doth dam up the spirit of peace and liberty, first within the heart, by filling it with slavish fears of others; secondly without, by giving the bodies of one to be imprisoned, punished and oppressed by the outward power of another. And this evil was brought upon us through his own covetousness, whereby he is blinded and made weak, and sees not the law of righteousness in his heart, which is the pure light of reason, but looks abroad for it, and thereby the creation is cast under bondage and curse, and the creator is slighted; first by the teachers and rulers that sets themselves down in the spirit's room, to teach and rule, where he himself is only king. Secondly by the other, that refuses the spirit, to be taught and governed by fellow creatures; and this was called Israel's sin in casting off the Lord and choosing Saul, one like themselves, to be their king, whenas they had had the same spirit of reason and government in themselves as he had, if they were but subject. And Israel's rejecting of outward teachers and rulers to embrace the Lord, and to be all taught and ruled by that righteous King that Jeremiah prophesied shall rule in the new heavens and new earth in the latter days, will be their restoration from bondage, Jer. 23.5,6.

But for the present state of the old world that is running

up like parchment in the fire, and wearing away, we see proud imaginary flesh, which is the wise serpent, rises up in flesh and gets dominion in some to rule over others, and so forces one part of the creation, man, to be a slave to another; and thereby the spirit is killed in both. The one looks upon himself as a teacher and ruler, and so is lifted up in pride over his fellow-creatures. The other looks upon himself as imperfect, and so is dejected in his spirit, and looks upon his fellow-creature of his own image as a lord above him.

And thus Esau, the man of flesh which is covetousness and pride, hath killed Jacob, the spirit of meekness and righteous government in the light of reason, and rules over him: and so the earth, that was made a common treasury for all to live comfortably upon, is become through man's unrighteous actions one over another to be a place wherein one torments another.

Now the great creator, who is the spirit reason, suffered himself thus to be rejected and trodden underfoot by the covetous proud flesh for a certain time limited; therefore, saith he, *The seed out of whom the creation did proceed, which is myself, shall bruise this serpent's head and restore my creation again from this curse and bondage; and when I the King of righteousness reigns in every man, I will be the blessing of the earth, and the joy of all nations.*

And since the coming in of the stoppage, or the A-dam, the earth hath been enclosed and given to the elder brother Esau, or man of flesh, and hath been bought and sold from one to another; and Jacob, or the younger brother, that is to succeed or come forth next, who is the universal spreading power of righteousness that gives liberty to the whole creation, is made a servant.

And this elder son, or man of bondage, hath held the earth in bondage to himself not by a meek law of righteousness, but by subtle selfish counsels and by open and violent force; for wherefore is it that there is such wars and rumours of wars in the nations of the earth? And wherefore are men so mad to destroy one another? but only to uphold civil property of honour, dominion and riches one over another, which is the curse the creation groans under, waiting for deliverance.

But when once the earth becomes a common treasury again, as it must, for all the prophecies of Scriptures and reason are circled here in this community, and mankind must have the law of righteousness once more writ in his heart, and all must be made of one heart and one mind:

Then this enmity in all lands will cease, for none shall dare to seek a dominion over others, neither shall any dare to kill another, nor desire more of the earth than another; for he that will rule over, imprison, oppress and kill his fellow creatures, under what pretence so ever, is a destroyer of the creation, and an actor of the curse, and walks contrary to the rule of righteousness: *Do as you would have others do to you; and love your enemies, not in words but in actions.*

Therefore, you powers of the earth, or Lord Esau the elder brother, because you have appeared to rule the creation, first take notice that the power that sets you to work is selfish covetousness and an aspiring pride, to live in glory and ease over Jacob, the meek spirit; that is, the seed that lies hid in and among the poor common people or younger brother, out of whom the blessing of deliverance is to rise and spring up to all nations.

And reason, the living King of righteousness, doth only look on and lets thee alone, that whereas thou counts thyself an angel of light, thou shalt appear in the light of the sun to be a devil, A-dam, and the curse that the creation groans under; and the time is now come for thy downfall and Jacob must rise, who is the universal spirit of love and righteousness that fills and will fill all the earth.

Thou teaching and ruling power of flesh, thou hast had three periods of time to vaunt thyself over thy brother. The first was from the time of thy coming in, called A-dam or a stoppage, till Moses came; and there thou, that wast a self-lover in Cain, killed thy brother Abel, a plain-hearted man that loved righteousness. And thou by thy wisdom and beastly government made the whole earth to stink till Noah came, which was a time of the world like the coming in of the watery seed into the womb, towards the bringing forth of the man-child.

And from Noah till Moses came thou still hast ruled in vaunting, pride and cruel oppression: Ishmael against Isaac, Esau against Jacob; for thou hast still been the man of flesh that hath ever persecuted the man of righteousness, the spirit reason.

And secondly, from Moses till the Son of Man came, which was a time of the world that the man-child could not speak like a man, but lisping, making signs to shew his meaning; as we see many creatures that cannot speak do. For Moses's law was a language lapped up in types, sacrifices, forms and customs, which was a weak time. And in this time likewise, O thou teaching and ruling power, thou wast an oppressor; for look into Scriptures and see if Aaron and the priests were not the first that deceived the people. And the rulers, as kings and governors, were continually the ocean-head out of whose power burdens, oppressions and poverty did flow out upon the earth: and these two powers still hath been the curse, that hath led the earth (mankind) into confusion and death by their imaginary and selfish teaching and ruling, and it could be no otherwise; for while man looks upon himself as an imperfect creation, and seeks and runs abroad for a teacher and a ruler, he is all this time a stranger to the spirit that is within himself.

But though the earth hath been generally thus in darkness since the A-dam rise up, and hath owned a light and a law without them to walk by, yet some have been found as watchmen in this night-time of the world, that have been taught by the spirit within them and not by any flesh without them, as Abraham, Isaac, Jacob and the prophets: and these and such as these have still been the butt at whom the powers of the earth in all ages of the world, by their selfish laws, have shot their fury.

And then thirdly, from the time of the Son of Man, which

was a time that the man-child began to speak like a child growing upward to manhood, till now that the spirit is rising up in strength, O thou teaching and ruling power of the earthy man, thou hast been an oppressor, by imprisonment, impoverishing and martyrdom; and all thy power and wit hath been to make laws and execute them against such as stand for universal liberty, which is the rising up of Jacob; as by those ancient enslaving laws not yet blotted out, but held up as weapons against the man-child.

O thou powers of England, though thou hast promised to make this people a free people, yet thou hast so handled the matter through thy self-seeking humour that thou hast wrapped us up more in bondage, and oppression lies heavier upon us; not only bringing thy fellow-creatures, the commoners, to a morsel of bread, but by confounding all sorts of people by thy government of doing and undoing.

First, thou hast made the people to take a covenant and oaths to endeavour a reformation and to bring in liberty every man in his place; and yet while a man is in pursuing of that covenant, he is imprisoned and oppressed by thy officers, courts and justices, so called.

Thou hast made ordinances to cast down oppressing, popish, episcopal, self-willed and prerogative laws; yet we see that self-will and prerogative power is the great standing law that rules all in action, and others in words.

Thou hast made many promises and protestations to make the land a free nation: and yet at this very day the same people, to whom thou hast made such protestations of liberty, are oppressed by thy courts, sizes,* sessions, by thy justices and clerks of the peace (so called), bailiffs, committees, are imprisoned and forced to spend that bread that should save their lives from famine.

And all this because they stand to maintain an universal liberty and freedom, which not only is our birthright which our maker gave us, but which thou hast promised to restore unto us, from under the former oppressing powers that are

* Assizes.

gone before, and which likewise we have bought with our money, in taxes, free-quarter and blood shed; all which sums thou hast received at our hands, and yet thou hast not given us our bargain.

O thou A-dam, thou Esau, thou Cain, thou hypocritical man of flesh, when wilt thou cease to kill thy younger brother? Surely thou must not do this great work of advancing the creation out of bondage; for thou art lost extremely, and drowned in the sea of covetousness, pride and hardness of heart. *The blessing shall rise out of the dust which thou treadest under foot, even the poor despised people, and they shall hold up salvation to this land and to all lands, and thou shalt be ashamed.*

Our bodies as yet are in thy hand, our spirit waits in quiet and peace upon our Father for deliverance; and if he give our blood into thy hand for thee to spill, know this, that he is our almighty captain. And if some of you will not dare to shed your blood * to maintain tyranny and oppression upon the creation, know this, that our blood and life shall not be unwilling to be delivered up in meekness to maintain universal liberty, that so the curse on our part may be taken off the creation.

And we shall not do this by force of arms, we abhor it, for that is the work of the Midianites, to kill one another; but by obeying the Lord of Hosts, who hath revealed himself in us and to us, by labouring the earth in righteousness together, to eat our bread with the sweat of our brows, neither giving hire nor taking hire but working together and eating together as one man or as one house of Israel restored from bondage. And so by the power of reason, the law of righteousness in us, we endeavour to lift up the creation from that bondage of civil property which it groans under.

We are made to hold forth this declaration to you that are the great council, and to you the great Army of the land of England, that you may know what we would have and what you are bound to give us by your covenants and pro-

* Read 'not spare to shed our blood'?

83

mises; and that you may join with us in this work and so
find peace. Or else, if you do oppose us, we have peace in our
work and in declaring this report: and you shall be left
without excuse.

The work we are going about is this, to dig up George
Hill and the waste ground thereabouts and to sow corn,
and to eat our bread together by the sweat of our brows.

And the first reason is this, that we may work in righteousness and lay the foundation of making the earth a common
treasury for all, both rich and poor, that everyone that is
born in the land may be fed by the earth his mother that
brought him forth, according to the reason that rules in the
creation. Not enclosing any part into any particular hand,
but all as one man working together and feeding together
as sons of one father, members of one family; not one lording over another, but all looking upon each other as equals
in the creation; so that our maker may be glorified in the
work of his own hands, and that everyone may see he is
no respecter of persons but equally loves his whole creation
and hates nothing but the serpent, which is covetousness,
branching forth into selfish imagination, pride, envy, hypocrisy, uncleanness; all seeking the ease and honour of flesh
and fighting against the spirit reason that made the creation;
for that is the corruption, the curse, the devil, the father of
lies, death and bondage, that serpent and dragon that the
creation is to be delivered from.

And we are moved hereunto for that reason and others
which hath been shewed us, both by vision, voice and
revelation.

For it is shewed us that so long as we or any other doth
own the earth to be the peculiar interest of lords and landlords, and not common to others as well as them, we own
the curse, and holds the creation under bondage; and so
long as we or any other doth own landlords and tenants,
for one to call the land his or another to hire it of him, or
for one to give hire and for another to work for hire; this is
to dishonour the work of creation; as if the righteous creator

should have respect to persons, and therefore made the earth for some and not for all. And so long as we or any other maintain this civil property, we consent still to hold the creation down under that bondage it groans under, and so we should hinder the work of restoration and sin against light that is given into us, and so through the fear of the flesh (man) lose our peace.

And that this civil property is the curse is manifest thus: those that buy and sell land, and are landlords, have got it either by oppression or murder or theft; and all landlords lives in the breach of the seventh and eighth commandments, *Thou shalt not steal nor kill*.

First by their oppression: they have by their subtle imaginary and covetous wit got the plain-hearted poor or younger brethren to work for them for small wages, and by their work have got a great increase; for the poor by their labour lifts up tyrants to rule over them; or else by their covetous wit they have outreached the plain-hearted in buying and selling, and thereby enriched themselves but impoverished others: or else by their subtle wit, having been a lifter up into places of trust, have enforced people to pay money for a public use, but have divided much of it into their private purses; and so have got it by oppression.

Then secondly for murder: they have by subtle wit and power pretended to preserve a people in safety by the power of the sword; and what by large pay, much free-quarter and other booties which they call their own, they get much monies, and with this they buy land and become landlords; and if once landlords, then they rise to be justices, rulers and state governors, as experience shews. But all this is but a bloody and subtle thievery, countenanced by a law that covetousness made; and is a breach of the seventh commandment, *Thou shalt not kill*.

And likewise thirdly a breach of the eighth commandment, *Thou shalt not steal*; but these landlords have thus stolen the earth from their fellow-creatures, that have an equal share with them by the law of reason and creation, as well as they.

And such as these rise up to be rich in the objects of the earth. Then by their plausible words of flattery to the plain-hearted people whom they deceive, and that lies under confusion and blindness, they are lifted up to be teachers, rulers and lawmakers over them that lifted them up; as if the earth were made peculiarly for them, and not for others' weal. If you cast your eye a little backward you shall see that this outward teaching and ruling power is the Babylonish yoke laid upon Israel of old, under Nebuchadnezzar; and so successively from that time the conquering enemy have still laid these yokes upon Israel to keep Jacob down. And the last enslaving conquest which the enemy got over Israel was the Norman over England; and from that time kings, lords, judges, justices, bailiffs and the violent bitter people that are freeholders, are and have been successively. The Norman bastard William himself, his colonels, captains, inferior officers and common soldiers, who still are from that time to this day in pursuit of that victory, imprisoning, robbing and killing the poor enslaved English Israelites.

And this appears clear. For when any trustee or state officer is to be chosen the freeholders or landlords must be the choosers, who are the Norman common soldiers, spread abroad in the land. And who must be chosen but some very rich man, who is the successor of the Norman colonels or high officers? And to what end have they been thus chosen but to establish that Norman power the more forcibly over the enslaved English, and to beat them down again whenas they gather heart to seek for liberty?

For what are all those binding and restraining laws that have been made from one age to another since that conquest, and are still upheld by fury over the people? I say, what are they but the cords, bonds, manacles and yokes that the enslaved English, like Newgate prisoners, wears upon their hands and legs as they walk the streets? by which those Norman oppressors and these their successors from age to age have enslaved the poor people by, killed their younger brother, and would not suffer Jacob to arise.

O what mighty delusion do you, who are the powers of England, live in! That while you pretend to throw down that Norman yoke and Babylonish power, and have promised to make the groaning people of England a free people, yet you still lift up that Norman yoke and slavish tyranny, and holds the people as much in bondage as the bastard Conqueror himself and his council of war.

Take notice that England is not a free people till the poor that have no land have a free allowance to dig and labour the commons, and so live as comfortably as the landlords that live in their enclosures. For the people have not laid out their monies and shed their blood that their landlords, the Norman power, should still have its liberty and freedom to rule in tyranny in his lords, landlords, judges, justices, bailiffs and state servants; but that the oppressed might be set free, prison doors opened, and the poor people's hearts comforted by an universal consent of making the earth a common treasury, that they may live together as one house of Israel, united in brotherly love into one spirit; and having a comfortable livelihood in the community of one earth, their mother.

If you look through the earth, you shall see that the landlords, teachers and rulers are oppressors, murderers and thieves in this manner. But it was not thus from the beginning. And this is one reason of our digging and labouring the earth one with another, that we might work in righteousness and lift up the creation from bondage. For so long as we own landlords in this corrupt settlement, we cannot work in righteousness; for we should still lift up the curse and tread down the creation, dishonour the spirit of universal liberty, and hinder the work of restoration.

Secondly, in that we begin to dig upon George Hill to eat our bread together by righteous labour and sweat of our brows, it was shewed us by vision in dreams and out of dreams that that should be the place we should begin

upon. And though that earth in view of flesh be very barren,
yet we should trust the spirit for a blessing. And that not
only this common or heath should be taken in and manured
by the people, but all the commons and waste ground in
England and in the whole world shall be taken in by the
people in righteousness, not owning any property; but taking
the earth to be a common treasury, as it was first made for
all.

Thirdly, it is shewed us that all the prophecies, visions
and revelations of scriptures, of prophets and apostles, concerning the calling of the Jews, the restoration of Israel, and
making of that people the inheritors of the whole earth,
doth all seat themselves in this work of making the earth a
common treasury; as you may read, Ezek. 24.26, 27, etc.
Jer. 33.7 to 12. Isaiah 49.17, 18, etc. Zech. 8. from 4 to 12
Dan. 2.44, 45. Dan. 7.27. Hos. 14.5, 6, 7. Joel 2.26, 27. Amos 9.
from 3 to the end, Obad. 17. 18, 21. Mic. 5. from 7 to the end.
Hab. 2.6, 7, 8, 13, 14. Gen. 18.18. Rom. 11.15. Zeph. 3. etc.
Zech. 14.9.

And when the Son of Man was gone from the apostles, his
spirit descended upon the apostles and brethren, as they were
waiting at Jerusalem; and the rich men sold their possessions
and gave part to the poor; and no man said that ought that
he possessed was his own, for they had all things common,
Acts 4.32.

Now this community was supressed by covetous proud
flesh, which was the powers that ruled the world; and the
righteous Father suffered himself thus to be suppressed for
a time, times and dividing of time,* or for 42 months, or for
three days and half, which are all but one and the same term
of time. And the world is now come to the half day; and the
spirit of Christ, which is the spirit of universal community
and freedom, is risen, and is rising, and will rise higher and
higher, till those pure waters of Shiloah, the well springs of
life and liberty to the whole creation, do overrun A-dam and
drown those banks of bondage, curse and slavery.

* See Daniel, 7.25.

Fourthly, this work to make the earth a common treasury was shewed us by voice in trance and out of trance, which words were these,

> 'Work together, eat bread together, declare this all abroad.'

Which voice was heard three times. And in obedience to the spirit we have declared this by word of mouth, as occasion was offered. Secondly, we have declared it by writing, which others may read. Thirdly, we have now begun to declare it by action, in digging up the common land and casting in seed, that we may eat our bread together in righteousness. And every one that comes to work shall eat the fruit of their own labours, one having as much freedom in the fruit of the earth as another. Another voice that was heard was this,

> 'Israel shall neither take hire nor give hire.'

And if so, then certainly none shall say, 'This is my land, work for me, and I'll give you wages.' For the earth is the Lord's, that is man's, who is lord of the creation, in every branch of mankind; for as divers members of our human bodies make but one body perfect; so every particular man is but a member or branch of mankind; and mankind living in the light and obedience to reason, the King of righteousness, is thereby made a fit and complete lord of the creation. And the whole earth is this Lord's man,* subject to the spirit: and not the inheritance of covetous proud flesh, that is selfish and enmity to the spirit.

And if the earth be not peculiar to any one branch or branches of mankind, but the inheritance of all: then is it free and common for all, to work together and eat together.

And truly, you councillors and powers of the earth, know this, that wheresoever there is a people thus united by common community of livelihood into oneness, it will become the strongest land in the world, for then they will be as one man to defend their inheritance; and salvation (which is

* Read 'Lord man's'?

liberty and peace) is the walls and bulwarks of that land or city.

Whereas on the other side, pleading for property and single interest divides the people of a land and the whole world into parties, and is the cause of all wars and bloodshed and contention everywhere.

Another voice that was heard in a trance was this,

> 'Whosoever labours the earth for any person or persons that are lifted up to rule over others, and doth not look upon themselves as equal to others in the creation: the hand of the Lord shall be upon that labourer: I the Lord have spoke it, and I will do it.'

This declares likewise to all labourers or such as are called poor people, that they shall not dare to work for hire for any landlord or for any that is lifted up above others; for by their labours they have lifted up tyrants and tyranny; and by denying to labour for hire they shall pull them down again. He that works for another, either for wages or to pay him rent, works unrighteously and still lifts up the curse; but they that are resolved to work and eat together, making the earth a common treasury, doth join hands with Christ to lift up the creation from bondage, and restores all things from the curse.

Fifthly, that which does encourage us to go on in this work is this: we find the streaming out of love in our hearts towards all, to enemies as well as friends; we would have none live in beggary, poverty or sorrow, but that everyone might enjoy the benefit of his creation: we have peace in our hearts and quiet rejoicing in our work, and filled with sweet content, though we have but a dish of roots and bread for our food.

And we are assured that in the strength of this spirit that hath manifested himself to us, we shall not be startled, neither at prison nor death while we are about his work; and we have been made to sit down and count what it may cost us in undertaking such a work, and we know the full sum and are resolved to give all that we have to buy this pearl which we see in the field.

For by this work we are assured, and reason makes it appear to others, that bondage shall be removed, tears wiped away, and all poor people by their righteous labours shall be relieved and freed from poverty and straits. For in this work of restoration there will be no beggar in Israel. For surely, if there was no beggar in literal Israel, there shall be no beggar in spiritual Israel the anti-type, much more.

Sixthly, we have another encouragement that this work shall prosper, because we see it to be the fulness of time. For whereas the Son of Man, the Lamb, came in the fulness of time, that is, when the powers of the world made the earth stink everywhere by oppressing others under pretence of worshipping the spirit rightly, by the types and sacrifices of Moses's law; the priests were grown so abominably covetous and proud that they made the people to loathe the sacrifices and to groan under the burden of their oppressing pride.

Even so now in this age of the world that the spirit is upon his resurrection, it is likewise the fulness of time in a higher measure. For whereas the people generally in former times did rest upon the very observation of the sacrifices and types, but persecuted the very name of the spirit: even so now professors * do rest upon the bare observation of forms and customs, and pretend to the spirit, and yet persecutes, grudges and hates the power of the spirit; and as it was then, so it is now: all places stink with the abomination of self-seeking teachers and rulers. For do not I see that everyone preacheth for money, counsels for money and fights for money, to maintain particular interests? And none of these three, that pretend to give liberty to the creation, do give liberty to the creation; neither can they, for they are enemies to universal liberty; so that the earth stinks with their hypocrisy, covetousness, envy, sottish ignorance and pride.

The common people are filled with good words from pul-

* i.e. those who claim to be religious.

pits and council tables, but no good deeds; for they wait and wait for good and for deliverances, but none comes. While they wait for liberty, behold greater bondage comes instead of it; and burdens, oppressions, task-masters, from sessions, lawyers, bailiffs of hundreds, committees, impropriators, clerks of peace and courts of justice (so called) does whip the people by old popish weather-beaten laws, that were excommunicate long ago by covenants, oaths and ordinances; but as yet are not cast out, but rather taken in again, to be standing pricks in our eyes and thorns in our side; beside freequartering, plundering by some rude soldiers, and the abounding of taxes; which if they were equally divided among the soldiery, and not too much bagged up in the hands of particular officers and trustees, there would be less complaining: besides the horrible cheating that is in buying and selling, and the cruel oppression of landlords and lords of manors and quarter sessions. Many that have been good housekeepers (as we say) cannot live, but are forced to turn soldiers and so to fight to uphold the curse, or else live in great straits and beggary. O you A-dams of the earth, you have rich clothing, full bellies, have your honours and ease, and you puff at this; but know, thou stout-hearted Pharaoh, that the day of judgment is begun, and it will reach to thee ere long. Jacob hath been very low, but he is rising, and will rise, do the worst thou canst; and the poor people whom thou oppresses shall be the saviours of the land. For the blessing is rising up in them, and thou shalt be ashamed.

And thus, you powers of England and of the whole world, we have declared our reasons why we have begun to dig upon George Hill in Surrey. One thing I must tell you more, in the close, which I received *in voce* likewise at another time; and when I received it, my eye was set towards you. The words were these:

Let Israel go free.

Surely, as Israel lay 430 years under Pharaoh's bondage, before Moses was sent to fetch them out: even so Israel (the elect spirit spread in sons and daughters) hath lain three times so long already, which is the anti-type, under your bondage and cruel task-masters. But now the time of deliverance is come, and thou proud Esau and stout-hearted covetousness, thou must come down and be lord of the creation no longer. For now the King of righteousness is rising to rule in and over the earth.

Therefore, if thou wilt find mercy, *Let Israel go free*; break in pieces quickly the bond of particular property, disown this oppressing murder, oppression and thievery of buying and selling of land, owning of landlords and paying of rents, and give thy free consent to make the earth a common treasury, without grumbling: that the younger brethren may live comfortably upon earth, as well as the elder: that all may enjoy the benefit of their creation.

And hereby thou wilt *Honour thy father and thy mother*: thy father, which is the spirit of community, that made all and that dwells in all; thy mother, which is the earth, that brought us all forth: that as a true mother loves all her children. Therefore do not thou hinder the mother earth from giving all her children suck, by thy enclosing it into particular hands, and holding up that cursed bondage of enclosure by thy power.

And then thou wilt repent of thy theft, in maintaining the breach of the eighth commandment, by stealing the land as I say from thy fellow-creatures, or younger brothers: which thou and all thy landlords have and do live in the breach of that commandment.

Then thou wilt *own no other God*, or ruling power, but one, which is the King of righteousness, ruling and dwelling in every one and in the whole; whereas now thou hast many gods: for covetousness is thy god, pride and an envious murdering humour (to kill one by prison or gallows that crosses thee, though their cause be pure, sound and good reason) is thy god, self-love and slavish fear (lest others serve thee as thou hast served them) is thy god, hypocrisy, fleshly imagination, that keeps no promise, covenant nor protestation, is thy god: love of money, honour and ease is thy god. And all these, and the like ruling powers, makes thee blind and hard-hearted, that thou does not nor cannot lay to heart the affliction of others, though they die for want of bread in that rich city, undone under your eyes.

Therefore once more, *Let Israel go free*, that the poor may labour the waste land and suck the breasts of their mother earth, that they starve not. And in so doing thou wilt *keep the Sabbath day*, which is a day of rest, sweetly enjoying the peace of the spirit of righteousness; and find peace, by living among a people that live in peace. This will be a day of rest which thou never knew yet.

But I do not entreat thee, for thou art not to be entreated, but in the name of the Lord that hath drawn me forth to speak to thee, I, yea I say, I command thee to *let Israel go free* and quietly to *gather together into the place where I shall appoint; and hold them no longer in bondage.*

And thou A-dam that holds the earth in slavery under the curse: if thou wilt not *let Israel go free* (for thou being the antitype will be more stout and lusty than the Egyptian Pharaoh of old, who was thy type), then know that whereas I brought ten plagues upon him, I will multiply my plagues upon thee, till I make thee weary and miserably ashamed. *And I will bring out my people with a strong hand and stretched-out arm.*

Thus we have discharged our souls in declaring the cause of our digging upon George Hill in Surrey, that the great council and army of the land may take notice of it, that there is no intent of tumult or fighting, but only to get bread to eat with the sweat of our brows; working together in righteousness and eating the blessings of the earth in peace.

And if any of you that are the great ones of the earth, that have been bred tenderly and cannot work, do bring in your stock into this common treasury as an offering to the work of righteousness, we will work for you, and you shall receive as we receive. But if you will not, but Pharaoh-like cry, *Who is the Lord that we should obey him?* and endeavour to oppose, then know that he that delivered Israel from Pharaoh of old is the same power still, in whom we trust and whom we serve; for this conquest over thee shall be got, *not by sword or weapon, but by my Spirit, saith the Lord of Hosts.*

William Everard,	*Gerrard Winstanley,*
John Palmer,	*Richard Goodgroome,*
John South,	*Thomas Starre,*
John Courton,	*William Hoggrill,*
William Taylor,	*Robert Sawyer,*
Christopher Clifford,	*Thomas Eder,*
John Barker.	*Henry Bickerstaffe,*
	John Taylor, &c.

FINIS.

A
DECLARATION
FROM THE
Poor oppressed People
OF
ENGLAND

DIRECTED
To all that call themselves,
or are called

Lords of Manors,

through this NATION;
That have begun to cut, or that
through fear and covetousness, do
intend to cut down the Woods
and Trees that grow upon the
Commons and Waste Land.

A
DECLARATION
FROM THE
Poor oppressed People of *England*.

We whose names are subscribed do in the name of all the poor oppressed people in England declare unto you that call yourselves lords of manors and lords of the land that in regard the King of righteousness, our maker, hath enlightened our hearts so far as to see that the earth was not made purposely for you to be lords of it, and we to be your slaves, servants and beggars; but it was made to be a common livelihood to all, without respect of persons: and that your buying and selling of land and the fruits of it, one to another, is the cursed thing, and was brought in by war; which hath and still does establish murder and theft in the hands of some branches of mankind over others, which is the greatest outward burden and unrighteous power that the creation groans under. For the power of enclosing land and owning property was brought into the creation by your ancestors by the sword; which first did murder their fellow-creatures, men, and after plunder or steal away their land, and left this land successively to you, their children. And therefore, though you did not kill or thieve, yet you hold that cursed thing in your hand by the power of the sword; and so you justify the wicked deeds of your fathers; and that sin of your fathers shall be visited upon the head of you and your children, to the third and fourth generation, and longer too, till your bloody and thieving power be rooted out of the land.

And further, in regard the King of righteousness hath made us sensible of our burdens, and the cries and groanings of our hearts are come before him: we take it as a testimony of love from him, that our hearts begin to be freed from slavish fear of men, such as you are; and that we find resolutions in us, grounded upon the inward law of love one towards another, to dig and plough up the commons and waste lands through England; and that our conversation shall be so unblameable that your laws shall not reach to oppress us any longer, unless you by your laws will shed the innocent blood that runs in our veins.

For though you and your ancestors got your property by murder and theft, and you keep it by the same power from us that have an equal right to the land with you by the righteous law of creation, yet we shall have no occasion of quarrelling (as you do) about that disturbing devil, called particular property. For the earth, with all her fruits of corn, cattle and such like, was made to be a common storehouse of livelihood to all mankind, friend and foe, without exception.

And to prevent all your scrupulous objections, know this, that we must neither buy nor sell; money must not any longer (after our work of the earth's community is advanced) be the great god that hedges in some, and hedges out others. For money is but part of the earth: and surely, the righteous creator, who is King, did never ordain that unless some of mankind do bring that mineral (silver and gold) in their hands to others of their own kind, that they should neither be fed, nor be clothed. No surely, for this was the project of tyrant-flesh (which landlords are branches of) to set his image upon money. And they make this unrighteous law, that none should buy or sell, eat or be clothed or have any comfortable livelihood among men, unless they did bring his image stamped upon gold or silver in their hands.

And whereas the Scriptures speak, that the mark of the Beast is 666, the number of a man; and that those that do not bring that mark in their hands or in their foreheads, they should neither buy nor sell, Revel. 13.16: and seeing the numbering letters round about the English money make 666,* which is the number of that kingly power and glory (called a man); and seeing the age of the creation is now come to the image of the Beast or half day, and seeing 666 is his mark, we expect this to be the last tyrannical power that shall reign; and that people shall live freely in the enjoyment of the earth, without bringing the mark of the Beast in their hands or in their promise; and that they shall buy wine and milk without money or without price, as Isaiah speaks.

For after our work of the earthly community is advanced, we must make use of gold and silver, as we do of other metals, but not to buy and sell withal; for buying and selling is the great cheat that robs and steals the earth one from another. It is that which makes some lords, others beggars, some rulers, others to be ruled; and makes great murderers and thieves to be imprisoners and hangers of little ones, or of sincere-hearted men.

And while we are made to labour the earth together, with one consent and willing mind; and while we are made free that every one, friend and foe, shall enjoy the benefit of their creation, that is, to have food and raiment from the earth, their mother; and every one subject to give account of his thoughts, words and actions to none, but to the one only righteous judge and Prince of Peace; the spirit of righteousness that dwells, and that is now rising up to rule in, every creature and in the whole globe. We say, while we are made to hinder no man of his privileges given him in his creation, equal to one as to another; what law then can you make to take hold upon us, but laws of oppression and tyranny, that shall enslave or spill the blood of the innocent? And so yourselves, your judges, lawyers and justices, shall be found to be the greatest transgressors in and over mankind.

But to draw nearer to declare our meaning, what we

* For an attempt to work out the mathematics of this, see S., p. 270.

would have and what we shall endeavour to the uttermost to obtain, as moderate and righteous reason directs us; seeing we are made to see our privileges, given us in our creation, which have hitherto been denied to us and our fathers since the power of the sword began to rule and the secrets of the creation have been locked up under the traditional, parrot-like speaking from the universities and colleges for scholars, and since the power of the murdering and thieving sword, formerly as well as now of late years, hath set up a government and maintains that government; for what are prisons, and putting others to death, but the power of the sword to enforce people to that government which was got by conquest and sword and cannot stand of itself, but by the same murdering power? That government, that is got over people by the sword and kept by the sword, is not set up by the King of righteousness to be his law, but by covetousness, the great god of the world; who hath been permitted to reign for a time, times and dividing of time, and his government draws to the period of the last term of his allotted time. And then the nations shall see the glory of that government that shall rule in righteousness, without either sword or spear;

And seeing further the power of righteousness in our hearts, seeking the livelihood of others as well as ourselves, hath drawn forth our bodies to begin to dig and plough in the commons and waste land for the reasons already declared;

And seeing and finding ourselves poor, wanting food to feed upon while we labour the earth to cast in seed and to wait till the first crop comes up; and wanting ploughs, carts, corn and such materials to plant the commons withal, we are willing to declare our condition to you, and to all that have the treasury of the earth locked up in your bags, chests and barns, and will offer up nothing to this public treasury; but will rather see your fellow-creatures starve for want of bread, that have an equal right to it with yourselves by the law of creation. But this by the way we only declare to you and to all that follow the subtle art of buying and selling the earth with her fruits, merely to get the treasury thereof into their hands, to lock it up from them to whom it belongs; that so such covetous, proud, unrighteous, selfish flesh may be left without excuse in the day of judgment.

And therefore the main thing we aim at, and for which we declare our resolutions to go forth and act, is this: to lay hold upon, and as we stand in need to cut and fell and make the best advantage we can of the woods and trees that grow upon the commons, to be a stock for ourselves and our poor brethren, through the land of England, to plant the commons withal; and to provide us bread to eat, till the fruit of our labours in the earth bring forth increase. And we shall meddle with none of your properties (but what is called commonage) till the spirit in you make you cast up your lands and goods, which were got and still is kept in your hands by murder and theft; and then we shall take it from the spirit that hath conquered you, and not from our swords, which is an abominable and unrighteous power, and a destroyer of the creation. But the Son of Man comes not to destroy, but to save.

And we are moved to send forth this declaration abroad, to give notice to every one whom it concerns, in regard we hear and see that some of you, that have been lords of manors, do cause the trees and woods that grow upon the commons, which you pretend a royalty unto, to be cut down and sold for your own private use; whereby the common land, which your own mouths do say belongs to the poor, is impoverished, and the poor oppressed people robbed of their rights; while you give them cheating words by telling some of our poor oppressed brethren that those of us that have begun to dig and plough up the commons will hinder the poor; and so blind their eyes, that they see not their privilege, while you and the rich freeholders make the most profit of the commons, by your over-stocking of them with sheep and cattle; and the poor that have the name to own the commons have the least share therein. Nay, they are checked by you if they cut wood, heath, turf or furzes in places about the common where you disallow.

Therefore we are resolved to be cheated no longer, nor be held under the slavish fear of you no longer, seeing the earth was made for us as well as for you. And if the common land belongs to us who are the poor oppressed, surely the woods that grow upon the commons belong to us likewise? Therefore we are resolved to try the uttermost in the light of reason to know whether we shall be free men or slaves. If we lie still and let you steal away our birthrights, we perish; and if we petition we perish also, though we have paid taxes, given free-quarter and ventured our lives to preserve the nation's freedom as much as you, and therefore by the law of contract with you, freedom in the land is our portion as well as yours, equal with you. And if we strive for freedom, and your murdering, governing laws destroy us, we can but perish.

Therefore we require and we resolve to take both common land and common woods to be a livelihood for us, and look upon you as equal with us, not above us, knowing very well that England, the land of our nativity, is to be a common treasury of livelihood to all, without respect of persons.

So then, we declare unto you that do intend to cut our common woods and trees, that you shall not do it; unless it be for a stock for us, as aforesaid, and we to know of it by a public declaration abroad, that the poor oppressed that live thereabouts may take it and employ it for their public use. Therefore take notice, we have demanded it in the name of the commons of England and of all the nations of the world, it being the righteous freedom of the creation.

Likewise we declare to you that have begun to cut down our common woods and trees, and to fell and carry away the same for your private use, that you shall forbear and go no farther, hoping that none that are friends to the commonwealth of England will endeavour to buy any of those common trees and woods of any of those lords of manors (so called) who have, by the murdering and cheating law of the sword, stolen the land from younger brothers, who have by the law of creation a standing portion in the land, as well and equal with others. Therefore we hope all woodmongers will disown all such private merchandise, as being a robbing of the poor oppressed, and take notice that they have been told our resolution. But if any of you that are wood-mongers will buy it of the poor, and for their use to stock the commons, from such as may be appointed by us to sell it, you shall have it quietly, without diminution; but if you will slight us in this thing, blame us not if we make stop of the carts you send and convert the woods to our own use, as need requires, it being our own, equal with him that calls himself the lord of the manor, and not his peculiar right, shutting us out, but he shall share with us as a fellow-creature.

For we say our purpose is to take those common woods to sell them, now at first to be a stock for ourselves, and our children after us, to plant and manure the common land withal. For we shall endeavour by our righteous acting not to leave the earth any longer entangled unto our children by self-seeking proprietors; but to leave it a free store-house and common treasury to all, without respect of persons. And this we count is our duty, to endeavour to the uttermost, every man in his place (according to the National Covenant which the Parliament set forth) * a reformation, to preserve the people's liberties, one as well as another: as well those as have paid taxes and given free-quarter, as those that have either borne the sword or taken our monies to dispose of them for public use. For if the reformation must be according to the Word of God, then every one is to have the benefit and freedom of his creation, without respect of persons. We count this our duty, we say, to endeavour to the uttermost, and so shall leave those that rise up to oppose us without excuse in their day of judgment; and our precious blood, we hope, shall not be dear to us, to be willingly laid down at the

* The Solemn League and Covenant was adopted by Parliament on 25 September 1643.

door of a prison, or foot of a gallows, to justify this righteous cause, if those that have taken our money from us, and promised to give us freedom for it, should turn tyrants against us: for we must not fight, but suffer.

And further we intend that not one, two or a few men of us shall sell or exchange the said woods, but it shall be known publicly in print or writing to all, how much every such and such parcel of wood is sold for, and how it is laid out, either in victuals, corn, ploughs or other materials necessary.

And we hope we may not doubt (at least we expect) that they that are called the great council and powers of England, who so often have declared themselves, by promises and covenants, and confirmed them by multitude of fasting days and devout protestations to make England a free people, upon condition they would pay monies and adventure their lives against the successor of the Norman conqueror, under whose oppressing power England was enslaved: and we look upon that freedom promised to be the inheritance of all, without respect of persons. And this cannot be, unless the land of England be freely set at liberty from proprietors, and become a common treasury to all her children, as every portion of the land of Canaan was the common livelihood of such and such a tribe, and of every member in that tribe, without exception, neither hedging in any, nor hedging out.

We say we hope we need not doubt of their sincerity to us herein, and that they will not gainsay our determinate course; howsoever, their actions will prove to the view of all either their sincerity or hypocrisy. We know what we speak is our privilege, and our cause is righteous and if they doubt of it, let them but send a child for us to come before them, and we shall make it manifest four ways.

First, by the National Covenant, which yet stands in force to bind Parliament and people to be faithful and sincere before the Lord God Almighty, wherein every one in his several place hath covenanted to preserve and seek the liberty each of other, without respect of persons.

Secondly, by the late victory over King Charles, we do claim this our privilege, to be quietly given us out of the hands of tyrant-government, as our bargain and contract with them; for the Parliament promised, if we would pay taxes and give free-quarter and adventure our lives against Charles and his party, whom they called the common enemy, they would make us a free people. These three being all done by us, as well as by themselves, we claim this our bargain by the law of contract from them, to be a free people with them, and to have an equal privilege of common livelihood with them, they being chosen by us but for a peculiar work and for an appointed time, from among us, not to be our oppressing lords, but servants to succour us. But these two are our weakest proofs. And yet by them (in the light of reason and equity that dwells in men's hearts) we shall with ease cast down all those former enslaving Norman reiterated laws, in every king's reign since the conquest, which are as thorns in our eyes and pricks in our sides, and which are called the ancient government of England.

Thirdly, we shall prove that we have a free right to the land of England, being born therein as well as elder brothers, and that it is our right equal with them, and they with us, to have a comfortable livelihood in the earth, without owning any of our own kind to be either lords or landlords over us. And this we shall prove by plain text of Scripture, without exposition upon them, which the scholars and great ones generally say is their rule to walk by.

Fourthly, we shall prove it by the righteous law of our creation, that mankind in all his branches is the lord of the earth and ought not to be in subjection to any of his own kind without him, but to live in the light of the law of righteousness and peace established in his heart.

And thus in love we have declared the purpose of our hearts plainly, without flattery, expecting love and the same sincerity from you, without grumbling or quarrelling, being creatures of your own image and mould, intending no other matter herein but to observe the law of righteous action, endeavouring to shut out of the creation the cursed thing, called particular property, which is the cause of all wars, bloodshed, theft and enslaving laws, that hold the people under misery.

Signed for and in the behalf of all the poor oppressed people of England and the whole world.

Gerrard Winstanley	*James Manley*	*John Ash*
John Coulton	*Thomas Barnard*	*Ralph Ayer*
John Palmer	*John South*	*John Pra*
Thomas Star	*Robert Sayer*	*John Wilkinson*
Samuel Webb	*Christopher Clifford*	*Anthony Spire*
John Hayman	*John Beechee*	*Thomas East*
Thomas Edcer	*William Coomes*	*Allen Brown*
William Hogrill	*Christopher Boncher*	*Edward Parret*
Daniel Weeden	*Richard Taylor*	*Richard Gray*
Richard Wheeler	*Uriah Worthington*	*John Mordy*
Nathaniel Yates	*Nathaniel Holcombe*	*John Bachilor*
William Clifford	*Giles Childe,* senior	*William Childe*
John Harrison	*John Webb*	*William Hatham*
Thomas Hayden	*Thomas Yarwel*	*Edward Wicher*
James Hall	*William Bonnington*	*William Tench*

FINIS.

AN
APPEAL

To the House of

COMMONS,

Desiring their ANSWER:

Whether the Common-people
shall have the quiet enjoyment of
the *Commons* and *Waste Land*;

Or whether they shall be under
the will of *Lords* of *Manors* still.

Occasioned by an Arrest, made by
Thomas Lord Wenman, Ralph Verney
Knight, and Richard Winwood Esq;
upon the Author hereof, for a Trespass,
in Digging upon the Common-Land at
George Hill in Surrey.

By Gerrard Winstanley, John Barker,
and Thomas Star, In the Name of all
the poor oppressed in the Land of
England.

Unrighteous Oppression kindles a flame;
but Love, Righteousness and
Tenderness of heart quenches it again.

AN
Appeal to the House of Commons,

Desiring their ANSWER;

Whether the Common-People shall have the quiet enjoyment of the

Commons and *Waste Lands*:

Or whether they shall be under the will of

Lords of *Manors* still.

SIRS,

The cause of this our presentment before you is an appeal to you, desiring you to demonstrate to us and the whole land the equity or not equity of our cause; and that you would either cast us by just reason under the feet of those we call task-masters or lords of manors, or else to deliver us out of their tyrannical hands: in whose hands, by way of arrest, we are for the present, for a trespass to them (as they say) in digging upon the common land. The settling whereof according to equity and reason will quiet the minds of the oppressed people; it will be a keeping of our National Covenant; it will be peace to yourselves, and make England the most flourishing and strongest land in the world, and the first of nations that shall begin to give up their crown and sceptre, their dominion and government, into the hands of Jesus Christ.

The cause is this: we, amongst others of the common people, that have been ever friends to the Parliament, as we are assured our enemies will witness to it, have ploughed and digged upon George Hill in Surrey, to sow corn for the succour of man, offering no offence to any, but do carry ourselves in love and peace towards all, having no intent to meddle with any man's enclosures or property, till it be freely given to us by themselves, but only to improve the commons and waste lands to our best advantage, for the relief of ourselves and others, being moved thereunto by the reason hereafter following, not expecting any to be much offended, in regard the cause is so just and upright.

Yet notwithstanding, there be three men (called by the people lords of manors) viz. Thomas Lord Wenman, Ralph Verney Knight, and Richard Winwood Esquire,* have arrested us for a trespass in digging upon the commons, and upon the arrest we made our appearance in Kingston court, where we understood we were arrested for meddling with other men's rights; and secondly, they were encouraged to arrest us upon your act of Parliament † (as they tell us) to maintain the old laws. We desired to plead our own cause, the court denied us, and to fee a lawyer we cannot, for divers reasons, as we may shew hereafter.

Now Sirs, our case is this, for we appeal to you, for you are the only men that we are to deal withal in this business: whether the common people, after all their taxes, free-quarter and loss of blood to recover England from under the Norman yoke, shall have the freedom to improve the commons and waste lands free to themselves, as freely their own as the enclosures are the property of the elder brothers? Or whether the lords of manors shall have them, according to their old custom from the kings' will and grant, and so remain task-masters still over us, which was the people's slavery under conquest.

We have made our appeal to you, to settle this matter in

* It is not clear why these three brought the action since the manor of St George's Hill belonged to Francis Drake. See S., pp. 319–20 and pp. 123, 130 below.
† Of 17 February 1649.

the equity and reason of it, and to pass the sentence of freedom to us, you being the men with whom we have to do in this business, in whose hands there is power to settle it; for no court can end this controversy but your court of Parliament, as the case of this nation now stands.

Therefore we entreat you to read over this following declaration, wherein we have declared our reason that the commons and waste lands is the common people's, and that in equity you ought to let them quietly enjoy them, as the elder brothers quietly enjoy their enclosures. The profit of this business to the nation, the quieting of the hearts of the poor oppressed that are groaning under burdens and straits, and the peace of your own hearts, to see the peace of the nation settled in his * platform, will much countervail the spending of so much time.

Sirs, you know that the land of England is the land of our nativity, both yours and ours, and all of us by the righteous law of our creation ought to have food and raiment freely by our righteous labouring of the earth, without working for hire or paying rent one to another.

But since the fall of man from that righteous law, the nations of the world have rise up in variance one against another, and fought against, murdered and stolen the land of their nativity one from another, and by their power of their conquests have still set up some to rule in tyranny over others, and thereby have enslaved the conquered, which is a burden the whole creation hath and yet does groan under. The teeth of all nations hath been set on edge by this sour grape, the covetous murdering sword.

England, you know, hath been conquered and enslaved divers times, and the best laws that England hath (viz. Magna Charta) were got by our forefathers' importunate petitioning unto the kings, that still were their task-masters; and yet these best laws are yokes and manacles, tying one sort of people to be slaves to another. Clergy and gentry have got their freedom, but the common people still are

* this?

and have been left servants to work for them, like the Israelites under the Egyptian task-masters.

The last enslaving yoke that England groaned under (and yet is not freed from) was the Norman, as you know; and since William the Conqueror came in, about six hundred years ago, all the kings that still succeeded did confirm the old laws, or else make new ones, to uphold that Norman conquest over us; and the most favouring laws that we have doth still bind the hands of the enslaved English from enjoying the freedom of their creation.

You of the gentry, as well as we of the comonalty, all groaned under the burden of the bad government and burdening laws under the late King Charles, who was the last successor of William the Conqueror: you and we cried for a Parliament, and a Parliament was called, and wars, you know, presently begun, between the King, that represented William the Conqueror, and the body of the English people that were enslaved.

We looked upon you to be our chief council, to agitate business for us, though you were summoned by the King's writ, and chosen by the freeholders, that are the successors of William the Conqueror's soldiers. You saw the dangers so great, that without a war England was like to be more enslaved, therefore you called upon us to assist you with plate, taxes, free-quarter and our persons; and you promised us, in the name of the Almighty, to make us a free people; thereupon you and we took the National Covenant with joint consent, to endeavour the freedom, peace and safety of the people of England.

And you and we joined purse and person together in this common cause; and William the Conqueror's successor, which was Charles, was cast out; and thereby we have recovered ourselves from under that Norman yoke; and now unless you and we be merely besotted with covetousness, pride and slavish fear of men, it is and will be our wisdom to cast out all those enslaving laws, which was the tyrannical power that the kings pressed us down by. O shut not your eyes against the light, darken not knowledge by dispute about particular men's privileges when universal freedom is brought to be tried before you, dispute no further when truth appears, but be silent and practise it.

Stop not your ears against the secret mourning of the oppressed under these expressions, lest the Lord see it and be offended and shut his ears against your cries, and work a deliverance for his waiting people some other way than by you.

The main thing that you should look upon is the land, which calls upon her children to be freed from the entanglement of the Norman task-masters; for one third part lies waste and barren, and her children starve for want, in regard the lords of manors will not suffer the poor to manure it.

When William the Conqueror came in, he took the land from the English, both the enclosures from the gentry, and the commons and waste lands from the common people, and gave our land to his Norman soldiers.

Therefore seeing we have with joint consent of purse and person conquered his successor, Charles, and the power now is in your hand, the nation's representative: O let the first thing you do be this, to set the land free. Let the gentry have their enclosures free from all Norman enslaving entanglements whatsoever, and let the common people have their commons and waste lands set free to them from all Norman enslaving lords of manors, that so both elder and younger brother, as we spring successively one from another, may live free and quiet one by and with another, not burdening one another in this land of our nativity.

And this thing you are bound to see done, or at least to endeavour it, before another representative succeed you; otherwise you cannot discharge your trust to God and man, for these reasons:

First, if you free not the land from entaglement of all Norman yokes, or rather bondages, so that the people, one as well as another, may enjoy the benefit of their creation: that is, to have the land free to work upon, that they may eat their bread in righteousness; that is to say, let the freeholders have their freedom to work quietly in their enclosures, and let the common people have their commons and waste lands quiet to themselves. If you establish not this, seeing power now is in your hand, you will be the first that break covenant with Almighty God.

For you swore in your National Covenant to endeavour a reformation according to the Word of God, which reformation is to restore us to that primitive freedom in the earth, in which the earth was first made and given to the sons of men, and that is to be a common treasury of livelihood to all, without working for hire or paying rent to any, for this is the reformation according to the Word of God before the Fall of man, in which there is no respect of persons.

And seeing in particular you swore to endeavour the freedom, peace and safety of this people of England, shutting out no sort from freedom; therefore you cannot say that the gentry and clergy were only comprehended, but without exception all sorts of people in the land are to have freedom, seeing all sorts have assisted you in person and purse, and the common people more especially, seeing their estates were weakest, and their misery in the wars the greatest.

Therefore let the gentry and freeholders have their enclosures freed from all entanglements of fines, heriots and other burdens, and let the common people have their commons and waste lands freed from entanglements of the Norman lords of manors, and pluck up all Norman tyranny by the roots, and so keep your covenant, that you and all sorts of people may live in peace one among another.

Secondly, if this freedom be not granted quietly, you will pull the blood and cries of the poor oppressed upon your heads: first, because you have taken their money in taxes and free-quarter from them, whereby they are made worse able to live than before the wars. Secondly, because in your low estate, when you called upon us to come and help a bleeding dying nation, and we did come with purse and person and underwent great hardship, and you still promised us freedom in the end, if in case you and we prevailed over the Norman successor; and we have prevailed.

And if now, while the price is in your hand, you should still leave us under the Norman lords of manors, and will not quietly suffer us to plant ourselves upon the commons and waste land, which is ours by the law of our creation, and which is ours now by conquest from under our oppressor, for which we have paid taxes, given free-quarter, and adventured our lives; the common land now is as freely the common people's, as you can say the enclosures are your property.

If you deny this freedom, then you justly pull the blood and cries of the poor oppressed upon you, and are covenant-breakers and will be proved double hypocrites: first to Almighty God, in breaking covenant with him, for in his name you made the Covenant. Secondly to men, in breaking covenant with them, for the matter of the Covenant was the freedom, peace and safety of the people of England, taking in all sorts of people.

Thirdly, if you do not set us free from the Norman yoke, now after you have taken our taxes and free-quarter from us, whereby we have dearly bought our freedom, and you thereupon promised freedom, and you have power now to give it, for if you speak the word the Norman yokes will be broke, and all sorts will rejoice in freedom and righteousness; but if you will not, you give a just occasion to the common people of England never to trust the fair words of a Parliament any more, as you were always very slow in trusting the King when he swore by the word of a king, because you found that subtlety and self lay under, and no reality.

And truly the hearts of people are much falling from you, for your breach of promises when you have power to keep them, and for your neglect of giving them their freedom and removing burdens; and what danger may ensue by that to yourselves and the nations, you know how to judge; and for our parts we are sorry to hear the muttering of the people against you.

O that there were a heart in you to consider of these things, and act righteousness, how sweetly might you and the people live together. If you grant this freedom we speak of, you gain the hearts of the nation; if you neglect this, you will fall as fast in their affections as ever you rise. I speak what I see, and do you observe; slight not that love that speaks feelingly, from the sense of the nation's burdens.

Fourthly, if still you should establish the old Norman laws and confirm lords of manors in their ancient custom and oppressing power over the common people, you would now at length, after the wars with King Charles are over, take part with such (as is known very well) as have been either flat enemies or ambidexters all along the wars, and will cast such as have been your true friends at the feet of the nation's enemies, to be still oppressed by their cruelty. Surely if these lords and freeholders have their enclosures established to them in peace, is not that freedom enough? Must they needs have the common land likewise? As Ahab, that was restless till he had Naboth's vineyard; and so in the midst of their abundance, yet will eat the bread out of the poor's mouths. O, the land mourns in her children, under the hard-hearted covetousness of these men.

Fifthly, if you establish the old Norman laws, that lords of manors shall still have the commons and waste lands, then you are the maintainers of the old Norman murder and theft still; for lords of manors came to be tyrants over the poor enslaved English by the murder and theft of William the Conqueror, and downwards to this day they have held title to their royalties therefrom, and from the will of the king; for when he had conquered, he turned the English out and gave their land to his Norman soldiers.

Sixthly, if you establish the old Norman laws, and this especially, that the lords of manors shall still be lords of the common land, and the common people be still enslaved to them, then you pull the guilt of King Charles his blood upon your own heads. For then it will appear to the view of all men that you cut off the King's head that you might establish yourselves in his chair of government, and that your aim was not to throw down tyranny, but the tyrant. But alas, the King's blood was not our burden, it was those oppressing Norman laws, whereby he enslaved us, that we groaned under.

Let it not be said in the ears of posterity that the gentry of England assembled in Parliament proved covenant-breakers, oaths-, protestations- and promise-breakers to God and the common people, after their own turn was served; and killed the King for his power and government, as a thief kills a true man for his money. I do not say you have done so; but for shame dally no longer, but cut off the bad laws with the King's head, and let the poor oppressed go free as well as the gentry and clergy, and you will find more peace. Let the common land be set free, break the Norman yoke of lords of manors; and pull not the cries and blood of the poor oppressed upon you.

Seventhly, know this, that if ever you, or any Parliament of England, do England good, you must make all your laws in the light of equity and reason, respecting the freedom of all sorts of people; but if you respect some sort of people (to wit the gentry and clergy) and give freedom to them; for they, by virtue of your act of Parliament establishing the old Norman laws, do arrest and trouble me and others for digging upon the commons, whereas by virtue of the victory over the King, in regard I have to my estate given free-quarter and taxes for England's liberty, as they have done, I have as much right to the common land as they; therefore I say, if the gentry and clergy must have their Norman power established to them, and the common people, that are more considerable for number and necessities, be left still under the yoke, you will be proved the foolish builders.

Surely if you found out the Court of Wards to be a burden, and freed lords of manors and gentry from paying fines to the king; and freed their children from the slavery of falling ward:* let the common people be set free too from paying homage to lords of manors; and let all sorts have freedom by virtue of this conquest over the Norman successor. And seeing you took away the will of the king from enslaving lords of manors, take away the will of lords of manors from enslaving the common people.

Thus, Sirs, we have made our appeal to you, as the only men that must and can give sentence of freedom in this controversy, and that you will not leave us in the cruel hands of lords of manors, the successors of the Norman task-masters. For there are but three ways that lords of manors can lay claim to the common land, and yet all three are too weak to build a just title upon.

First, if they can prove that the earth was made by Almighty God peculiarly for them, and not for others equal with them, then we have trespassed in digging upon their rights; but the earth was made as free for us as for them; therefore they have trespassed against us their fellow-creatures, in troubling us by their tyrannical arrest, and hindering us from our righteous labour.

Secondly, if they say that others sold or gave them the title to the commons, by way of inheritance: they are to prove by what authority any other had from the pure law of our creation to give away or sell the earth from the use of any of their fellow-creatures, it being the common store-house of livelihood for all, without respect of persons.

He that sells the earth, and he that buys, doth remove the land-mark from the third person, because the land that is bought and sold belongs to the third man as well as to the other two that buys and sells; and they two persons that buys and sells, and leaves the land that is bought for an inheritance to their children, excluding others, they murder the third man, because they steal away his livelihood from him; for after a man hath bought the land, and paid money for it to another, he saith, 'this is my land, I have paid for it'.

* Wardship and the Court of Wards were abolished by Parliamentary Ordinance on 24 February 1646.

But the third man comes in and saith, 'the land is mine, equal with you by the law of creation'. And so he that is the buyer, he begins to draw his sword, and to fight; and if he conquer, he rejoices, and says, 'the land is now mine indeed, I have bought and I have conquered'. But thou covetous person, so long as there is another man in the world besides thee and him whom thou hast killed, the earth belongs to him as well as to thee. And this is the case of the nations of the world, and thus property came in, and hath been left as an inheritance to children; which is the burden the creation groans under.

Here we see who are thieves and murderers: even the buyers and sellers of land with her fruits, these are they that take away another man's right from him; and that over-throws righteous property, to uphold particular property, which covetousness the god of this world hath set up.

But thirdly, if lords of manors say, as it is truth, that they hold title to the commons by custom, from the king's will, as they do, this is as bad as the other; for we know the king came in by conquest and gave the land to these forefathers, to be task-masters over the conquered English. But if you say that these later kings were chosen by the people, it is possible it might be so, but surely it was when his greatness over-awed them, or else they would never have chosen him to enslave them and to set task-masters over them.

But seeing the common people have joined person and purse with you, to recover yourselves from under the tyranny of kings, and have prevailed: the common people now have more truer title to the common lands than the lords of manors, for they held title by conquest and sword of the king (we now the common people have recovered the land again by conquest and sword in casting out the king) so that the title of lords of manors is broke.

Therefore now the common people have more true title to the common land than lords of manors have, in regard they have recovered themselves out of slavery by taxes, free-quarter and conquest, yet we shut them not out, but let them take part with us as fellow-creatures, and we with them, and so honour our creator in the work of his own hands.

Thus we have declared our cause without flattery to you; if you leave us in the hands of oppression, and under the power of the old tyrannical laws, know this, that we suffer in pursuit of our National Covenant, endeavouring a reformation in our place and calling, according to the Word of God, and you shall be left without excuse.

Set the land free from oppression, and righteousness will be the laws, government and strength of that people.

These are some of the NORMAN Laws which William the Conquueror brought into *ENGLAND*.

First, he turned the English out of their lands, and placed his Norman soldiers therein, and made those that had the greatest portion lords and barons, and gave them a royalty to the commons, to hold from his will, as a custom whereby the common people should not plant themselves anywhere in the land, upon any common land, but some lord of manor or other should know of it and hinder them, as these three that have arrested us, viz. Wenman, Verney and Winwood, lord, knight and esquire, the three estates of the Norman gentry, will not suffer us to dig quietly upon George Hill, but seek to drive us off, having no more claim thereunto but an ancient custom which they hold from the king's will, whereby they have and still would tyrannize over the people: and this is the rise and standing of lords of manors.

Secondly, another Norman law is this: William the Conqueror caused the laws to be written in the Norman and French tongue, and then appointed his own Norman people to expound and interpret those laws, and appointed the English people to pay them a fee for their pains, and from hence came in the trade of lawyers. He commanded likewise that no man should plead his own cause, but those lawyers should do it for them.

Thirdly, William the Conqueror broke that good and quiet course of ending controversies in a neighbourhood, and commanded the people to come up to Westminster to the four terms every year to have their causes tried.

Fourthly, William the Conqueror brought in the paying of tithes to the clergy, in thankfulness to the pope and clergy's good services in preaching for him, and so to persuade the people to embrace him.

These are some of the Norman laws and burdens, which if removed, it would be much ease and quiet to this nation.

FINIS.

A

WATCH-WORD

TO

The City of London,

AND THE

ARMY:

WHEREIN

You may see that England's freedom, which should be the result of all our Victories, is sinking deeper under the Norman power, as appears by this relation of the unrighteous proceedings of Kingston Court against some of the Diggers at George Hill, under colour of Law; but yet thereby the cause of the Diggers is more brightened and strengthened: so that every one singly may truly say what his freedom is, and where it lies.

By Gerrard Winstanley.

When these clay-bodies are in grave, and children
stand in place,
This shews we stood for truth and peace and
freedom in our days;
And true born sons we shall appear of England
that's our mother,
No Priests nor Lawyers wiles t'embrace, their
slavery we'll discover.

To the City of London, Freedom and Peace desired.

Thou City of London, I am one of thy sons by freedom, and I do truly love thy peace; while I had an estate in thee, I was free to offer my mite into thy public treasury, Guildhall, for a preservation to thee and the whole land; but by thy cheating sons in the thieving art of buying and selling, and by the burdens of and for the soldiery in the beginning of the war, I was beaten out both of estate and trade, and forced to accept of the good will of friends crediting of me, to live a country life; and there likewise by the burden of taxes and much free-quarter, my weak back found the burden heavier than I could bear. Yet in all the passages of these eight years' troubles I have been willing to lay out what my talent was, to procure England's peace inward and outward, and yet all along I have found such as in words have professed the same cause to be enemies to me. Not a full year since, being quiet at my work, my heart was filled with sweet thoughts, and many things were revealed to me which I never read in books, nor heard from the mouth of any flesh, and when I began to speak of them, some people could not bear my words, and amongst those revelations this was one: that the earth shall be made a common treasury of livelihood to whole mankind, without respect of persons; and I had a voice within me bade me declare it all abroad, which I did obey, for I declared it by word of mouth wheresoever I came. Then I was made to write a little book called *The new Law of righteousness*, and therein I declared it; yet my mind was not at rest, because nothing was acted, and thoughts run in me that words and writings were all nothing and must die, for action is the life of all, and if thou dost not act, thou dost nothing. Within a little time I was made obedient to the word in that particular likewise; for I took my spade and went and broke the ground upon George Hill in Surrey, thereby declaring freedom to the creation, and that the earth must be set free from entanglements of lords and landlords, and that it shall become a common treasury to all, as it was first made and given to the sons of men. For which doing the dragon presently casts a flood of water to drown the man-child, even that freedom that now is declared, for the old Norman prerogative lord of that manor, Mr Drake, caused me to be arrested for a trespass against him, in digging upon that barren heath, and the unrighteous proceedings of Kingston court in this business I have here declared to thee and to the whole land, that you may consider the case that England is in. All men have stood for freedom, thou hast kept fasting days and prayed in morning exercises for freedom; thou hast given thanks for victories, because hopes of freedom; plenty of petitions and promises thereupon have been made for freedom; and now the common enemy is gone, you are all like men in a mist, seeking for freedom and know not where nor what it is: and those of the richer sort of you that see it are ashamed and afraid to own it, because it comes clothed in a clownish garment, and open to the best language that scoffing Ishmael can afford, or that railing Rabsheka can speak, or furious Pharoah can act against him. For freedom is the man that will turn the world upside down, therefore no wonder he hath enemies.

And assure yourselves, if you pitch not right now upon the right point of freedom in action, as your Covenant hath it in words, you will wrap up your children in greater slavery than ever you were in. The Word of God is love, and when all thy actions are done in love to the whole creation, then thou advancest freedom, and freedom is Christ in you and Christ among you; bondage is Satan in you and Satan among you. No true freedom can be established for England's peace, or prove you faithful in covenant, but such a one as hath respect to the poor as well as the rich; for if thou consent to freedom to the rich in the City and givest freedom to the freeholders in the country, and to priests and lawyers and lords of manors and impropriators, and yet allowest the poor no freedom, thou art then a declared hypocrite, and all thy prayers, fasts and thanksgivings are and will be proved an abomination to the Lord, and freedom himself will be the poor's portion when thou shalt lie groaning in bondage.

I have declared this truth to the Army and Parliament, and now I have declared it to thee likewise, that none of you that are the fleshly strength of this land may be left without excuse, for now you have been all spoken to, and because I have obeyed the voice of the Lord in this thing, therefore do the freeholders and lords of manors seek to oppress me in the outward livelihood of the world, but I am in peace. And London, nay England, look to thy freedom! I'll assure thee, thou art very near to be cheated of it, and if thou lose it now after all thy boasting, truly thy posterity will curse thee for thy unfaithfulness to them. Every one talks of freedom, but there are but few that act for freedom, and the actors for freedom are oppressed by the talkers and verbal professors of freedom; if thou wouldst know what true freedom is, read over this and other my writings, and thou shalt see it lies in the community in spirit, and community in the earthly treasury; and this is Christ the true man-child spread abroad in the creation, restoring all things into himself. And so I leave thee,

August 26 1649.

> Being a free denizen of thee, and a true
> lover of thy peace,
>
> *Gerrard Winstanley.*

A Watch-word to the
City of London, and the Army.*

Whereas we Henry Bickerstaffe, Thomas Star and Gerrard Winstanley, were arrested into Kingston court by Thomas Wenman, Ralph Verney and Richard Winwood for a trespass in digging upon George Hill in Surrey, being the rights of Mr Drake, the lord of that manor (as they say), we all three did appear the first court day of our arrest, and demanded of the court what was laid to our charge, and to give answer thereunto ourselves. But the answer of your court was this, that you would not tell us what the trespass was, unless we would fee an attorney to speak for us. We told them we were to plead our own cause, for we knew no lawyer that we could trust with this business: we desired a copy of the declaration, and proffered to pay for it; and still you denied us, unless we would fee an attorney. But in conclusion, the Recorder of your court told us the cause was not entered. We appeared two court days after this, and desired to see the declaration, and still you denied us, unless we will fee an attorney: so greedy are these attorneys after money, more than to justify a righteous cause. We told them we could not fee any, unless we would wilfully break our National Covenant, which both Parliament and people have taken jointly together to endeavour a reformation: and unless we would be professed traitors to this nation and commonwealth of England, by upholding the old Norman tyrannical and destructive laws, when they are to be cast out if equity and reason be the moderator.

Then seeing you would not suffer us to speak, one of us

* The next nine pages reproduce a document which Winstanley had submitted to the court at Kingston.

brought this following writing into your court, that you might read our answer; because we would acknowledge all righteous proceedings in law, though some slander us and say we deny all law, because we deny the corruption in law and endeavour a reformation in our place and calling, according to that National Covenant: and we know if your laws be built upon equity and reason, you ought both to have heard us speak and read our answer. For that is no righteous law whereby to keep a commonwealth in peace, when one sort shall be suffered to speak and not another, as you deal with us, to pass sentence and execution upon us before both sides be heard to speak.

This principle in the forehead of your laws foretells destruction to this commonwealth: for it declares that the laws that follow such refusal are selfish and thievish and full of murder, protecting all that get money by their laws, and crushing all others.

The writer hereof does require Mr Drake, as he is a Parliament-man, therefore a man counted able to speak rationally, to plead this cause of digging with me; and if he shew a just and rational title that lords of manors have to the commons, and that they have a just power from God to call it their right, shutting out others; then I will write as much against it as ever I writ for this cause. But if I shew by the law of righteousness that the poorest man hath as true a title and just right to the land as the richest man, and that undeniably the earth ought to be a common treasury of livelihood for all, without respecting persons: then I shall require no more of Mr Drake but that he would justify our cause of digging, and declare abroad that the commons ought to be free to all sorts, and that it is a great trespass before the Lord God Almighty for one to hinder another of his liberty to dig the earth, that he might feed and clothe himself with the fruits of his labour therefrom freely, without owning any landlord, or paying any rent to any person of his own kind.

I sent this following answer to the arrest in writing into Kingston court. In four passages your court hath gone contrary to the righteousness of your own statute laws: for first it is mentioned in 36. Ed. 3. 15. that no process, warrant or arrest should be served till after the cause was recorded and entered; but your bailiff either could not or would not tell us the cause when he arrested us, and Mr Rogers your Recorder told us the first court day we appeared that our cause was not entered.

Secondly, we appeared two other court days, and desired a copy of the declaration, and proffered to pay for it, and you denied us. This is contrary to equity and reason, which is the foundation your laws are or should be built upon, if you would have England to be a commonwealth and stand in peace.

Thirdly, we desired to plead our own cause, and you denied us, but told us we must fee an attorney to speak for us, or else you would mark us for default in not appearance. This is contrary to your own laws likewise, for in 28. Ed. 1. 11. chap. there is freedom given to a man to speak for himself, or else he may choose his father, friend or neighbour to plead for him, without the help of any other lawyer.

Fourthly, you have granted a judgment against us and are proceeding to an execution, and this is contrary likewise to your own laws, which say that no plaint ought to be received or judgment passed, till the cause be heard and witnesses present to testify the plaint to be true, as Sir Edward Coke, 2. Part of Institutes upon the 29. chap. of Magna Charta, fol. 51. 52. 53; The Mirror of Justice.

But that all men may see we are neither ashamed nor afraid to justify that cause we are arrested for, neither to refuse to answer to it in a righteous way, therefore we have here delivered this up in writing, and we leave it in your hands, disavowing the proceedings of your court because you uphold prerogative oppression though the kingly office be taken away, and the Parliament hath declared England a commonwealth; so that prerogative laws cannot be in force, unless you be besotted by your covetousness and envy.

We deny that we have trespassed against those three men,

or Mr Drake either, or that we should trespass against any if we should dig up or plough for a livelihood upon any the waste land in England, for thereby we break no particular law made by any act of Parliament, but only an ancient custom, bred in the strength of kingly prerogative, which is that old law or custom by which lords of manors lay claim to the commons, which is of no force now to bind the people of England since the kingly power and office was cast out: and the common people, who have cast out the oppressor by their purse and person, have not authorized any as yet to give away from them their purchased freedom; and if any assume a power to give away or withhold this purchased freedom, they are traitors to this commonwealth of England: and if they imprison, oppress or put to death any for standing to maintain the purchased freedom, they are murderers and thieves, and no just rulers.

Therefore in the light of reason and equity, and in the light of the National Covenant which Parliament and people have taken with joint consent: all such prerogative customs, which by experience we have found to burden the nation, ought to be cast out with the kingly office, and the land of England now ought to be a free land and a common treasury to all her children, otherwise it cannot properly be called a commonwealth.

Therefore we justify our act of digging upon that hill, to make the earth a common treasury. First, because the earth was made by Almighty God to be a common treasury of livelihood for whole mankind in all his branches, without respect of persons; and that not any one according to the Word of God (which is love), the pure law of righteousness, ought to be lord or landlord over another, but whole mankind was made equal and knit into one body by one spirit of love, which is Christ in you the hope of glory; even [as] all the members of man's body, called the little world, are united into equality of love to preserve the whole body.

But since the Fall of man therefrom, which came in by the rising up of covetousness in the heart of mankind (to which serpent the man consented) and from thence mankind was called A-dam: for this covetousness makes mankind to be a stoppage of freedom in the creation, and by this covetous power one branch of mankind began to lift up himself above another, as Cain lifted up himself and killed his brother Abel: and so one branch did kill and steal away the comfortable use of the earth from another, as it is now: the elder brother lives in a continual thievery, stealing the land from the younger brother. And the plain truth is, thieves and murderers (upheld by preaching witches and deceivers) rule the nations: and for the present, the laws and government of the world are laws of darkness, and the devil's kingdom, for covetousness rules all. And the power of the sword over brethren in armies, in arrests, in prisons, in gallows and in other inferior torments inflicted by some upon others, as the oppression of lords of manors hindering the poor from the use of the common land, is Adam fallen, or Cain killing Abel to this very day.

And these prerogative oppressors are the Adamites and Cainites that walk contrary to the Word of God (which is love) by upholding murder and theft, by laws which their fathers made and which they now justify. For in the conquests that kings got, their ancestors did murder and kill and steal away the earth, and removed the landmark from the conquered, and made laws to imprison, torment or put to death all that would adventure to take the land from them again, and left both that stolen land and murdering laws to their children, the lords of manors and freeholders, who now with violence do justify their fathers' wickedness, by holding fast that which was left them by succession.

For what are all the laws of the nations, in this corrupt covetous government, lifting up one branch of Adam (mankind) above another, the conqueror above the conquered, or those that have power above them that are weak, I say what are they but laws of murder and theft, yea enmity itself, against the law of righteousness (which is love), which makes people do as they would be done unto?

And so all kingly power (in one or many men's hands) reigning by the sword, giving the use of the earth to some of mankind (called by him his gentry) and denying the free use of the earth to others, called the younger brothers or common people, is no other but Cain lifted up above Abel; the prerogative laws is Beelzebub, for they are the strength of covetousness and bondage in the creation, lifting up one and casting down another: the attorneys and priests and lawyers and bailiffs are servants to Beelzebub, and are devils; their prisons, whips and gallows are the torments of this hell, or government of darkness; for mind it all along, and you shall see that covetousness and bitter envy gets freedom by these laws; but the sincere and meek in spirit is trod underfoot.

And this is that power that hath made such havoc in the creation, it is that murderer and devil that is to be cast out. This power of covetousness is he that does countenance murder and theft in them that maintains his kingdom by the sword of iron, and punishes it in others: and so that which is called a sin in the common people, if they act such things, is counted no sin in the action of kings, because they have the power of the sword in their hands, the fear whereof makes people to fear them.

But since this kingly office by the Parliament is cast out of England, and England by them is declared to be a free state or commonwealth, we are in the first place thereby set free from those bonds and ties that the kings laid upon us. Therefore this tyranny of one over another, as of lords of manors over the common people, and for people to be forced to hire lawyers to plead their causes for them when they are able to plead themselves, ought to be taken away with the kingly office, because they are the strength of the ancient prerogative custom.

Secondly we justify our digging upon George Hill to make the earth a common treasury, because all sorts of people have lent assistance of purse and person to cast out the kingly office, as being a burden England groaned under;

therefore those from whom money and blood was received ought to obtain freedom in the land to themselves and posterity, by the law of contract between Parliament and people.

But all sorts, poor as well as rich, tenant as well as landlord, have paid taxes, free-quarter, excise, or adventured their lives to cast out that kingly office.

Therefore all sorts of people ought to have freedom in the land of this their nativity, without respecting persons, now the kingly office is cast out by their joint assistance. And those that do imprison, oppress and take away the livelihood of those that rise up to take possession of this purchased freedom are traitors to this nation and enemies to righteousness. And of this number are those men that have arrested or that may arrest the diggers that endeavour to advance freedom; therefore I say all sorts ought to have their freedom.

And that in regard they have not only joined persons and purses together, but in regard likewise they took the National Covenant with joint consent together, which the Parliament did make, of whom Mr Drake that caused us to be arrested was one; which Covenant likewise the ministers in their sermons most vehemently pressed upon the people to take, the intent whereof was this: that everyone in his several place and calling should endeavour the peace, safety and freedom of England, and that the Parliament should assist the people and the people the Parliament, and everyone that had taken it should assist those that had taken it, while they were in pursuit thereof, as in the sixth article of the National Covenant.

But now Mr Drake that was one that made this Covenant, and the Surrey Ministers that took it with great zeal at Kingston (which I was eye witness to and shall be of their hypocrisy therein) have set up a lecturer * at Cobham on purpose to drive off the diggers to forsake the pursuit of their covenant, are the most vehement to break covenant and to

* A preacher.

hinder them that would keep it, neither entering into peace themselves nor suffering them that are entering in to enter.

But in regard some of us did dig upon George Hill, thereby to take possession of that freedom we have recovered out of the hands of the kingly office, and thereby endeavour a reformation in our place and calling according to the Word of God (which is love): and while we are in pursuit of this our Covenant we expect both Parliament (that made the Covenant) and the officers of this court and parish ministers and lords of manors themselves, and especially Mr Drake, to assist us herein, against all that shall oppose us in this righteous work of making the earth a common treasury; and not to beat us, imprison us or take away our estates or lives, unless they will wilfully break covenant with God and man to please their own covetous froward heart ,and thereby declare themselves to be the worst of devils.

Therefore, in that we do dig upon that hill, we do not thereby take away other men's rights, neither do we demand of this court, or from the Parliament, what is theirs and not ours. But we demand our own to be set free to us and them out of the tyrannical oppression of ancient custom of kingly prerogative; and let us have no more gods to rule over us, but the King of righteousness only.

Therefore as the freeholders claim a quietness and freedom in their enclosures, as it is fit they should have, so we that are younger brothers or the poor oppressed, we claim our freedom in the commons, that so elder and younger brother may live quietly and in peace, together freed from the straits of poverty and oppression in this land of our nativity.

Thus we have in writing declared in effect what we should say if we had liberty to speak before you, declaring withal, that your court cannot end this controversy in that equity and reason of it, which we stand to maintain. Therefore we have appealed to the Parliament, who have received our appeal and promised an answer, and we wait for it. And we leave this with you, and let reason and righteousness be our judge; therefore we hope you will do nothing rashly, but seriously consider of this cause before you proceed to execution upon us.

You say God will blast our work, and you say you are in the right and we are in the wrong. Now if you be Christians, as you say you are, then do you act love to us, as we do to you; and let both sides wait with patience on the Lord, to see who he blesses. But if you oppose by violence, arrest us, judge, condemn and execute us, and yet will not suffer us to speak for ourselves, but you will force us to give money to our enemies to speak for us, surely you cannot say your cause is right; but hereby you justify our cause to be right, because you are the persecutors of a loving meek-spirited people, and so declare that the god you say that will blast us is covetousness, whom you serve by your persecuting power.

> *Covetous might may overcome rational right for a time.*
> *But rational right must conquer covetous might, and that's*
> *the life of mine.*

> *The law is righteous, just and good when reason is the*
> *rule,*
> *But whoso rules by the fleshly will declares himself*
> *a fool.*

Well, this same writing was delivered into their court, but they cast it away and would not read it, and all was because I would not fee an attorney; and then the next court day following, before there was any trial of our cause, for there was none suffered to speak but the plaintiff, they passed a judgment and after than an execution.

Now their jury was made of rich freeholders and such as stand strongly for the Norman power: and though our digging upon that barren common hath done the common good, yet this jury brings in damages of ten pounds a man, and the charges of the plaintiff in their court, twenty nine shilling and a penny; and this was their sentence and the passing of the execution upon us.

And two days after (for in this case they can end a cause speedily in their court; but when the attorney and lawyer get money they keep a cause depending seven years, to the utter undoing of the parties, so unrighteous is the law and lawyers) I say, two days after they sent to execute the execution, and they put Henry Bickerstaffe in prison, but after three days, Mr Drake released him again, Bickerstaffe not knowing of it till the release came. They seek after Thomas Star to imprison his body, who is a poor man not worth ten pounds.

Then they came privately by day to Gerrard Winstanley's house, and drove away four cows, I not knowing of it; and some of the lord's tenants rode to the next town shouting the diggers were conquered, the diggers were conquered. Truly it is an easy thing to beat a man and cry conquest over him, after his hands are tied as they tied ours. But if their cause be so good, why will they not suffer us to speak, and let reason and equity, the foundation of righteous laws, judge them and us? But strangers made rescue of those cows and drove them astray out of the bailiffs' hands, so that the bailiffs lost them; but before the bailiffs had lost the cows, I hearing of it went to them and said, 'Here is my body, take me that I may come to speak to those Normans that have stolen our land from us; and let the cows go, for they are none of mine'; and after some time, they telling me that they had nothing against my body, it was my goods they were to have; then said I, 'Take my goods, for the cows are not mine'; and so I went away and left them, being quiet in my heart and filled with comfort within myself, that the King of righteousness would cause this to work for the advancing of his own cause, which I prefer above estate or livelihood.

Saying within my heart as I went along, that if I could not

get meat to eat, I would feed upon bread, milk and cheese; and if they take the cows, that I cannot feed on this, or hereby make a breach between me and him that owns the cows, then I'll feed upon bread and beer till the King of righteousness clear up my innocence and the justice of his own cause: and if this be taken from me for maintaining his cause, I'll stand still and see what he will do with me, for as yet I know not.

Saying likewise within my heart as I was walking along, 'O thou King of righteousness shew thy power, and do thy work thyself, and free thy people now from under this heavy bondage of misery, Pharaoh the covetous power'. And the answer in my heart was satisfactory and full of sweet joy and peace: and so I said 'Father, do what thou wilt, this cause is thine, and thou knowest that the love to righteousness makes me do what I do'.

I was made to appeal to the Father of life in the speakings of my heart likewise thus: 'Father, thou knowest that what I have writ or spoken concerning this light, that the earth should be restored and become a common treasury for all mankind without respect of persons, was thy free revelation to me, I never read it in any book, I heard it from no mouth of flesh till I understood it from thy teaching first within me. I did not study nor imagine the conceit of it; self-love to my own particular body does not carry me along in the managing of this business; but the power of love flowing forth to the liberty and peace of thy whole creation, to enemies as well as friends: nay towards those that oppress me, endeavouring to make me a beggar to them. And since I did obey thy voice, to speak and act this truth, I am hated, reproached and oppressed on every side. Such as make profession of thee, yet revile me. And though they see I cannot fight with fleshly weapons, yet they will strive with me by that power. And so I see, Father, that England yet does choose rather to fight with the sword of iron and covetousness than by the sword of the spirit (which is love): and what thy purpose is with this land or with my body, I know not;

but establish thy power in me, and then do what pleases thee'.

These and such like sweet thoughts dwelt upon my heart as I went along, and I feel myself now like a man in a storm, standing under shelter upon a hill in peace, waiting till the storm be over to see the end of it, and of many other things that my eye is fixed upon. But I will let this pass,

And return again to the dragon's den, or hornet's nest, the selfish murdering fleshly laws of this nation, which hangs some for stealing and protects others in stealing. Lords of manors stole the land from their fellow-creatures formerly in the conquests of kings, and now they have made laws to imprison and hang all those that seek to recover the land again out of their thieving murdering hands.

They took away the cows which were my livelihood, and beat them with their clubs, that the cows' heads and sides did swell, which grieved tender hearts to see: and yet these cows never were upon George Hill, nor never digged upon that ground, and yet the poor beasts must suffer because they gave milk to feed me. But they were driven away out of those devils' hands (the bailiffs), and were delivered out of hell at that time.

And thus lords of manors, their bailiffs (the true upholders of the Norman power) and some freeholders that do oppose this public work, are such as the country knows have been no friends to that cause the Parliament declared for, but to the kingly power. And now if they get the foot fast in the stirrup, they will lift themselves again into the Norman saddle; and they do it secretly; for they keep up the Norman laws and thereby traitors to freedom get into places of law and power, and by that will enslave England more than it was under the kingly power.

Therefore England beware; thou art in danger of being brought under the Norman power more than ever. The King Charles that was successor to William the Conqueror thou hast cast out: and though thy Parliament have declared against the kingly office, and cast it out and proclaimed England a commonwealth,* that is to be a free land for the liberty and livelihood of all her children;

Yet William the Conqueror's army begins to gather into head again, and the old Norman prerogative law is the place of their rendez-vous: for though their chief captain Charles be gone, yet his colonels, which are lords of manors, his councillors and divines, which are our lawyers and priests, his inferior officers and soldiers, which are the freeholders and landlords, all which did steal away our land from us when they killed and murdered our fathers in that Norman conquest: and the bailiffs, that are slaves to their covetous lusts, and all the ignorant bawling women against our digging for freedom, are the snapsack boys and the ammunition sluts that follow the Norman camp.

These are all striving to get into a body again, that they may set up a new Norman slavery over us; and the place of their rendez-vous, prerogative power, is fenced already about with a line of communication: an act made by a piece of the Parliament to maintain the old laws, which if once this camp be fortified in his full strength, it will cost many a sighing heart and burdened spirit before it be taken.

And this Norman camp are got into so numerous a body already, that they have appointed their sutlers to drive away the cows which were my livelihood, and some of them they would sell to make money of to pay the attorney (Gilder) and lawyers their fees, for denying the diggers our privilege to plead our own cause; for as it is clearly seen that if we be suffered to speak we shall batter to pieces all the old laws, and prove the maintainers of them hypocrites and traitors to this commonwealth of England, and then the attorneys' and lawyers' trade goes down, and lords of manors must be reckoned equal to other men. And this covetous flesh and blood cannot endure.

And other of the cows were to be killed to victual the

* Monarchy was abolished by act of Parliament on 19 March 1649. England was declared a free commonwealth – i.e. a republic – by act of 19 May 1649.

camp, that is to feed those Normans, Will Star and Ned Sutton, both freeholders, and others the snapsack boys and ammunition drabs that helped to drive away the cows, that they might be encouraged by a bellyful of stolen goods to stick the closer to the business another time. Or else the price of these cows were to pay for the sack and tobacco which the Norman officers of knights, gentlemen and rich freeholders did spend at the White Lion at Cobham, when they met the 24. of August 1649, to advise together what course they should take to subdue the diggers. For, say they, 'If the cause of the diggers stand, we shall lose all our honour and titles, and we that have had the glory of the earth shall be of no more account than those slaves our servants and younger brothers that have been footstools to us and our fathers ever since the Norman William our beloved general took this land (not by love but) by a sharp sword, the power by which we stand: and though we own Christ by name, yet we will not do as he did to save enemies, but by our sword we will destroy our enemies, and do we not deserve the price of some of the diggers' cows to pay us for this our good service? And do not our reverend ministers tell us that William the Conqueror and the succeeding kings were God's anointed? And do not they say that our enclosures which were got by that murdering sword and given by William the Conqueror to our fathers, and so successively from them the land is our inheritance, and that God gave it us, and shall these broken fellows and beggarly rogues take our rights from us, and have the use of the land equal with us?' Thus do these Norman gentlemen comfort their hearts and support themselves with broken reeds, when they meet together in their councils.

But stay, you Norman gentlemen, let me put in a word amongst you: doth the murderer's sword make any man to be God's anointed? Surely, Jesus Christ was called God's anointed not because he conquered with a sword of iron, but because he conquered by love and the spirit of patience: therefore your general was not God's anointed, as Christ was.

And then the earth was not made to be the successive inheritance of children of murderers, that had the strongest arm of flesh and the best sword, that can tread others underfoot with a bold brazen forehead under colour of the law of justice, as the Norman power does. But it was made for all by the law of righteousness, and he gives the whole earth to be the inheritance of every single branch of mankind without respect of persons, and he that is filled with the love of this righteous King, doing as he would be done by, is a true anointed one.

Therefore that god whom you serve, and which did entitle you lords, knights, gentlemen and landlords, is covetousness, the god of this world, which always was a murderer, a devil and father of lies, under whose dark governing power both you and all the nations of the world for the present are under. But the King of righteousness or God of love whom I serve did not call the earth your inheritance, shutting out others, but gave the earth to be a common treasury to whole mankind (who is the lord of it) without respect of person.

This power of love is the King of righteousness, the Lord God Almighty that rules the whole creation in peace, that is the seed that breaks covetousness the serpent's head; he is the restoring power, that is now rising up to change all things into his own nature, he will be your judge, for vengeance is his; and for any wrong you have done me, as I can tell you of many, yet I have given all matters of judgment and vengeance into his hand, and I am sure he will do right and discover him that is the true trespasser that takes away my rights from me.

And take notice of this, you lords of manors and Norman gentry, though you should kill my body or starve me in prison, yet know that the more you strive, the more troubles your hearts shall be filled with; and do the worst you can to hinder public freedom, you shall come off losers in the latter end, I mean you shall lose your kingdom of darkness, though I lose my livelihood, the poor cows that is my living, and should be imprisoned. You have been told this 12 months ago, that you should lose ground by striving, and will you not take warning, will you needs shame yourselves, to let the poor diggers take away your kingdom from you? Surely, the power that is in them will take the rule and government from you, and give it a people that will make better use of it.

Alas! you poor blind earth-moles, you strive to take away my livelihood and the liberty of this poor weak frame my body of flesh, which is my house I dwell in for a time; but I strive to cast down your kingdom of darkness, and to open hell gates, and to break the devil's bonds asunder wherewith you are tied, that you my enemies may live in peace; and that is all the harm I would have you to have.

Therefore you lords of manors, you freeholders, you Norman clergy, oppressing tithe-mongers and you of the Parliament-men that have played fast and loose with this poor nation, for what is past let it go; hereafter advance freedom and liberty and pluck up bondage; and sin no more by lording it over your lords and masters, that set you upon those Parliament seats, lest worse things befall you than yet hath.

But to return again to Mr Gilder's advice (the attorney of Kingston court), and the proceeding of that court with the cows: you hear how they did judge, condemn and execute me, not suffering me to speak; and though those four cows were rescued out of their hands by strangers, not by me; and so by their own law they should have looked after the rescuers, yet contrary to their own law they came again to Winstanley's dwelling a fortnight after, and drove away seven cows and a bull in the night time, some of the cows being [a] neighbour's that had hired pasture. And yet the damage which their Norman jury and their covetous besotted ignorant attorney Mr Gilder had judged me to pay for a trespass in digging upon that barren George Hill was but eleven pound nine shillings and a penny (charges and all), which they are like never to have of me, for an empty carrier will dance and sing before these Norman thieves and pick-purses. And thus you see they judged and passed sentence upon me but once at their prerogative pleasure, which they call England's law: but they executed me twice, that they might be sure to kill me. But yet these cows likewise are brought home again, and the heart of my enemies is put into the pound of vexation because the cows are set free. Surely these lords of manors and the attorney Mr Gilder, that gave advice to arrest us for digging, have burned their Bibles long ago, because they have so quite and clean forgotten that petition in the Lord's prayer, *forgive us our trespasses as we forgive them*; for they make this a trespass against them, for digging upon the waste land of our mother the land of England for a livelihood, whenas their law itself saith that the commons and wastes belong to the poor.

So that you see the Norman camp is grown very numerous and big, that they want much beef to victual them; and they are such hungry ones that they will eat poor lean cows, that are little better than skin and bone; and poor cows, if I keep them in the winter they are like to be poorer for want of hay; for before the report of our digging was much known, I bought three acres of grass of a lord of a manor, whom I will not here name because I know the counsel of others made him prove false to me; for when the time came to mow, I brought money to pay him beforehand. But he answered me, I should not have it, but sold it to another before my face. This was because his parish priest and the Surrey ministers (and sorry ones too they are that have set up a lecture at Cobham for a little time to preach down the diggers) have bid the people neither to buy nor sell with us, but to beat us, imprison us or banish us; and thereby they prove themselves to be members of the Beast that had two horns like a lamb and yet spake like a dragon; and so they fulfil that scripture in Rev. 13.16, *that no man might buy and sell, save he that had the mark of the Beast*. Or else surely they do it on purpose to quicken us to our work and to drive us to plant the commons with all speed as may be.

But though the cows were poor, yet they care not, so the

skins will but pay the lawyers' and attorney Gilder his fees, and the flesh to feed the snapsack boys, either to eat and make merry with, or else to sell to make money of, to pay those that drive away the cows for their pains or charges they have been at in this 18 weeks striving to beat the diggers off their work. But the bone will serve the bailiffs to pick, because their action will be both proved thievery in stealing another man's cattle, and their trespass very great against the same man, in opening all the gates round about the ground where Winstanley dwells, and let hogs and common cattle into the standing barley and other corn, which the right owner will seek satisfaction for.

So that the fury of this Norman camp against the diggers is so great that they would not only drive away all the cows upon the ground but spoil the corn too, and when they had done this mischief the bailiffs and the other Norman snapsack boys went hollowing and shouting as if they were dancing at a whitsun ale: so glad they are to do mischief to the diggers, that they might hinder the work of freedom.

And why are they so furious against us? but because we endeavour to dig up their tithes, their lawyers' fees, their prisons and all that art and trade of darkness, whereby they get money under colour of law; and to plant the pleasant fruit trees of freedom in the room of that cursed thornbush, the power of the murdering sword. For they say, they do all they do by the law of the land which the Parliament hath confirmed to them by an act: and if so, then soldiers, where is the price of your blood? and countrymen and citizens, where is the price of your taxes and free-quarter? If this be the freedom you are like to have, to be beaten and not be suffered to say 'Why do you so?' and shall have no remedy, unless you will fee a lawyer (an enemy) to plead for you, when you are able to plead your own cause better yourself, and save that charge and have your cause ended sooner and with more peace and quietness.

And you zealous preachers and professors of the City of London, and you great officers and soldiery of the Army, where are all your victories over the Cavaliers, that you made such a blaze in the land in giving God thanks for, and which you begged in your fasting days and morning exercises? Are they all sunk into the Norman power again, and must the old prerogative laws stand; what freedom then did you give thanks for? Surely, that you had killed him that rid upon you, that you may get up into his saddle to ride upon others. O thou City, thou hypocritical City! Thou blindfold drowsy England, that sleeps and snorts in the bed of covetousness, awake, awake, the enemy is upon thy back, he is ready to scale the walls and enter possession, and wilt thou not look out?

Does not the streams of bondage run in the same river that it did, and with a bigger stream of Norman power? So that if you awaken not betimes, the flood of the Norman prerogative power will drown you all. Here's more rivers comes into the main stream since the storm fell, and the waters of fury rises very high, banked in by laws; and while you are talking and disputing about words, the Norman soldiers are secretly working among you to advance their power again; and so will take away the benefit of all your victories by a subtle act of intricate laws, which the sword in the field could not do against you. And when you have lost that freedom, which you boasted of that you will leave to your posterity, then who must give thanks, you that vapoured in words, or they that lay close in action, waiting to trip up your heels by policy, when the sword could not do it?

I tell thee, thou England, thy battles now are all spiritual, dragon against the Lamb, and the power of love against the power of covetousness; therefore all that will be soldiers for Christ, the law of righteousness, join to the Lamb. He that takes the iron sword now shall perish with it, and would you be a strong land and flourish in beauty, then fight the Lamb's battles, and his strength shall be thy walls and bulwarks.

You knights, gentlemen and freeholders, that sat in council at the White Lion in Cobham to find out who are our backers and who stirs us up to dig the commons, I'll tell you plainly who it is: it is love, the King of righteousness in our hearts, that makes us thus to act that the creation may be set at liberty. And now I have answered your inquiry, do what you can to him and us his servants. And we require you in his name to let our cause have a public trial, and do not work any longer in darkness, set not your bailiffs and slaves to come by night to steal away the cows of poor men under colour of justice, whenas the cause was never yet heard in open court.

He that backs you, and that sets you to work to deny to us your younger brother the use of the common land, is covetousness, which is Beelzebub, the greatest devil; so that there is the two generals known, which you and we fight under, the two great princes of light and darkness, bondage and freedom, that does act all flesh in the great controversies of the world. These are the two men that stir in this business, that is the wicked man that counsels and backs you to be so envious and furious against us, and the righteous man Christ that backs and counsels us to love you our enemies. And do we not see that Gebal, Ammon and Amalek,* and all the rabble of the nations, lords, knights, gentlemen, lawyers, bailiffs, priests and all the Norman snapsack boys and ammunition women to the old Norman camp, do all combine together in the art of unrighteous fury, to drive the poor diggers off from their work, that the name of community and freedom, which is Christ, may not be known in earth. Thus I have dealt plainly with you all, and I have not flattered Parliament, Army, City nor country, but have declared in this and other writings the whole light of that truth revealed to me by the word of the Lord: and I shall now wait to see his hand to do his own work in what time and by what instruments he pleases. And I see the poor must first be picked out and honoured in this work, for they begin to receive the word of righteousness, but the rich generally are enemies to true freedom.

* See Psalm 83.7.

The work of digging still goes on and stops not for a rest;*
The cows were gone but are returned, and we are all at rest.
No money's paid, nor never shall, to lawyer or his man
To plead our cause, for therein we'll do the best we can.
In Cobham on the little heath our digging there goes on.
And all our friends they live in love, as if they were but one.

Thus you gentlemen, that will have no law to rule over you, but your prerogative will must be above law and above us that are the younger brothers in the land; but if you say, No, your will shall be subject to law: then I demand of you, Mr Drake, Mr Gilder, and other the bailiffs and officers of Kingston court, why will you arrest us and trouble us and say we trespass against you, and though we came to answer to your arrest and to plead our own cause, yet contrary to the equity, nay contrary to the bare letter that † the law, as I shewed you before, you denied me that privilege, but went on and did condemn and execute a forcible power upon body and goods, is not your will here above law? Do you not hereby uphold the Norman conquest?

Mr Drake, you are a Parliament-man, and was not the beginning of the quarrel between King Charles and your House? This the King pleaded to uphold prerogative, and you were against it, and yet must a Parliament-man be the first man to uphold prerogative, who are but servants to the nation for the peace and liberty of everyone, not conquering kings to make their will a law? Did you not promise liberty to the whole nation, in case the Cavalier party were cast out? And why now will you seek liberty to yourself and gentry, with the denial of just liberty and freedom to the common people, that have borne the greatest burden?

You have arrested us for digging upon the common land, you have executed your unrighteous power in distraining cattle, imprisoning our bodies, and yet our cause was never publicly heard, neither can it be proved that we have broke any law that is built upon equity and reason, therefore we wonder where you had your power to rule over us by will,

* arrest?   † of?

more than we to rule over you by our will. We request you before you go too far, not to let covetousness be your master, trample not others under your feet under colour of law, as if none knew equity of law but you; for we and our estates shall be thorns in your eyes and pricks in your sides, and you may curse that counsel bid you beg our estates or imprison our persons. But this we request, that you would let us have a fair open trial, and do not carry on the course of law in secret, like Nicodemus that is afraid to have his business come to light; therefore I challenge you once more, seeing you profess yourselves Christians, to let us be brought to a trial of our cause. Let your ministers plead with us in the Scriptures, and let your lawyers plead with us in the equity and reason of your own law; and if you prove us transgressors, then we shall lay down our work and acknowledge we have trespassed against you in digging upon the commons, and then punish us. But if we prove by Scripture and reason that undeniably the land belongs to one as well as another; then you shall own our work, justify our cause, and declare that you have done wrong to Christ, who you say is your Lord and master, in abusing us his servants and your fellow-creatures, while we are doing his work. Therefore I, knowing you to be men of moderation in outward show, I desire that your actions towards your fellow-creatures may not be like one beast to another, but carry yourselves like man to man; for your proceeding in your pretence of law hitherto against us is both unrighteous, beastly and devilish, and nothing of the spirit of man seen in it. You attorneys and lawyers, you say you are ministers of justice, and we know that equity and reason is or ought to be the foundation of law; if so, then plead not for money altogether, but stand for universal justice and equity. Then you will have peace; otherwise both you with the corrupt clergy will be cast out as unsavoury salt.

FINIS.

Preface to
SEVERAL PIECES
GATHERED
INTO ONE VOLUME

To all rational and meek-spirited readers, who are men most fit to judge.

Friends, I do not write this epistle to set up myself, as if there were something more in me than other men; I tell you plain, I have nothing but what I do receive from a free discovery within, therefore I write it to set forth the spirit's honour, and to cast a word of comfort into a broken and empty heart. Sometimes my heart hath been full of deadness and uncomfortableness, wading like a man in the dark and slabby * weather; and within a little time I have been filled with such peace, light, life and fulness, that if I had had two pair of hands, I had matter enough revealed to have kept them writing a long time; and such matter as hath been my own experience in by-past or present time, which hath filled my heart with abundance of sweet joy and rest.

Then I took the opportunity of the spirit and writ, and the power of self at such over-flowing times was so prevalent in me, that I forsook my ordinary food whole days together; and if my household-friends would persuade me to come to meat, I have been forced with that inward fulness of the power of life to rise up from the table and leave them to God, to write. Thus I have been called in from my ordinary labour, and the society of friends sometimes hath been a burden to me, and best I was when I was alone. I was so filled with that love and delight in the life within that I have sat writing whole winter days from morning till night and the cold never offended me, though when I have risen I was so stark with cold that I was forced to rise by degrees and hold by the table, till strength and heat came into my legs,

* Slushy.

and I have been secretly sorry when night came, which forced me to rise. The joy of that sweet anointing was so precious and satisfactory within my spirit that I could truly say, *O that I had a tabernacle builded here, that I might never know or seek any other frame of spirit!*

But within some time my heart hath been shut up again, and then I have laid aside my pen, and could not for chillness sit in the cold as I did, if it had been for never so great advantage, so that my flesh was willing to be at ease.

And sometimes by reason of the great opposition I have met with in the world, because of the words I have spoke or writ, the fear and trouble within me hath said, 'I will never write nor speak more in these matters of my inward life; for since I began to write or speak the light that is in me, I am the more hated, therefore I will lie still'; this purpose hath continued a little time.

But then hath the power of that overflowing anointing taken hold upon me, and I have been made another man immediately, and my heart hath been opened, as if a man should open a door and carry a light[ed] candle into a dark room; and the power of love, joy, peace and life hath so over-powered me, that I could not forbear, but must speak and go write again. And when I obeyed, I had quiet rest; and when I neglected any opportunity, and did not empty myself either by words or writing but kept the light to myself, I was troubled afterwards for it.

And though I have set myself to study to fetch back to mind those things I neglected, it was as difficult for me to do as to carry a steeple upon my back, I was so dead and my spirit so unhandy in the business. But by such experiences I learned to wait upon the spirit, and to deliver that to the creation which he revealed in me; and I have a settled peace by that obedience.

And therefore though some have said I had done well if I had left writing when I had finished *The Saints' Paradice*: surely such men know little of the spirit's inward workings; and truly what I have writ since or before that time, I was carried forth in the work by the same power, delivering it to others as I received it, and I received it not from books nor study.

And all that I have writ concerning the matter of digging, I never read it in any book, nor received it from any mouth; though since the light was given me, I have met with divers to whom the same light of truth is revealed; but never heard any speak of it before I saw the light of it rise up within myself: and I was restless in my spirit till I had delivered all abroad that which was declared within me. And now I have peace.

Thus I have given you account, where I had what I have writ. I received it not from man, but from the light of life rising up within me: therefore I shall leave my writings in all your hands; read and judge; and give the spirit of righteousness the glory, whom I strive to advance, and cast what dirt you will upon my particular flesh; and so farewell.

Decemb. 20th 1649.   Resting in peace,
                                     being one branch of mankind.

                                             Gerrard Winstanley.

A New-year's Gift for the

PARLIAMENT

AND

ARMY:

SHEWING,

What the KINGLY *Power is;*

And that the CAUSE of those They call

DIGGERS

Is the life and marrow of that Cause the Parliament hath Declared for, and the Army Fought for;

The perfecting of which Work, will prove England to be the first of Nations, or the tenth part of the city Babylon, that falls off from the Beast first, and that sets the Crown upon Christ's head, to govern the World in Righteousness:

By Gerrard Winstanley a lover of England's freedom and Peace.

Die Pride and Envy; Flesh, take the poor's advice
Covetousness be gone: Come, Truth and Love arise.
Patience take the Crown; throw Anger out of doors:
Cast out Hypocrisy and Lust, which follows whores:
Then England sit in rest; Thy sorrows will have end;
Thy Sons will live in peace, and each will be a friend.

A
New year's Gift
SENT TO THE
PARLIAMENT
AND
ARMY.

Gentlemen of the Parliament and Army: you and the common people have assisted each other to cast out the head of oppression which was kingly power seated in one man's hand, and that work is now done; and till that work was done you called upon the people to assist you to deliver this distressed bleeding dying nation out of bondage; and the people came and failed you not, counting neither purse nor blood too dear to part with to effect this work.

The Parliament after this have made an act to cast out kingly power, and to make England a free commonwealth. These acts the people are much rejoiced with, as being words forerunning their freedom, and they wait for their accomplishment that their joy may be full; for as words without action are a cheat and kills the comfort of a righteous spirit, so words performed in action does comfort and nourish the life thereof.

Now Sirs, wheresoever we spy out kingly power, no man I hope shall be troubled to declare it, nor afraid to cast it out, having both act of Parliament, the soldiers' oath and the common people's consent on his side; for kingly power is like a great spread tree, if you lop the head or top bough, and let the other branches and root stand, it will grow again and recover fresher strength.

If any ask me what kingly power is? I answer, there is a twofold kingly power. The one is the kingly power of righteousness, and this is the power of Almighty God, ruling the whole creation in peace and keeping it together. And this is the power of universal love, leading people into all truth, teaching everyone to do as he would be done unto: now once more striving with flesh and blood, shaking down everything that cannot stand, and bringing everyone into the unity of himself, the one spirit of love and righteousness, and so will work a thorough restoration. But this kingly power is above all and will tread all covetousness, pride, envy and self-love, and all other enemies whatsoever, under his feet, and take the kingdom and government of the creation out of the hand of self-seeking and self-honouring flesh, and rule the alone King of righteousness in the earth; and this indeed is Christ himself, who will cast out the curse. But this is not that kingly power intended by that act of Parliament to be cast out, but pretended to be set up, though this kingly power be much fought against both by Parliament, Army, clergy and people; but when they are made to see him, then they shall mourn because they have persecuted him.

But the other kingly power is the power of unrighteousness, which indeed is the devil. And O that there were such a heart in Parliament and Army as to perform your own act. Then people would never complain of you for breach of covenant, for your covetousness, pride and too much self-seeking that is in you. And you on the other side would never have cause to complain of the people's murmurings against you. Truly this jarring that is between you and the people is the kingly power; yea that very kingly power which you have made an act to cast out. Therefore see it be fulfilled on your part; for the kingly power of righteousness expects it, or else he will cast you out for hypocrites and unsavoury salt; for he looks upon all your actions, and truly there is abundance of rust about your actings, which makes them that they do not shine bright.

This kingly power is covetousness in his branches, or the power of self-love ruling in one or in many men over others and enslaving those who in the creation are their equals; nay, who are in the strictness of equity rather their masters. And this kingly power is usually set in the chair of government under the name of prerogative when he rules in one over other: and under the name of state privilege of Parliament when he rules in many over others: and this kingly power is always raised up and established by the sword, and therefore he is called the murderer, or the great red dragon which fights against Michael, for he enslaves the weakness of the people under him, denying an equal freedom in the earth to every one, which the law of righteousness gave every man in his creation. This I say is kingly power under darkness; and as he rules in men, so he makes men jar one against another, and is the cause of all wars and complainings. He is known by his outward actions, and his action at this very day fills all places; for this power of darkness rules, and would rule, and is that only enemy that fights against creation and national freedom. And this kingly power is he which you have made an act of Parliament to cast out. And now you rulers of England, play the men and be valiant for the truth, which is Christ: for assure yourselves God will not be mocked, nor the devil will not be mocked. For first you say and profess you own the Scriptures of prophets and apostles, and God looks that you should perform that word in action. Secondly you have declared against the devil, and if you do not now go through with your work but slack your hand by hypocritical self-love, and so suffer this dark kingly power to rise higher and rule, you shall find he will maul both you and yours to purpose.

The life of this dark kingly power, which you have made an act of Parliament and oath to cast out, if you search it to the bottom, you shall see it lies within the iron chest of cursed covetousness, who gives the earth to some part of mankind and denies it to another part of mankind: and that part that hath the earth, hath no right from the law of creation to take it to himself and shut out others; but he took it away violently by theft and murder in conquest. As when our Norman William came into England and conquered, he turned the English out and gave the land unto his Norman soldiers, every man his parcel to enclose; and hence rose up property. For this is the fruit of war from the beginning, for it removes property out of a weaker into a stronger hand, but still upholds the curse of bondage; and hereby the kingly power, which you have made an act and sworn to cast out, does remove himself from one chair to another. And so long as the sword rules over brethren (mind what I say) so long the kingly power of darkness rules, and so large as yet is his kingdom; which spreads from sea to sea and fills the earth; but Christ is rising who will take the dominion and kingdom out of his hand, and his power of righteousness shall rise and spread from east to west, from north to south and fill the earth with himself, and cast the other cursed power out. When covetousness sheathes his sword and ceases to rage in the field, he first makes sharp laws of bondage: that those that are conquered, and that by him are appointed not to enjoy the earth but are turned out, shall be servants, slaves and vassals to the conqueror's party: so those laws that upholds whips, prisons, gallows, is but the same power of the sword that raged and that was drunk with blood in the field.

King Charles, it is true, was the head of this kingly power in England, and he reigned as he was a successor of the last Norman conqueror: and whosoever you be that hath property of land, hath your titles and evidences made to you in his or his ancestors' name, and from his and their will and kingly power. I am sure he was not our creator, and therefore parcelled out the earth to some and denied it to others; therefore he must needs stand as a conqueror, and was the head of this kingly power that burdens and oppresses the people, and that is the cause of all our wars and divisions.

For if this kingly power of covetousness, which is the unrighteous divider, did not yet rule, both Parliament, Army
and rich people would cheerfully give consent that those we
call poor should dig and freely plant the waste and common
land for a livelihood (seeing there is land enough, and more
by half than is made use of), and not be suffered to perish for
want. And yet O ye rulers of England, you make a blazing
profession that you know and that you own God, Christ and
the Scriptures: but did Christ ever declare such hardness of
heart? Did not he bid the rich man go and sell all that he
hath and give to the poor? And does not the Scripture say,
If thou makest a covenant, keep it, though it be to thy loss?
But truly it will not be to your loss, to let your fellow-creatures, your equals in the creation, nay those that have been
faithful in your cause and so your friends: I say it will not
be to your loss to let them quietly improve the waste and
common land, that they may live in peace, freed from the
heavy burdens of poverty. For hereby our own land will be
increased with all sorts of commodities, and the people will
be knit together in love, to keep out a foreign enemy that
endeavours and that will endeavour as yet to come like an
army of cursed rats and mice to destroy our inheritance. So
that if this freedom be quietly granted to us, you grant it
but to yourselves, to Englishmen, to your own flesh and
blood: and you do but give us our own neither, which
covetousness in the kingly power hath and yet does hold
from us; for the earth in the first creation of it was freely
given to whole mankind, without respect of persons. Therefore you lords of manors, and you rulers of England, if you
own God, Christ and Scripture, now make restitution and
deliver us quiet possession of our land, which the kingly
power as yet holds from us.

  While this kingly power reigned in one man called
Charles, all sorts of people complained of oppression, both
gentry and common people, because their lands, enclosures
and copyholds were entangled, and because their trades were
destroyed by monopolizing patentees, and your troubles

were that you could not live free from oppression in the earth. Thereupon you that were the gentry, when you were assembled in Parliament, you called upon the poor common people to come and help you, and cast out oppression; and you that complained are helped and freed, and that top bough is lopped off the tree of tyranny, and kingly power in that one particular is cast out. But alas, oppression is a great tree still, and keeps off the sun of freedom from the poor commons still; he hath many branches and great roots which must be grubbed up, before everyone can sing Sion's songs in peace.

As we spy out kingly power we must declare it and cast it out, or else we shall deny the Parliament of England and their acts, and so prove traitors to the land by denying obedience thereunto. Now there are three branches more of kingly power, greater than the former, that oppresses this land wonderfully; and these are the power of the tithing priests over the tenths of our labours; and the power of lords of manors, holding the free use of the commons and waste land from the poor; and the intolerable oppression either of bad laws, or of bad judges corrupting good laws. These are branches of the Norman conquest and kingly power still, and wants a reformation.

For as for the first, William the Conqueror promised that if the clergy would preach him up, so that the people might be bewitched so as to receive him to be God's anointed over them, he would give them the tenths of the land's increase yearly; and they did it, and he made good his promise. And do we not yet see that if the clergy can get tithes or money, they will turn as the ruling power turns, any way: to popery, to protestantism; for a king, against a king; for monarchy, for state-government; they cry 'Who bids most wages?' They will be on the strongest side, for an earthly maintenance; yea, and when they are lifted up, they would rule too, because they are called spiritual men. It is true indeed, they are spiritual; but it is of the spiritual power of covetousness and pride; for the spiritual power of love and righteousness they know not; for if they knew it, they would not persecute and rail against him as they do.

The clergy will serve on any side, like our ancient laws that will serve any master. They will serve the papists, they will serve the protestants, they will serve the king, they will serve the states; they are one and the same tools for lawyers to work with under any government. O you Parliament-men of England, cast those whorish laws out of doors, that are so common, that pretend love to every one and is faithful to none: for truly, he that goes to law (as the proverb is) shall die a beggar: so that old whores and old laws picks men's pockets, and undoes them. If the fault lie in the laws (and much does), burn all your old law-books in Cheapside, and set up a government upon your own foundation. Do not put new wine into old bottles; but as your government must be new, so let the laws be new, or else you will run farther into the mud where you stick already, as though you were fast in an Irish bog; for you are so far sunk that he must have good eyes that can see where you are: but yet all are not blind, there are eyes that sees you. But if the fault lies in the judges of the law, surely such men deserve no power in a reforming commonwealth, that burdens all sorts of people.

And truly I'll tell you plain, your two acts of Parliament are excellent and righteous: the one to cast out kingly power, the other to make England a free commonwealth. Build upon these two, it is a firm foundation, and your house will be the glory of the world; and I am confident, the righteous spirit will love you. Do not stick in the bog of covetousness: let not self-love so bemuddy your brain that you should lose yourselves in the thicket of bramble-bush words, and set never a strong oak of some stable action for the freedom of the poor oppressed that helped you when you complained of oppression. Let not pride blind your eyes, that you should forget you are the nation's servants, and so prove Solomon's words good in yourselves, that servants ride on horseback and coaches, whenas princes, such as chose you and set you there, go on foot: and many of them, through their love to the nation, have so wasted themselves that now they can hardly get bread, but with great difficulty. I tell you this is a sore evil, and this is truth; therefore think upon it, it is a poor man's advice, and you shall find weight in it, if you do as well as say.

Then secondly for lords of manors, they were William the Conqueror's colonels and favourites, and he gave a large circuit of land to every one, called a lordship, that they might have a watchful eye that if any of the conquered English should begin to plant themselves upon any common or waste land, to live out of sight or out of slavery, that then some lord of manor or other might see and know of it, and drive them off, as these lords of manors nowadays endeavours to drive off the diggers from digging upon the commons. But we expect the rulers of the land will grant unto us their friends the benefit of their own acts against kingly power, and not suffer that Norman power to crush the poor oppressed who helped them in their straits, nor suffer that Norman power to bud fresher out, and so in time may come to over-top our dear-bought freedom more than ever.

Search all your laws, and I'll adventure my life (for I have little else to lose) that all lords of manors hold title to the commons by no stronger hold than the king's will, whose head is cut off; and the king held title as he was a conqueror. Now if you cast off the king who was the head of that power, surely the power of lords of manors is the same; therefore perform your own act of Parliament, and cast out that part of the kingly power likewise, that the people may see you understand what you say and do, and that you are faithful.

For truly the kingly power reigns strongly in the lords of manors over the poor. For my own particular, I have in other writings as well as in this declared my reasons that the common land is the poor people's property; and I have digged upon the commons, and I hope in time to obtain the freedom to get food and raiment therefrom by righteous labour, which is all I desire; and for so doing, the supposed lord of that manor hath arrested me twice; first, in an action of £20 trespass for ploughing upon the commons, which I never did; and because they would not suffer me to plead my own cause, they made shift to pass a sentence of execution against some cows I kept, supposing they had been mine, and took them away; but the right owner reprieved them, and fetched the cows back. So greedy are these thieves and murderers after my life for speaking the truth, and for maintaining the life and marrow of the Parliament's cause in my actions.

And now they have arrested me again in an action of £4 trespass for digging upon the commons, which I did, and own the work to be righteous and no trespass to any. This was the attorney of Kingston's advice, either to get money on both sides, for they love money as dearly as a poor man's dog do his breakfast in a cold morning (but regard not justice), or else that I should not remove it to a higher court, but that the cause might be tried there; and then they know how to please the lords of manors, that have resolved to spend hundreds of pounds but they will hinder the poor from enjoying the commons. For they will not suffer me to plead my own cause, but I must fee an enemy, or else be condemned and executed without mercy or justice as I was before, and so to put me in prison till I pay their unrighteous sentence; for truly attorneys are such neat workmen that they can turn a cause which way those that have the biggest purse will have them: and the country knows very well that Kingston court is so full of the kingly power that some will rather lose their rights than have their causes tried there. One of the officers of that court told a friend of mine that if the digger's cause was good, he would pick out such a jury as should overthrow him. And upon my former arrest they picked out such a jury as sentenced me to pay £10 damages for ploughing upon the commons, which I did not do, neither did any witness prove it before them. So that from

Kingston juries, lords of manors and kingly power, good Lord deliver us.

Do these men obey the Parliament's acts, to throw down kingly power? O no: the same unrighteous doing that was complained of in King Charles's days, the same doings is among them still. Monies will buy and sell justice still: and is our 8 years' wars come round about to lay us down again in the kennel of injustice as much or more than before? Are we no farther learned yet? O ye rulers of England, when must we turn over a new leaf? Will you always hold us in one lesson? Surely you will make dunces of us: then all the boys in other lands will laugh at us. Come, I pray, let us take forth and go forward in our learning.

You blame us who are the common people as though we would have no government; truly gentlemen, we desire a righteous government with all our hearts, but the government we have gives freedom and livelihood to the gentry to have abundance, and to lock up treasures of the earth from the poor, so that rich men may have chests full of gold and silver, and houses full of corn and goods to look upon; and the poor that works to get it can hardly live, and if they cannot work like slaves, then they must starve. And thus the law gives all the land to some part of mankind whose predecessors got it by conquest, and denies it to others who by the righteous law of creation may claim an equal portion; and yet you say this is a righteous government. But surely it is no other but selfishness, which is the great red dragon, the murderer.

England is a prison; the variety of subtleties in the laws preserved by the sword are bolts, bars and doors of the prison; the lawyers are jailors, and poor men are the prisoners; for let a man fall into the hands of any from the bailiff to the judge, and he is either undone or weary of his life.

Surely this power [of] the laws, which is the great idol that people dote upon, is the burden of the creation, a nursery of idleness, luxury and cheating, the only enemy of Christ the King of righteousness; for though it pretend justice, yet the judges and law-officers buy and sell justice for money, and wipes their mouths like Solomon's whore and says 'It is my calling', and never are troubled at it.

Two things must cast out this idol. First, let not people send their children to those nurseries of covetousness, the Inns of Court. Secondly, let not people live in contention, but fulfil Christ's last commandment, *Love*; and endeavour to practise that full point of the law and the prophets, *Do as you would be done by*, and so cast out envy and discontent. Woe to you lawyers, for your trade is the bane and misery of the world; your power is the only power that hinders Christ from rising. The destruction of your power will be the life of the world; it is full of confusion, it is Babylon, and surely its fall is near, in regard the light of truth is rising, who will consume your power but save your persons, by the words of his mouth and brightness of his coming.

The lawyer's trade is one of the false prophets, that says 'Lo here is Christ, I'll save you in this court; and lo there is Christ, I'll save you in that court'. But when we have tried all, we are lost and not saved, for we are either utterly made beggars by this saviour the law, or else we are nursed up in hardness of heart and cruelty against our fellow-creature whom we ought to love and preserve, and not destroy. This saviour jeers righteousness, and bids every man save himself and never regard what becomes of another, and so is a plain destroyer of the creation. Surely that woe pronounced against lawyers by the man Christ must be fulfilled, delay is no payment. Therefore you Parliament and Army that have power in your hands, reform the law; and suffer none to be called to practise law but reformed ones; nay suffer every man to plead his own cause and choose his own lawyer, where he finds the most ingenuous man. Well, every man's burden in this age fills their mouths with words of lamentation against law and lawyers sufficiently; therefore you that have an opportunity to ease the cry of the oppressed, shut not your eyes and ears, but cast out this covetous corruption whereby corrupt lawyers do oppress the people; it is another branch of the kingly power.

You gentlemen of Surrey and lords of manors, and you Mr Parson Platt * especially, that lay almost a fortnight waiting and tempting the Lord Fairfax to send soldiers to drive off the diggers: when he granted your desire, it was but to secure the sheriff, for he did not give them commission to beat us, which we thank him for; and we thank the soldiers for their moderation, that they would not strike poor worms, England's and the creation's faithful friends, though you would have moved them thereunto. My advice to you gentlemen is this, hereafter to lie still and cherish the diggers, for they love you, and would not have your finger ache if they could help it; and why should you be so bitter against them? O let them live by you; some of them have been soldiers, and some countrymen that were always friends to the Parliament's cause, by whose hardship and means you enjoy the creatures about you in peace; and will you now destroy part of them that have preserved your lives? O do not do so; be not so besotted with the kingly power; hereafter let not the attorneys or lawyers neatly counsel your money out of your purses, and stir you up to beat and abuse the diggers, to make all rational men laugh at your folly and condemn you for your bitterness. If you have yet so much money, give it not away to destroy men, but give it to some poor or other to be a stock, and bid them go and plant the common; this will be your honour, and your comfort. Assure yourselves you never must have true comfort till you be friends with the poor; therefore come, come, love the diggers, and make restitution of their land you hold from them; for what would you do if you had not such labouring men to work for you?

And you great officers of the Army and Parliament, love your common soldiers (I plead for equity and reason) and

* John Platt was lord of the manor of Cobham. He was a Presbyterian, ejected from his rectory of West Horsley in 1662.

do not force them by long delay of payment to sell you their dear-bought debentures * for a thing of nought, and then to go and buy our common land and crown land, and other land that is the spoil one of another, therewith. Remember you are servants to the commons of England, and you were volunteers in the wars; and the common people have paid you for your pains so largely that some of us have not left ourselves hardly bread to eat. And therefore if there be a spoil to be gathered of crown lands, deans', bishops', forest lands and commons, that is to come to the poor commons freely; and you ought to be content with your wages, unless you will deny Christ and the Scriptures; and you ought not to go and buy one of another that which is common to all the nation; for you ought neither to buy nor sell other men's property by the law of creation; for Christ gives you no such warrant. As soon as you have freed the earth from one entanglement of kingly power, will you entangle it more and worse by another degree of kingly power? I pray consider what you do, and do righteously. We that are the poor commons, that paid our money and gave you free-quarter, have as much right in those crown lands and lands of the spoil as you; therefore we give no consent that you should buy and sell our crown lands and waste lands, for it is our purchased inheritance from under oppression, it is our own, even the poor common people's of England. It was taken from us and hath been held from us by former conquests, whereof the Norman conquest was the last, which is cast out by yours and our joint assistance; therefore you cannot in equity take it from us, nor we cannot in equity take it from you, for it is our joint purchased inheritance. We paid you your wages to help us to recover it, but not to take it to yourselves and turn us out, and buy and sell it among yourselves; for this is a cheat of the kingly swordly power which you hold up; and we profess to all the world, in so doing you deny God, Christ and the Scriptures whom ye professed you own: for God,

* Claims to land issued to the troops in lieu of wages, which they often had to sell at a discount to obtain cash.

Christ and Scriptures own no such practice. Likewise we profess to all the creation that in so doing you rob us of our rights; and you kill us, by denying to give us our livelihood in our own inheritance freely, which is the crown land and common land and waste lands, bishops' and deans', which some of you begin to say you are not satisfied in your conscience to let us have. Aye, well spoke, tender-hearted covetousness! If you do so, you will uphold the kingly power, and so disobey both acts of Parliament and break your oath, and you will live in the breach of those two commandments, *Thou shalt not kill: Thou shalt not steal*, by denying us the earth which is our livelihood, and thereby killing us by a lingering death.

Well, the end of all my speech is to point out the kingly power where I spy it out; and you see it remains strongly in the hands of lords of manors, who have dealt discourteously with some who are sincere in heart, though there have some come among the diggers that have caused scandal, but we disown their ways.*

The lords of manors have sent to beat us, to pull down our houses, spoil our labours; yet we are patient, and never offered any violence to them again, this 40 weeks past, but wait upon God with love till their hearts thereby be softened; and all that we desire is but to live quietly in the land of our nativity, by our righteous labour upon the common land which is our own, but as yet the lords of the manor (so formerly called) will not suffer us, but abuse us. Is not that part of the kingly power? In that which follows I shall clearly prove it is, for it appears so clear that the understanding of a child does say, 'It is tyranny, it is the kingly power of darkness', therefore we expect that you will grant us the benefit of your act of Parliament that we may

* Some Ranters seem to have joined the Digger colony and caused trouble by their 'excessive community of women', which Winstanley attacked in *A Vindication of those ... called Diggers* (S., pp. 399–403). Cf. *Englands Spirit Unfounded*, ed. G. E. Aylmer, *Past and Present*, No. 40, pp. 14–15.

say, 'Truly England is a commonwealth, and a free people indeed.'

Sirs, though your tithing priests and others tell you that we diggers do deny God, Christ and the Scripture, to make us odious and themselves better thought of; yet you will see in time, when the King of righteousness whom we serve does clear our innocence, that our actions and conversation is the very life of the Scripture, and holds forth the true power of God and Christ. For is not the end of all preaching, praying and profession wrapped up in this action, namely, *Love your enemies and do to all men as you would they should do to you, for this is the very law and the prophets*. This is the new commandment that Christ left behind him. Now if any seem to say this and does not do this, but acts contrary, for my part I own not their ways; they are members that uphold the curse.

Bare talking of righteousness, and not acting, hath ruled and yet does rule king of darkness in the creation; and it is the cause of all this immoderate confusion and ignorance that is in men.

But the actings of righteousness from the inward power of love shall rule king of righteousness in the creation now in these latter days, and cast the other serpent and fiery scorpion out; for this is Christ the restoring power: and as he rises up, so multitude of words without action (which is hypocrisy) is to die; his judgment hastens apace.

If any sort of people hold the earth to themselves by the dark kingly power, and shut out others from that freedom, they deny God, Christ and Scriptures, and they overthrow all their preaching, praying and profession; for the Scriptures declare them to be hypocrites, scribes and Pharisees, *that say, and do not*. They have words and no deeds: like Parson Platt the preacher at Horsley in Surrey, a lord of manor (by marriage) of the place where we dig, who caused a poor old man's house that stood upon the common to be pulled down in the evening of a cold day, and turned the old man and his wife and daughter to lie in the open field, because he was a digger: and he and other lords of manors and gentlemen sent their servants up and down the town, to bid their tenants and neighbours neither to give the diggers lodging nor victuals, on pain of their displeasure. Though this Parson Platt preach the Scriptures, yet I'll affirm he denies God, Christ and Scriptures, and knows nothing of them; for covetousness, pride and envy hath blinded his eyes. A man knows no more of righteousness than he hath power to act; and surely this cruelty of preaching Platt is an unrighteous act.

If the diggers were enemies (O you lords of manors) as they are not, you ought to love them. I am sure they love you; and if you doubt it, put them to the trial; you shall find them more faithful than many of those pick-thank slaves and belly-god servants to whom your ears are open, when they bring tales full of envy to you against us.

We are told likewise that to make us who are called diggers odious, and to incense you against us, there came to the General and Council of State divers justices and others, and told you that we diggers were Cavaliers, and that we waited an opportunity and gathered together to stand up for the Prince.*

But all that know us can prove that to be a false report, to the dishonour of those justices; for we have been friends to the Parliament's cause, and so do continue and will continue; for this work of digging, to make England a free commonwealth, is the life and marrow of the Parliament's cause. And the two acts of Parliament, the one to cast out kingly power, the other to make England a free commonwealth, declares it: and we do obey those acts and will obey them, for they hold forth righteousness.

But for our rising in arms for the Prince or any other, let any come and see our strength and work, and they will say, it is a mere envious slander cast upon us, to incense you against us.

Besides, you shall see by and by that our principles are

* i.e. for Charles II.

wholly against kingly power in everyone, as well as in one. Likewise we hear that they told you that the diggers do steal and rob from others. This likewise is a slander: we have things stolen from us, but if any can prove that any of us do steal any man's proper goods, as sheep, geese, pigs (as they say), let such be made a spectacle to all the world. For my part I own no such doing, neither do I know any such thing by any of the diggers. Likewise they report that we diggers hold women to be common, and live in that bestialness. For my part I declare against it. I own this to be a truth, that the earth ought to be a common treasury to all; but as for women, *Let every man have his own wife, and every woman her own husband*; and I know none of the diggers that act in such an unrational excess of female community. If any should, I profess to have nothing to do with such people, but leave them to their own master, who will pay them with torment of mind and diseases in their bodies.

These and such like tales, we hear, are brought to you, to incense you against us: but we desire you to mark them that bring them, for we partly know who they be, and we can tell them to their faces, they were Cavaliers, and had hands in the Kentish rising, and in stirring up that offensive Surrey petition, which was the occasion of bloodshed in Westminster yard, and they would rejoice to see the Prince come in with an army to over-top you,* for we know, they love you not but from the teeth outwards, for their own ends. And these are the proud Hamans that would incense you against the Mordecais of the land, even your true-hearted friends, the diggers. Well, in the midst of our slanders we rejoice in the uprightness of our hearts, and we do *commit our cause to him that judgeth righteously*.

Upon these lying reports and importunity to the General, it seems the General granted the lords of manor to have some soldiers to go along with the sheriff, to pull down the diggers' houses; and so the soldiers did come. But they were

---

* There was a royalist rising in Kent in 1648. The royalist Surrey petition was presented to Parliament on 16 May 1648.

very moderate and rational men, and as they were sent to secure the sheriff, so they did: but there was no cause. For though the gentlemen possessed the General that they feared opposition from the diggers, yet the soldiers saw they lifted not up a finger in discontent, but fought against those dragons, the lords of manors, with the spirit of love and patience. For when the two lords of manor sat among the soldiers on horseback and coach, and commanded their fearful tenants to pull down one of the diggers' houses before their faces, and rejoiced with shouting at the fall; yet some of the diggers stood by and were very cheerful, and preached the gospel to those Turkish bashaws, which are words of life, and in time will prove words of terror to torment their awakened consciences.

And the poor tenants that pulled down the house durst do no other, because their landlords and lords looked on, for fear they should be turned out of service or their livings; as a poor honest man, because he looked with a cheerful countenance upon the diggers (though he was afraid to come near, or afraid to speak openly, lest his landlord's setting-dogs should smell the sound of his words and carry a pick-thank tale, which his lord's ears are much open to) a bailiff was sent presently to him, to warn him out of his house.

Can the Turkish bashaws hold their slaves in more bondage than these gospel-professing lords of manors do their poor tenants? And is not this the kingly power? O you rulers of England, I pray see that your own acts be obeyed, and let the oppressed go free.

And when the poor enforced slaves had pulled down the house, then their lords gave them ten shillings to drink, and there they smiled one upon another; being fearful, like a dog that is kept in awe when his master gives him a bone and stands over him with a whip; he will eat and look up and twinch his tail; for they durst not laugh out, lest their lords should hear they jeered them openly: for in their hearts they are diggers. Therefore you lords of manors, if you have none to stand for you but whom you force by threatening, then leave off striving against the spirit, and say you are fallen; and come in and embrace righteousness, that you may find mercy betimes.

The next day after this there came two soldiers and three countrymen to another house which the diggers had set up (which the sheriff the day before had let alone, for, as some say, he was grieved to see what was done). One of these soldiers was very civil, and walked lovingly with the diggers round their corn which they had planted and commended the work, and would do no harm (as divers others were of the same mind), and when he went his way gave the diggers 12*d*. to drink. But the other soldier was so rude that he forced those three countrymen to help him to pull down the house, and railed bitterly. The men were unwilling to pull it down; but for fear of their landlords and the threatening soldier, they did put their hands to pull it down.

And seeing Parson Platt (the lord of that manor) will not suffer the diggers to have a house (wherein he forgets his master Christ, that is persecuted in naked, hungry and houseless members), yet the diggers were mighty cheerful, and their spirits resolve to wait upon God, to see what he will do. And they have built them some few little hutches like calf-cribs, and there they lie a-nights, and follow their work a-days still with wonderful joy of heart, taking the spoiling of their goods cheerfully, counting it a great happiness to be persecuted for righteousness' sake by the priests and professors that are the successors of Judas and the bitter-spirited Pharisees that put the man Christ Jesus to death. And they have planted divers acres of wheat and rye, which is come up and promises a very hopeful crop, committing their cause to God and wait upon him, saying, 'O thou King of righteousness, do thine own work'.

O that you would search and try our ways narrowly, and see whether we deny God, Christ, Scriptures, as the priests slander us we do; and you shall find that the Scriptures warrant our action, and God in Christ is the life of our souls and the support of our spirits in the midst of this our sharp persecution from the hands of unreasonable men, who have not faith in Christ but uphold the kingly power, which you have voted down.

Likewise you shall see that we live in the performance of that work which is the very life and marrow of the Parliament's cause, whereby we honour the Parliament and their cause: as you shall see by this following declaration, unfolding the foundation whereupon England's laws are, or the freedom of a commonwealth ought to be, built; which is equity and reason.

In the time of the kings, who came in as conquerors and ruled by the power of the sword, not only the common land but the enclosures also were captivated under the will of those kings, till now of late that our later kings granted more freedom to the gentry than they had presently after the conquest: yet under bondage still. For what are prisons, whips and gallows in the times of peace but the laws and power of the sword, forcing and compelling obedience and so enslaving, as if the sword raged in the open field?

England was in such a slavery under the kingly power that both gentry and commonalty groaned under bondage; and to ease themselves, they endeavoured to call a Parliament, that by their counsels and decrees they might find some freedom.

But Charles the then king perceiving that the freedom they strove for would derogate from his prerogative tyranny, thereupon he goes into the north to raise a war against the Parliament; and took William the Conqueror's sword into his hand again, thereby to keep under the former conquered English, and to uphold his kingly power of self-will and prerogative, which was the power got by former conquests; that is, to rule over the lives and estates of all men at his will, and so to make us pure slaves and vassals.

Well, this parliament, that did consist of the chief lords, lords of manors and gentry, and they seeing that the King, by raising an army, did thereby declare his intent to enslave all sorts to him by the sword; and being in distress and in a low ebb, they call upon the common people to bring in their plate, monies, taxes, free-quarter, excise, and to adventure their lives with them, and they would endeavour to recover England from that Noman yoke, and make us a free people. And the common people assent hereunto, and call this the Parliament's cause, and own it and adventure person and purse to preserve it; and by the joint assistance of Parliament and people the king was beaten in the field, his head taken off and his kingly power voted down. And we the commons thereby virtually have recovered ourselves from the Norman conquest; we want nothing but possession of the spoil, which is a free use of the land for our livelihood.

And from hence we the common people, or younger brothers, plead our property in the common land, as truly our own by virtue of this victory over the King as our elder brothers can plead property in their enclosures; and that for three reasons in England's law.

First, by a lawful purchase or contract between the Parliament and us; for they were our landlords and lords of manors, that held the freedom of the commons from us while the King was in his power; for they held title thereunto from him, he being the head and they branches of the kingly power that enslaved the people by that ancient conqueror's sword, that was the ruling power. For they said, 'Come and help us against the King that enslaves us, that we may be delivered from his tyranny, and we will make you a free people'.

Now they cannot make us free unless they deliver us from the bondage which they themselves held us under; and that is, they held the freedom of the earth from us: for we in part with them have delivered ourselves from the King. Now we claim freedom from that bondage you have and yet do hold us under, by the bargain and contract between Parliament and us, who (I say) did consist of lords of manors and landlords, whereof Mr Drake, who hath arrested me for digging upon the common, was one at that time. Therefore by the law of bargain and sale we claim of them our freedom, to live comfortably with them in this land of our nativity; and this we cannot do so long as we lie under poverty, and must not be suffered to plant the commons and waste land for our livelihood. For take away the land from any people, and those people are in a way of continual death and misery; and better not to have had a body, than not to have food and raiment for it. But (I say) they have sold us our freedom in the common, and have been largely paid for it; for by means of our bloods and money they sit in peace: for if the King had prevailed, they had lost all, and been in slavery to the meanest Cavalier, if the King would. Therefore we the commons say, 'Give us our bargain: if you deny us our bargain, you deny God, Christ and Scriptures; and all your profession then is and hath been hypocrisy'.

Secondly, the commons and crown land is our property by equal conquest over the kingly power: for the Parliament did never stir up the people by promises and covenant to assist them to cast out the King and to establish them in the King's place and prerogative power. No, but all their declarations were for the safety and peace of the whole nation.

Therefore the common people being part of the nation, and especially they that bore the greatest heat of the day in casting out the oppressor: and the nation cannot be in peace so long as the poor oppressed are in wants and the land is entangled and held from them by bondage.

But the victory being obtained over the King, the spoil, which is properly the land, ought in equity to be divided now between the two parties, that is Parliament and common people. The Parliament, consisting of lords of manors and gentry, ought to have their enclosure lands free to them without molestation, as they are freed from the Court of Wards;

And the common people, consisting of soldiers and such as paid taxes and free-quarter, ought to have the freedom of all waste and common land and crown land equally among them. The soldiery ought not in equity to have all, nor the other people that paid them to have all; but the spoil ought to be divided between them that stayed at home and them that went to war; for the victory is for the whole nation.

And as the Parliament declared they did all for the nation, and not for themselves only; so we plead with the Army, they did not fight for themselves, but for the freedom of the nation: and I say, we have bought our freedom of them likewise by taxes and free-quarter. Therefore we claim an equal freedom with them in this conquest over the King.

Thirdly, we claim an equal portion in the victory over the King by virtue of the two acts of Parliament: the one to make England a free commonwealth, the other to take away kingly power. Now the kingly power (you have heard) is a power that rules by the sword in covetousness and self, giving the earth to some and denying it to others: and this kingly power was not in the hand of the King alone; but lords, and lords of manors, and corrupt judges and lawyers especially, held it up likewise. For he was the head and they, with the tithing priests, are the branches of that tyrannical kingly power; and all the several limbs and members must be cast out before kingly power can be pulled up root and branch. Mistake me not, I do not say, cast out the persons of men. No, I do not desire their fingers to ache: but I say, cast out their power whereby they hold the people in bondage, as the King held them in bondage. And I say, it is our own freedom we claim, both by bargain and by equality in the conquest; as well as by the law of righteous creation which gives the earth to all equally.

And the power of lords of manors lies in this: they deny the common people the use and free benefit of the earth, unless they give them leave and pay them for it, either in rent, in fines, in homages or heriots. Surely the earth was never made by God that the younger brother should not live in the earth unless he would work for and pay his elder brother rent for the earth. No; this slavery came in by conquest, and it is part of the kingly power; and England cannot be a free commonwealth till this bondage be taken away. You have taken away the King; you have taken away the House of Lords.* Now step two steps further, and take away the power of lords of manors and of tithing priests, and the intolerable oppressions of judges by whom laws are corrupted; and your work will be honourable.

Fourthly, if this freedom be denied the common people, to enjoy the common land; then Parliament, Army and judges will deny equity and reason, whereupon the laws of a well-governed commonwealth ought to be built. And if this equity be denied, then there can be no law but club law among the people: and if the sword must reign, then every party will be striving to bear the sword; and then fare-well peace; nay, farewell religion and gospel, unless it be made use of to entrap one another, as we plainly see some priests and others make it a cloak for their knavery. If I adventure my life and fruit of my labour equal with you, and obtain what we strive for; it is both equity and reason that I should equally divide the spoil with you, and not you to have all and I none. And if you deny us this, you take away our property from us, our monies and blood, and give us nothing for it.

Therefore, I say, the common land is my own land, equal with my fellow-commoners, and our true property, by the law of creation: it is everyone's, but not one single one's. Yea, the commons are as truly ours by the last excellent two acts of Parliament, the foundation of England's new righteous government aimed at, as the elder brothers can say the enclosures are theirs. For they adventured their lives and covenanted with us to help them to preserve their freedom: and we adventured our lives and they covenanted with us to purchase and to give us our freedom, that hath been hundreds of years kept from us.

Daemona non armis, sed morte subegit Jesus.

* By Act of Parliament, 17 March 1649.

> *By patient sufferings, not by death,*
> *Christ did the devil kill;*
> *And by the same, still to this day,*
> *his foes he conquers still.*

True religion and undefiled is this, to make restitution of the earth, which hath been taken and held from the common people by the power of conquests formerly and so *set the oppressed free*. Do not all strive to enjoy the land? The gentry strive for land, the clergy strive for land, the common people strive for land; and buying and selling is an art whereby people endeavour to cheat one another of the land. Now if any can prove from the law of righteousness that the land was made peculiar to him and his successively, shutting others out, he shall enjoy it freely for my part. But I affirm it was made for all; and true religion is to let every one enjoy it. Therefore, you rulers of England, make restitution of the lands which the kingly power holds from us: *set the oppressed free*, and come in and honour Christ, who is the restoring power, and you shall find rest.

The CURSE *and* BLESSING *that is in* MANKIND

In the beginning of time, the spirit of universal love appeared to be the father of all things. The creation of fire, water, earth and air came out of him and is his clothing. Love is the Word.

The creation is the house or garden in which this one spirit hath taken up his seat, and in which he manifests himself. For if ever love be seen or known, he appears either in the inward feeling within your hearts, loving all with tender love; or else appears towards you from outward objects, as from other men or other creatures.

There are two earths in which the spirit of love declares himself. First the living earth, called mankind: this is the creation or the living soul. And when this spirit of universal love rules king therein, this earth is then in peace, and is grown up to the perfection of a man anointed. But when self or particular love rules, which is called the sin covetousness, then this earth is brought into bondage, and sorrow fills all places. This is the dark side of the cloud, in which there is no true peace.

Secondly, in the great body of earth, in which all creatures subsist, the spirit of universal love appears to preserve his creation in peace: for universal love unites not only mankind into an oneness, but unites all other creatures into a sweet harmony of willingness to preserve mankind. And this spirit of love spread abroad is the same spirit of love that is supreme in man: and this is the righteous man.

But when covetousness or particular love began to work, then not only mankind was divided amongst themselves but all creatures were divided, and enmity rose up amongst them, setting one against another; and this power is the wicked man: mark him where you see him, which is the murderer and must be cast out.

Well, in the beginning universal love appeared to be the father of all things (though self-love in our experience rules in man first); and as he made mankind to be the lord of the earth, so he made the earth to be a common treasury of livelihood to whole mankind without respect of persons; and for all other creatures likewise that were to proceed from the earth.

Mankind is the chief creature, and the spirit of universal love in his branches is the lord of all the earth; and this spirit in man unfolds himself in light and darkness. His face is called the universal power of love: his back parts is called the selfish power: or thus, the one is called the son of bondage which causes shame, the other is called the son of freedom which brings peace and honour. These two strive in the womb of the earth, which shall come forth first and which shall rule; the fleshy man hath got the start; but the other will prove the stronger and cast him out with honour.

While this spirit of lordship in the last day-time of mankind was universal love and righteousness, leading every single branch of mankind to do to another as he would be done unto; then every thing was in peace, and there was a sweet communion of love in the creation: and as the spirit was a common treasury of unity and peace within, so the earth was a common treasury of delight for the preservation of their bodies without; so that there was nothing but peace upon the face of the whole earth.

This was man's estate before the Fall, or the day-time of mankind; for since the time that our Bibles speak of Adam on this day is about 6000 years; and this time hath been the night-time of mankind: and Isaiah's time was about midnight, when in one of his words he cries, *Watchman, what of the night? Watchman, what of the night?* The seventh thousand year which is now dawning will be the rising of the son of universal love again, and of the dispersing of the night or darkness; for as the night and day, sun and moon, hath their exchanges, so hath these two powers, called sons of God in mankind; and in this age wherein we now live is the expiring of the selfish power, and the rising up of the blessing which hath been spoke of in all ages, but now appearing like lightning from east to west, casting out the mystery of iniquity or self-power by the word of his mouth and by the brightness of his coming, and so bringing peace.

So that, as there is the power of light which is universal love, called the blessing which brings peace; so there is the power of darkness which is particular or self-love, and this is called the curse, for it brings sorrow: and while this rules king in the earth, as it doth at this day visibly through the whole earth, few are saved, that is, few enter into rest and peace; for this power hath filled all places with his stinking self-seeking government and troubles everybody.

As there is light and darkness, day and night, clouds and clearness, moving upon the face of the great earth; and as there is earth and waters in the great world which runs round: so mankind is called sometimes earth, sometimes waters; and as the sun in the skies moves upon the great earth and makes that fruitful which seemed dead, while the sun is under the dark cloudy winter quarter:

Even so the son of universal love who is the spirit and power of universal freedom, he moves upon the living waters (mankind) and makes him (who all the dark time past was a chaos of confusion, lying under types, shadows, ceremonies, forms, customs, ordinances and heaps of waste words, under which the spirit of truth lay buried) now to enlighten, to worship in spirit and truth, and to bring forth fruit of righteousness in action.

In our present experience, the darkness or self-love goeth before, and light or universal love follows after; the flesh runs hasty and quick and loses himself in unrational excessive action; the true spirit comes slowly after and takes the crown.

Darkness and bondage doth oppress liberty and light;

and the power of universal love appears most sweet and full of glory when the power of self-love or covetousness hath tortured the creation (mankind) with bitter tyranny: for this is the dragon or murderer that must be cast out before the creation (man) can sing Hallelujah in peace.

So then you may see that the innocence, light and purity of mankind is this, when the spirit of universal love lives in him and he lives in love, enjoying the sweet union and communion of spirit, each with other.

When they enjoy the sweet delight of the unity of one spirit, and the free content of the fruits and crops of this outward earth upon which their bodies stand: this was called the man's innocence or pleasure in the garden before his fall, or the day-time of mankind; and day is more glorious than night: and greater honour to be a child of the day than of the night.

The fall of mankind or his darkness is this, when that son of universal love, which was the seed out of which the creation sprung forth, did begin to go behind the cloud of flesh, and to let self-seeking flesh which would needs be a god stand alone by his imaginary light (as we see, while the sun is in the skies, a man sees and knows his footsteps, but when the sun is set under the cloud of the dark night, then he imagines his way and oft times stumbles and falls):

Even so when universal love shines in his glory in mankind, he stumbles not, he walks in the light because the light is in him; but when the light within withdraws and lets flesh stand alone, flesh (that is, the selfish power) will not wait in peace and acknowledge himself in a loss and in darkness till the sun rise again:

But will fain be a god, and calls his weakness strength; and though there appears nothing but deformity, yet he would have it called beauty; and because his inward power is not suitable to his outward profession, he is tormented: he is a saint without but a devil within. But if thou wouldest have peace, act as thou art, shew thyself abroad in action what thou art secretly; but when thou beginst to imagine a content and happiness to thyself by thy hypocritical self-invention, then thou art tormented, or shalt be.

And by this imagination mankind tears himself in pieces; as one of of your colonels of the Army said to me that the diggers did work upon George Hill for no other end but to draw a company of people into arms; and says 'our knavery is found out, because it takes not that effect'.

Truly, thou colonel, I tell thee, thy knavish imagination is thereby discovered, which hinders the effecting of that freedom which by oath and covenant thou hast engaged to maintain: for my part and the rest, we had no such thought. We abhor fighting for freedom, it is acting of the curse and lifting him up higher; and do thou uphold it by the sword, we will not: we will conquer by love and patience, or else we count it no freedom. Freedom gotten by the sword is an established bondage to some part or other of the creation; and this we have declared publicly enough; therefore thy imagination told thee a lie, and will deceive thee in a greater matter, if love doth not kill him. Victory that is gotten by the sword is a victory that slaves gets one over another; and hereby *men of the basest spirit* (saith Daniel) *are set to rule*: but victory obtained by love is a victory for a king.

But by this you may see what a liar imagination is, and how he makes bate * and tears the creation in pieces; for after that self-love hath subdued others under him, then imagination studies how to keep himself up and keep others down.

This is your very inward principle, O ye present powers of England, you do not study how to advance universal love; if you did, it would appear in action. But imagination and self-love mightily disquiets your mind and makes you call up all the powers of darkness to come forth and help to set the crown upon the head of self, which is that kingly power you have oathed and vowed against, and yet uphold it in your hands.

Imagination begets covetousness after pleasure, honour

* Contention, strife.

and riches. Covetousness begets fear, lest others should cross them in their design; or else begets a fear of want, and this makes a man to draw the creatures to him by hook or crook and to please the strongest side, looking what others do, not minding what himself doth.

Like some of your great officers, that told me that we diggers took away other men's property from them by digging upon the common; yet they have taken mine and other men's property of money (got by honest labour) in taxes and free-quarter to advance themselves and not allow us that [which] they promised us; for it [is] this beam in their own eyes they cannot see.

This fear begets hypocrisy, subtlety, envy and hardness of heart, which makes a man to break all promises and engagements, and to seek to save himself in others' ruin, and to suppress and oppress every one that does not say as he says and do as he does.

And this hardness of heart begets pride and security, and this begets luxury and lust of the flesh, and this runs into all excess with greediness and being in discontent against any that crosses his pleasure, till his heart become fully like the heart of a beast, as it is apparent in some at this day.

And thus by the power of self-love being advanced by the covetous sword against universal love, that power of darkness rises up to perfection in mankind; and so he makes one branch to tear and devour another by divisions, evil surmisings, envious fightings and killing, and by oppressing the meek in spirit, by unrighteous laws or by his self-will managing good laws unrighteously, as corrupt judges know how to do it and think none sees them; whereby part of mankind hath freedom and another part is cast out and thrown under bondage.

And all this falling out or quarrelling among mankind is about the earth, who shall and who shall not enjoy it; when indeed it is the portion of every one and ought not to be striven for, nor bought nor sold, whereby some are hedged in and others hedged out. For better not to have had a body, than to be debarred the fruit of the earth to feed and clothe it; and if every one did but quietly enjoy the earth for food and raiment, there would be no wars, prisons nor gallows; and this action which man calls theft would be no sin, for universal love never made it a sin, but the power of covetousness made that a sin, and made laws to punish it, though he himself live in that sin in a higher manner than [those] he hangs or punisheth. Those very men that punish others for theft do thieve and rob, as judges and lawyers that take bribes or that takes their clients' money and through neglect lose their cause. Parliament and Army lives in theft, whenas they take the commoners' money and free-quarter, and tell them what they do is to make England a free commonwealth; and yet all they do is to make the gentry free and leaves the commoners under bondage still. Or else why do you send your soldiers to beat a few naked spademen off from digging the commons for a livelihood, why do you not let the oppressed go free? Have they not bought it of you by their monies and blood as well as the gentry, and will not you make good your contract? Well, he that made the earth for us as well as for you will set us free though you will not. When will the veil of darkness be drawn off your faces? Will you not be wise, O ye rulers?

Well, this power of darkness is man's fall, or the night-time of mankind.

But universal love hath declared that he will rise again, and he himself who is the seed will bruise that serpent's head and reconcile mankind to himself again, and restore him to that innocence and peace which he is fallen from. When this son arises in more strength, and appears to be the saviour indeed, he will then make mankind to be all of one heart and one mind, and make the earth to be a common treasury, though for the present in outward view there is nothing but darkness and confusion upon the face of the earth, mankind.

When self-love began to arise in the earth, then man began to fall; this is Adam or the power of darkness that stops up the waters and well springs of life, or the clouds that hide the son of righteousness from man.

This Adam or dark power was small at the first, but he is risen to great strength, and the whole earth is now filled with him, as Isaiah saith, *Darkness hath covered the earth*, mankind. For let any that hath eyes look either to them above or them below, and they see darkness or the devil rule, and this curse destroys the earth. The creation sits like Rachel sighing, mourning and groaning under his oppressing power, and will not be comforted because they see no saviour to appear for their deliverance.

Indeed there are many saviours in word, but none in deed, and these great false Christs and false prophets does destroy the creation under the colour of saving it; and the people sees them not, but looks upon them as saviours, calling others false Christs and false prophets that speak against them.

The first false Christ that promises to save the creation is covetous kingly power, resting in the hand of one man or in the hand of many; but this power saves but part, and holds another part of the creation in bondage; and any government that rules by swordly power doth so throughout all lands: therefore he is a false Christ, and no true saviour.

The preaching clergy or universative * power promises to save the creation declaratively; but he is a false Christ, he saith and doth not, Pharisee-like, but will force people to maintain him from the earth by their labours for his sayings, by the laws of the kingly power. He saith some are elected to salvation and others are reprobated; he puts some into heaven, thrusts others into hell never to come out, and so he is not a universal saviour. That is no salvation to the creation, mankind, while any part groans for the true saviour; when he comes he will wipe away all tears, he comes not to destroy any but to save all.

Then the power of the lawyers, he saith he will save the creation, and this false Christ proves the greatest devourer and tearer of the creation of any other; for while he carries

* University?

193

burdened men from one court to another promising to save them, he at last saves himself and destroys others and laughs at others' loss, and throws men further from peace than he found them before he meddled with them. Well, from the bailiff to the judge, these are the creations of this Egyptian task-master, and no burden of cheating like to it; for he promises justice, but behold nothing but oppression is in his hands.

Then next the art of buying and selling promises to save the creation and bring it into peace; but this is a hypocritical false cheating Christ too. For hereby covetous self-love with his flattering tongue cheats honest-hearted ones and casts them under tyranny, and gets the fulness of the earth into his hands, and lock[s] it up in chests and barns from others, and saith this is righteous and God gave it him. But thou cheater, thou liest; God the King of righteousness gave it thee not, he bids thee sell all that thou hast and give to the poor, he doth not bid thee lock it up from the poor. Therefore thou trading art, thou art no true saviour neither, but a devil, thou savest part, and destroyest another part, yea and afterwards destroyest that part which at first thou seemedst to save.

Now all these saviours are linked together, if one truly fall all must fall; they all promise to save the creation but destruction is in their hands and actions, they all seek to set up self and particular power, and so to save but part of the creation, for every one are destroyers of universal love. They that sit in these seats would be called men of public spirits, but truly you are all selfish, you are afraid to own public-spirited men, nay you are ashamed some of you to be seen walking or talking with true public-spirited men called Levellers.

But well, yet there is a promise of restoration and salvation to the whole creation, and this must be wrought by a power contrary to darkness; for all those former saviours lie under darkness, nay are branches of the power of darkness itself, and darkness can never kill darkness; but now the true saviour must be a power quite opposite to darkness. And this is the power of universal love, light and righteousness; and if ever the creation be wholly saved, this power must be the saviour; for this is the blessing and he will declare himself the true saviour indeed, the other is but the curse. This is the true restorer, the true seed with us; as he arises and spreads, he will bruise the serpent's head in everyone and bring peace to all, and wipe away all tears from the creation, and make a thorough salvation of it through the whole earth and leave none under bondage.

This is the sun of righteousness; when he ariseth, he disperseth darkness and will make all ashamed that had hands in promoting of the other false saviours' power. But I must leave this and speak a little more of the present condition mankind lies under, and this is darkness or the Fall; and in this estate ignorant enslaved flesh would ever run round in it and never come out, but counts it freedom; but they that know the burden of this estate hunger after freedom.

This darkness is twofold. First inward, and that is the power of darkness in his branches, as covetousness, envy, pride, hypocrisy, self-love; this is the curse in man, and this darkness hath and yet doth cover the earth; this power would be as God, and makes one to rule over another; and he is so proud that he will hasten to rule though he kill others for honour, and this is he that stirs up wars and dissension and thereby he destroys himself.

Secondly this inward power sets one against another, and so fills the earth with dark actions, and causeth some part of mankind to tread others under foot and puts them into bondage. And they that act this power calls it the power and ordinance of God, which is true: it is God indeed, but it is the god of the world, the prince of darkness, not the King of righteousness. It is the power of the Beast, who is limited to rule for a time, times and dividing of time; and England is under that dividing of time, therefore I hope England shall be the tenth part of the city Confusion that shall fall from the Beast first.

And this dark power or imaginary covetousness hath

raised a platform of oppression in the creation, under which the creation groans and waits to be delivered; and it is raised thus:

First this dark power within makes every one to love himself with others' loss, just like beasts of the field; and this made mankind to begin to loathe or envy each other's freedom and peace, and hereby the union and communion of love within is broke, and mankind is fallen from it. Then this inward covetousness makes mankind to fight one against another for the earth, and breaks communion in that, and falls from content therein likewise; and everyone seeks to save himself, to take the earth to himself, but none or few seeks the things of Christ, or of universal love.

Nay covetousness is such a god, that where he rules he would have all the earth to himself, and he would have all to be his servants; and his heart swells most against community, calling community a thief, that takes other men's rights and property from them. But community will force nothing from anyone, but take what is given in love, of that which others have wrought for; but no man yet hath bestowed any labour upon the commons that lies waste; therefore the diggers doth take no man's proper goods from them in so doing, but those that by force spoils their labours takes their proper goods from them, which is the fruit of their own labours.

Well, you see how covetousness would have all the earth to himself, though he let it lie waste: he stirs up divisions among men and makes parties fight against parties; and all is but for this: who shall enjoy the earth and live in honour and ease and rule over others: and the stronger party always rules over the weaker party.

And hence came in kingly power to rule outwardly, dividing between members of that one body, mankind, giving the earth to that party called gentry, who are the successors of some late conquests, and denying the earth to the poor commoners who are the successors of some that were last conquered.

So that by kingly power the earth is divided as it is now at this day: but as the Scriptures say, *Kings were given for a plague to the people, not a blessing.* And I believe the nations have found this very true to their great sorrow: and the way to cast out kingly power again is not to cast them out by the sword, for this doth but set him in more power and removes him from a weaker to a stronger hand: but the only way to cast him out is for the people to leave him to himself, to forsake fighting and all oppression, and to live in love one towards another. This power of love is the true saviour.

The party that is called a king was but the head of an army, and he and his army having conquered shuts the conquered out of the earth, and will not suffer them to enjoy it, but as a servant and slave to him; and by this power the creation is divided, and part are cast into bondage. So that the best you can say of kingly power that rules by the sword is this: he is a murderer and a thief.

And by this power the earth is thus divided:

The several nations of the earth where kings rule are the several situation of such grand thieves and murderers, that will rule over others by the sword, upholding a forced property, which is the curse; and persecuting the community of love, which is Christ the blessing.

And under them they have their chief favourites or nearest soldiers in office to himself; and to these he allows the greatest portion of the earth, every one his part, called a lordship: and next to them the inferior officers or soldiers are appointed out lesser parcels of the earth, called freeholders, paying no slavish rent or homage to any, but only acknowledgment that the king is their general or head still.

And these lords of manors and freeholders, having thus seated themselves in the earth by taking other men's proper labours from them by the sword, are appointed by the king as watchmen, that if any of the conquered slaves seek to plant the common waste earth without their leave, they may be known and beaten off. So that the god from whom they claim title to the land as proper to them, shutting out others, was covetousness the murderer, the swordly power, that great red dragon who is called the god of the world.

But the King of righteousness, who is universal love, who is the Lord God Almighty, bidding every one *do as they would be done by*, made the earth for all, without respect of person, and shuts out none from enjoying a peaceable livelihood that hath a body. Therefore they that build upon the power of the sword, upholding covetous property, are enemies to the law of righteousness, which is *Love your enemies, do as you would be done by*.

But one of your officers told me: 'What?' (saith he) 'If we grant to every one to have the land of England in common, we do not only destroy property but we do that which is not practised in any nation in the world.'

I answered, it was true. Property came in you see by the sword, therefore the curse; for the murderer brought it in and upholds him by his power; and it makes a division in the creation, casting many under bondage; therefore it is not the blessing or the promised seed.

And what other lands do, England is not to take pattern; for England (as well as other lands) hath lain under the power of that Beast, kingly property. But now England is the first of nations that is upon the point of reforming: and if England must be the tenth part of the city Babylon that falls off from the Beast first, and would have that honour, he must cheerfully (and dally no longer) cast out kingly covetous property, and set the crown upon Christ's head, who is the universal love or free community, and so be the leader of that happy restoration to all the nations of the world. And if England refuse, some other nation may be chosen before him, and England then shall lose his crown, for if ever the creation be restored, this is the way which lies in this twofold power:

First community of mankind, which is comprised in the unity of spirit of love, which is called Christ in you or the

law written in the heart, leading mankind into all truth and
to be of one heart and one mind;

The second is community of the earth, for the quiet livelihood in food and raiment without using force or restraining
one another. These two communities, or rather one in two
branches, is that true levelling which Christ will work at his
more glorious appearance, for Jesus Christ the saviour of all
men is the greatest, first and truest Leveller that ever was
spoke of in the world.

Therefore you rulers of England, be not ashamed nor
afraid of Levellers, hate them not, Christ comes to you
riding upon these clouds. Look not upon other lands to be
your pattern, all lands in the world lie under darkness. So
doth England yet, though the nearest to light and freedom
of any other; therefore let no other land take your
crown.

You have set Christ upon his throne in England by your
promises, engagements, oaths and two acts of Parliament:
the one to cast out kingly power, the other to make England
a free commonwealth. Put all these into sincere action, and
you shall see the work is done, and you with others shall
sing Hallelujah to him that sits upon the throne, and to the
Lamb for evermore.

But if you do not, the Lamb shall shew himself a lion, and
tear you in pieces for your most abominable dissembling
hypocrisy, and give your land to a people who better deserves
it. I have varied a little, therefore I will return to what I was
speaking.

I told you that the murdering and thieving sword hath
found out a platform of tyrannical government called
kingly power.

First here is the king, the head of the murdering power
or great red dragon.

Then there are lords of manors, who have the greatest
circuit of land because the next in power to the head.

Then there are freeholders, that took the particular enclosures which they found in a land when they conquered

it, and had turned out those that had bestowed labour upon it by force of the sword in the field, or else by sequestering afterwards. These several parcels of land are called freehold land because the enjoyers or their ancestors were soldiers and helped the king to conquer; and if any of latter years came to buy these freeholds with money got by trading, it doth not alter the title of the conquest; for evidences are made in the king's name, to remove the freeholds so bought from one man's hand to another.

But now copyhold lands are parcels hedged in and taken out of the common waste land since the conquest, acknowledging homage, fines and heriots to the lord of that manor or circuit in which that enclosure by his leave is made: this homage still confirms the power of the conquests.

The lords of manors acknowledged homage to the king in that Court of Wards which you have taken away to ease yourselves.

But the copyholders you will have to acknowledge homage to lords of manors still; and is not this partiality? O you rulers, make the poor as free to the earth as your selves, and honour righteousness.

Now for the drawing in of the people to yield obedience to this platform of kingly tyrannical power to which people are made subject through fear:

The kingly power sets up a preaching clergy to draw the people by insinuating words to conform hereunto, and for their pains kingly power gives them the tithes. And when the kingly power hath any design to lift up himself higher, then the clergy is to preach up that design, as of late in our wars the preachers most commonly in their sermons meddled with little but state matters: and then if people seem to deny tithes, then the kingly power by his laws doth force the people to pay them: so that there is a confederacy between the clergy and the great red dragon. The sheep of Christ shall never fare well so long as the wolf or red dragon pays the shepherd their wages.

Then next after this the kingly power sets up a law and

rule of government to walk by: and here justice is pretended, but the full strength of the law is to uphold the conquering sword and to preserve his son property. Therefore if any one steal, this law will hang them, and this they say is of God; and so this kingly power hath power over the lives and labours of men at his pleasure. For though they say the law doth punish, yet indeed that law is but the strength, life and marrow of the kingly power, upholding the conquest still, hedging some into the earth, hedging out others; giving the earth to some and denying the earth to others, which is contrary to the law of righteousness, who made the earth at first as free for one as for another.

Yea that kingly power in the laws appointed the conquered poor to work for them that possess the land, for three pence and four pence a day; and if any refused, they were to be imprisoned; and if any walked a-begging and had no dwelling, he was to be whipped; and all was to force the slaves to work for them that had taken their property of their labours from them by the sword, as the laws of England are yet extant. And truly most laws are but to enslave the poor to the rich, and so they uphold the conquest and are laws of the great red dragon.

And at this very day poor people are forced to work in some places for 4, 5 and 6 pence a day; in other places for 8, 10 and 12 pence a day, for such small prizes now (corn being dear) that their earnings cannot find them bread for their family. And yet if they steal for maintenance, the murdering law will hang them; whenas lawyers, judges and court officers can take bribes by wholesale to remove one man's property by that law into another man's hands: and is not this worse thievery than the poor man's that steals for want? Well, this shews that if this be law, it is not the law of righteousness; it is a murderer, it is the law of covetousness and self-love; and this law that frights people and forces people to obey it by prisons, whips and gallows is the very kingdom of the devil and darkness which the creation groans under at this day.

And if any poor enslaved man that dares not steal begins to mourn under that bondage and saith, 'We that work most have least comfort in the earth, and they that work not at all, enjoy all'; contrary to the Scripture which saith, *The poor and the meek shall inherit the earth*:

Presently the tithing priest stops his mouth with a slam and tells him that is meant of the inward satisfaction of mind which the poor shall have, though they enjoy nothing at all; and so poor creatures, it is true, they have some ease thereby, and [are] made to wait with patience, while the kingly power swims in fulness and laughs at the other's misery: as a poor Cavalier gentlewoman presented a paper to the General in my sight, who looked upon the woman with a tender countenance; but a brisk little man and two or three more colonels pulled back the paper, not suffering the General to receive it, and laughed at the woman, who answered them again: 'I thought,' said she, 'you had not sat in the seat of the scornful'. This was done in Whitehall upon the 12 of December, 1649.

Well, all that I shall say to these men that will enjoy the earth in reality, and tell others they must enjoy it in conceit, surely your judgment from the most High sleepeth not; the law of retaliation, like for like, laughing for laughing, may be your portion. For my part I was always against the Cavaliers' cause; yet their persons are part of the creation as well as you, and many of them may enter into peace before some of you scoffing Ishmaelites. I am sure you act contrary to the Scripture which bids you *love your enemies, and do as you would be done by*, and this Scripture you say you own. Why then do you not practise it, and do to the Cavaliers as the prophet Elijah bid the king of Israel do to his enemies whom he had taken prisoners: *Set bread and water* (saith he) *before them, and send them to their master in peace.*

Come, make peace with the Cavaliers your enemies, and let the oppressed go free, and let them have a livelihood; and love your enemies, and do to them as you would have had them done to you if they had conquered you. Well, let them go in peace, and let love wear the crown.

For I tell you and your preachers, that Scripture which saith *The poor shall inherit the earth*, is really and materially to be fulfilled. For the earth is to be restored from the bondage of sword property, and it is to become a common treasury in reality to whole mankind; for this is the work of the true saviour to do, who is the true and faithful Leveller, even the spirit and power of universal love, that is now rising to spread himself in the whole creation, who is the blessing, and will spread as far as the curse had spread, to take it off and cast him out, and who will set the creation in peace.

This powerful saviour will not set up his kingdom nor rule his creation with sword and fighting, as some think and fear; for he hath declared to you long since that they that take the sword to save themselves shall perish with the sword.

But this shall be the way of his conquest: even as in the days of the Beast, the whole world wondered after him, set him up and was subject to him, and did persecute universal love and made war against him and his saints, and overcame them for a time:

Even so the spirit of love and blessing shall arise and spread in mankind like the sun from east to west, and by his inward power of love, light and righteousness shall let mankind see the abomination of the swordly kingly power, and shall loathe themselves in dust and ashes, in that they have owned and upheld him so long; and shall fall off from him, loathe him and leave him.

And this shall be your misery, O you covetous oppressing tyrants of the earth, not only you great self-seeking powers of England but you powers of all the world. The people shall all fall off from you, and you shall fall on a sudden like a great tree that is undermined at the root. And you powers of England, you cannot say: 'another day'; but you had warning, this falling off is begun already, divisions shall tear and torture you till you submit to community. O come in, come in to righteousness that you may find peace.

You or some of you hate the name Leveller, and the chiefest of you are afraid and ashamed to own a Leveller, and you laugh and jeer at them. Well, laugh out, poor blind souls; the people and common soldiers both lets you alone, but they laugh in their hearts at you, and yet desire that you did know the things that concern your peace.

The time is very near that the people generally shall loathe and be ashamed of your kingly power, in your preaching, in your laws, in your counsels, as now you are ashamed of the Levellers. I tell you Jesus Christ who is that powerful spirit of love is the head Leveller; and *as he is lifted up, he will draw all men after him*, and leave you naked and bare, and make you ashamed in yourselves. His appearance will be with power; therefore kiss the son, O ye rulers of the earth, lest his anger fall upon you. The wounds of conscience within you from him shall be sharper than the wounds made by your sword, he shook heaven and earth when Moses's law was cast out, but he will shake heaven and earth now to purpose much more, and nothing shall stand but what is lovely. Be wise, scorn not the counsel of the poor, lest you be whipped with your own rod.

This great Leveller, Christ our King of righteousness in us, shall cause men to beat their swords into ploughshares and spears into pruning hooks, and nations shall learn war no more; and every one shall delight to let each other enjoy the pleasures of the earth, and shall hold each other no more in bondage: then what will become of your power? Truly he must be cast out for a murderer; and I pity you for the torment your spirit must go through, if you be not fore-armed, as you are abundantly fore-warned from all places. But I look upon you as part of the creation who must be restored, and the spirit may give you wisdom to foresee a danger, as he hath admonished divers of your rank already to leave those high places, and to lie quiet and wait for the breakings forth of the powerful day of the Lord. Farewell, once more. *Let Israel go free.*

*A bill of account of the most remark-
able sufferings that the diggers have met
with from the great red dragon's power
since April 1, 1649, which was the
first day that they began to dig and to
take possession of the commons for the poor
on George Hill in Surrey.*

1 The first time, divers of the diggers were carried prisoners into Walton church, where some of them were struck
in the church by the bitter professors * and rude multitude;
but after some time freed by a justice.

2 They were fetched by above a hundred rude people,
whereof John Taylor was the leader, who took away their
spades, and some of them they never had again: and carried
them first to prison at Walton and then to a justice at Kingston, who presently dismissed them.

3 The dragonly enemy pulled down a house which the
diggers had built upon George Hill, and cut their spades and
hoes to pieces.

4 Two troops of horse were sent from the General to fetch
us before the Council of War, to give account of our digging.

5 We had another house pulled down and our spades cut
to pieces.

6 One of the diggers had his head sore wounded, and a
boy beaten and his clothes taken from him: divers being by.

7 We had a cart and wheels cut in pieces, and a mare cut

* See note on p. 91 above.

205

over the back with a bill, when we went to fetch a load of wood from *Stoke* common to build a house upon *George Hill.*

8 *Divers of the diggers were beaten upon the hill by William Star and John Taylor, and by men in women's apparel, and so sore wounded that some of them were fetched home in a cart.*

9 *We had another house pulled down, and the wood they carried to Walton in a cart.*

10 *They arrested some of us, and some they cast into prison; and from others they went about to take away their goods, but that the goods proved another man's, which one of the diggers was servant to.*

11 *And indeed at divers times besides we had all our corn spoiled; for the enemy was so mad that they tumbled the earth up and down, and would suffer no corn to grow.*

12 *Another cart and wheels was cut to pieces, and some of our tools taken by force from us, which we never had again.*

13 *Some of the diggers were beaten by the gentlemen, the sheriff looking on, and afterwards five of them were carried to White Lion Prison and kept there about 5 weeks, and then let out.*

14 *The sheriff, with the lords of manors and soldiers standing by, caused two or three poor men to pull down another house: and divers things were stolen from them.*

15 *The next day two soldiers and two or three countrymen sent by Parson Platt pulled down another house, and turned a poor old man and his wife out of doors to lie in the field in a cold night.*

And this is the last hitherto; and so you priests, as you were the last that had a hand in our persecution, so it may be that misery may rest in your hand; for assure yourselves, God in Christ will not be mocked by such hypocrites that pretend to be his nearest and dearest servants as you do, and yet will not suffer his hungry, naked and houseless members to live quiet by you in the earth, by whose blood and monies in these wars you are in peace.

And now those diggers that remain have made little hutches to lie in like calf-cribs, and are cheerful; taking the spoiling of their goods patiently, and rejoicing that they are counted worthy to suffer persecution for righteousness' sake. And they follow their work close, and have planted divers acres of wheat and rye, which is come up and promises a very fruitful crop, and resolves to preserve it by all the diligence they can. And nothing shall make them slack but want of food, which is not much now, they being all poor people, and having suffered so much in one expense or other since they began; for poverty is their greatest burden, and if anything do break them from the work, it will be that.

> *You lordly foes you will rejoice*
> *   this news to hear and see;*
> *Do so, go on; but we'll rejoice*
> *   much more the truth to see.*
> *For by our hands truth is declared,*
> *   and nothing is kept back;*
> *Our faithfulness much joy doth bring,*
> *   though victuals we may lack.*
> *This trial may our God see good,*
> *   to try, not us, but you;*
> *That your profession of the truth*
> *   may prove either false or true.*

And these are the troubles and persecutions that the diggers have gone through since they began, besides many particular abuses from rude spirits, and multitudes of slanders, lies and bad names, that the mouths of the scoffing Ishmaelites are filled with, and the secret enmity that hath come from close hypocrites that go for great professors.

> *But now profession, thou art tried*
> *   to purpose, all shall see;*
> *And verbal talk it will appear*
> *   a devil for to be.*

> *For actions pure holds forth the life*
>   *of God and Christ most dear:*
> *And false dissembling now must die,*
>   *if Scriptures you will hear.*
> *You preaching men, if truth you'll own,*
>   *see truth be acted too,*
> *Or else to Christ you will appear*
>   *to be his mortal foe.*
> *Scribes, Pharisees and the thief,*
>   *that Judas was by name,*
> *Great preachers were, but for no deeds,*
>   *the truth they much did stain.*
> *'No deeds', you'll say! 'Yes, that they had':*
>   *it's true they had indeed;*
> *But what deeds were they you can see?*
>   *No herb, but stinking weed.*
> *For persecution ever was*
>   *the work that came from them,*
> *And deadly foes they ever were*
>   *to Christ and righteous men.*

And here I end, having put my arm as far as my strength will go to advance righteousness. I have writ, I have acted, I have peace: and now I must wait to see the spirit do his own work in the hearts of others, and whether England shall be the first land, or some other, wherein truth shall sit down in triumph.

But O England, England, would God thou didst know the things that belong to thy peace before they be hid from thine eyes. The spirit of righteousness hath striven with thee, and doth yet strive with thee, and yet there is hope. Come in, thou England, submit to righteousness before the voice go out, 'My spirit shall strive no longer with flesh; and let not covetousness make thee oppress the poor.'

We have declared our reasons for our digging plentifully enough; and you rulers of England, will you always be like deaf adders, etc.? We have received many affronts from lords of manors and their servants divers times; yet nothing makes us be at a stand, whether England shall be the first land that shall fall off from the Beast, and set righteousness upon the throne or no, but the late action of the head of the soldiery, in granting a party of horse to come and weaken us.

Gentlemen of the soldiery, be not offended, for you promised me in Whitehall Gallery that you would not meddle with us but leave us to the law of the land and the country gentlemen to deal with us; and so you did a long time, and we hope in time that love and patience will conquer our furious enemies.

Yet we understand, which a little troubles us, yet content: that the General gave his consent that the soldiers should come to help to beat off the diggers, and to pull down their houses. It is true, the soldiers with the gentlemen our enemies came and caused others to pull down our houses, but the soldiers did not meddle, none but one, but expressed sorrow to see the passages.

But though they were modest and expressed tenderness, yet the General's grant and the soldiers' presence was a great crush to our business. Gentlemen of the Army, we have spoke to you, we have appealed to the Parliament, we have declared our cause with all humility to you all, and we are Englishmen, and your friends that stuck to you in your miseries; and these lords of manors that oppose us were wavering on both sides: yet you have heard them and answered their request to beat us off, and yet you would not afford us an answer.

Yet love and patience shall lie down and suffer. Let pride and covetousness stretch themselves upon their beds of ease and forget the afflictions of Joseph, and persecute us for righteousness' sake; yet we will wait to see the issue, the power of rightousness is our God. The globe runs round, the longest sunshine day ends in a dark night; and therefore to thee, O thou King of righteousness, we do commit our cause; judge thou between us and them that strive against us, and those that deal treacherously with thee and us, and do thine own work, and help weak flesh in whom the spirit is willing.

FINIS.

FIRE

IN THE

BUSH.

THE

SPIRIT BURNING, NOT CON-
suming, but purging Mankind.

OR,

The great Battle of God Almighty, between
Michael the Seed of Life, and the great red
Dragon, the Curse, fought within the Spirit of
Man.

With several other Declarations, and Testimonies of the Power of Life.

By GERRARD WINSTANLEY.

---

*The righteous Law a government will give to
    whole mankind,
How he should govern all the Earth, and therein
    true peace find;
This government is Reason pure, who will fill
    man with Love,
And wording Justice without deeds is judged by
    this Dove.*

TO

all the several societies of people called churches, in the Presbyterian, Independent or any other form of profession in the service of God.

Brethren and fellow-members of mankind: this following declaration of the word of life was a free gift to me from the the Father himself; and I received it not from men. When I had writ it, I was moved to send it to you immediately; but I delayed it by almost a fortnight, and thought not of it: then one night as I waked out of sleep the voice was in my very heart and mouth, ready to come forth: 'Go send it to the churches.' Thereupon I was filled with great love to you, my heart panting with love towards you, pitying your condition; in that there is a great striving as it were for life among you, and yet you lie under the power of death and bondage, and knows not, or at least doth not actually hold forth that you know, that spirit which in words you seem to profess.

You speak and preach of the life of love. But you have not the power of it; your verbal profession, without the pure righteous action, shews you generally to be outlandish men, of several nations, under the government of darkness, and that you are not yet the true inhabitants of the land of love. Before you live you must die, and before you be bound up into one universal body all your particular bodies and societies must be torn to pieces; for the true light is coming now once more, not only to shake the earth (that is, Moses's worship) but heaven also. That which you call gospel-worship and the kingdom without shall fall, that so the kingdom within may be established. For all your particular churches are like the enclosures of land which hedges in some to be heirs of life, and hedges out others; one saying Christ is here with them; another saying no, but he is there with them. But truly brethren, you shall see and find that Christ who is the universal power of love is not confined to parties or private chambers; but he is the power of life, light and truth now rising up to fill the earth (mankind) with himself.

Well, I have obeyed the voice; and I have sent this to you, with a heart free and full of love towards you. Some of you will receive this with gentleness; others will be offended. To some it will be refreshing, but others will storm and prepare war against it. And the Ishmaelites they will scoff, but be it so; yet my armour is tried, I am sure it will keep off the blow.

You shall find I speak of the garden of Eden, which is the spirit of man, not the spirit of beasts. And in that garden there are weeds and herbs. The weeds are these: self-love, pride, envy, covetousness after riches, honours, pleasures, imagination, thinking he cannot live in peace unless he enjoy this or that outward object; and sometimes the joy of envy when he obtains his end, and sometimes the sorrow of covetousness when he is crossed, rules as king in the garden. And the stinking weeds over-spreads the sweet flowers and herbs, which are the lights of the spirit of truth.

There is likewise the most venomous weed called hypocrisy, attended with evil-surmising, grudgings, speaking and promising, nay, swearing one thing yet doing another, inventing much show of holiness to compass his selfish ends. And while he rules king, as he doth rule at this day, he is assisted with vain-glory, fear of being disthroned, oppressing others, unmerciful; careless of former promises and engagements; persecuting those who doth such things as he promised and vowed to do whilst he was a servant, and such like.

And as you may call those by the name of weeds; so likewise you may call them outlandish men; for they are not the true native inhabitants of the heart, but strangers to the righteous spirit. And all these with their fellows make up but one power of darkness, devil or father of lies. And this power is the night-time of mankind, or the absence of the son of righteousness from the heart. This power is the reprobate which the word of life hath rejected, this shall never enter into true rest; this is the wicked man or dragon in you, which causes all wars and sorrows, and the son that causes shame; the son of bondage, which must not abide in the heart for ever but must be cast out.

Therefore, so long as you labour under this selfish, dark, imaginary power, you are strangers to the son of righteousness. If this dark power bear sway in you, it is he whom you profess, and it is he whom you call God and Christ; for that power that you hold forth in your actions is the spirit you profess. If your actions be full of self-love, as you may know it by your hasty anger when your religion is questioned, and by your snappish bitterness against those that differs from you, then this dark power is he you worship.

There is likewise in the garden of Eden (man's heart) sweet flowers and herbs, as joy, peace, love, humility, self-denial, patience, sincerity, truth or equity. These are the true inhabitants in the righteous land; and all these make up but one power or body, which is the seed or tree of life in you. And this power is the day-time of mankind, or the presence of the son of righteousness in the heart. This power is the elect, the son of the Father in whom he delights; this son shall live for ever in rest, peace, and in the power of eternal life. This is the righteous man, this is Michael, the seed Christ or blessing.

Therefore, consider what spirit you profess, and live not in darkness any longer. Babes and sucklings do see, and can say, that in your established forms you worship and profess you know not what; you say one thing and do another; you make God and Christ a very cheat to the world, as if he were all words and no deeds. Indeed your king hypocrisy is so; but the King of righteousness which your established forms hath and do dishonour before the nations is not so; and you all must and shall be torn in pieces and scattered and shamed. For your excessive pride, covetousness, hardness of heart, self-love and hypocrisy, and your verbal profession, shall be loathed by all and be cast out, as stinking, imaginary dung of false-hearted ones, who professes love in words and in actions deny love, but lifts up the devil and covetousness and bondage.

If you truly own Christ, you will cheerfully hold forth the restoring spirit in your actions. Christ the anointing spirit doth not enslave any, but comes to set all free; he comes not to destroy but to save; he comes not to put sackcloth and mourning weeds upon mankind, but to pull them off and to wipe away all tears.

So long as the earth is entangled and appropriated into particular hands, and kept there by the power of the sword – as it is, and your profession holds it up: so long the creation lies under bondage. And the devil, who is the power of covetousness or murderer, doth rule and is the god whom you generally profess; for you acknowledge Christ in words and the dragon in your actions; and so hypocrisy reigns king in the earth at this very day.

But if any of you will truly acknowledge Christ, now in the end of your days, come join hands and hearts together and set the earth free; nothing now stands in the way of Englishmen but inward covetousness. Be not like the rats and mice, that draws the treasures of the earth into your holes to look upon, whilst your fellow-members, to whom it belongs as well as to you by the law of creation, do starve for want. But you have no warrant from the law of righteousness so to do; whensoever you lock up the treasure of the earth and desires more than food and raiment, you do evil.

When you know the son within, as you can talk much of him without, then the son will set you free; and truly he is coming on amain, to break down all your pinfolds * and to lay all open to the common; the rough ways he will make

* Pounds for stray cattle.

smooth, and crooked ways straight; and level mountains and valleys.

And covetous, proud self-love, and ruling and teaching hypocrisy, shall tie up or restrain his spirit no longer; for the voice is gone out, 'Freedom, freedom, freedom.' He that hath ears to hear, let him hear; he that is filthy, let him be filthy still, till he be cast out as dung and unsavory salt. And so I leave this with you, as I was commanded, and bid you farewell.

> Being a friend to love, wading through
> the bondage of the world

Gerrard Winstanley.

The Matters contained in the following
DISCOURSE.

With divers other testimonies of
like Nature.†

* are?

† Chapters 8–13 do not appear. The title of this pamphlet derives
from a contrast between the fruitful vine and the barren thorn bush,
worked out in *Truth Lifting up its Head above Scandals* (S., p. 124,
cf. 237; cf. also *The Saints Paradice*, pp. 45, 48, 129).

FIRE
IN THE
BUSH.

The spirit burning, not consuming
but purging mankind.

What the Garden of Eden *is.*

The whole Creation of fire, water, earth and air, and all the
varieties of bodies made up thereof, is the clothing of God:
so that all things, that is a substantial being, looked upon in
the lump, is the fulness of him that fills all with himself; he
is in all things and by him all things consist.

And this God or almighty ruler is universal love, strength
and life; and as he begets and brings forth everything in
their degree and kind, so he is the restorer of all things,
from the defilement, death and sorrow which they fall into,
and the alone deliverer from the oppressing power, preserving every one in peace. Therefore he is called the Lord God
Almighty; for he is the only and alone living spirit, which
dwells everywhere and can do what he will.

And of all those bodies that are called creatures or the
clothing of God, mankind is the chief. And because the
Father or spirit of all things manifests himself in mankind,

219

in life, strength and wisdom more than in any other creature, therefore mankind is made the lord of all. And the whole earth is this: the lord's.

For when all things were produced, and appeared very good in the liking and content of the creating spirit, the word of command was to whole mankind (not to one or a few single branches of mankind), 'Do thou take possession over the fish, fowl, beast; and do thou till the earth; and do thou multiply and fill the earth'. And no part or branch of mankind is shut out by him from this employment.

For as the great earth and the inferior creatures therein are as the commons, forests and delights of God in the out-coasts of the creation: even so mankind, the living earth, is the very garden of Eden, wherein that spirit of love did walk and delight himself principally, as being the head and lord of all the rest.

In this garden are five rivers: hearing, seeing, tasting, smelling, feeling; which we in our age of the world call five senses. And these five water springs do refresh and preserve the whole creation, both of the out-coasts and of the garden.

In this garden, mankind, and in every branch of him, there is a tree of knowledge of good and evil, called imagination; and the tree of life, called universal love or pure knowledge in the power.

When mankind, or the living soul, feeds upon or delights himself in the fruit of that tree of good and evil, which is selfish, unwarranted and unexperienced imagination which is his weakness and disease: then he loses his honour and strength and falls from his dominion, lordship, and becomes like the beasts of the field, void of understanding. For the lord of so great and vast a body as the creation is must know all things clearly, as they be, and not by blind imagination, that leads mankind sometimes astray, as well as sometimes in the right way.

When mankind is guided by imagination, he runs a great hazard upon life and death. This power is he that calls good evil, and evil good, this knows not the creating spirit in inward feeling, but does fancy him to be sometimes one thing, sometimes another; and still dwells in the dark chamber of uncertainty.

And while mankind eats of this tree and delights himself here, he is driven out of the garden, that is, out of himself; he enjoys not himself, he knows not himself; he lives without the true God or ruler, and is like the beasts of the field, who live upon objects without them; and does not enjoy the kingdom within himself, but seeks after a kingdom and peace without him, as the beasts do.

This imagination is he that fills you with fears, doubts, troubles, evil surmisings and grudges; he it is that stirs up wars and divisions; he makes you lust after every thing you see or hear of, and promises delight to you in the enjoyment, as in riches, places of government, pleasures, society of strange women: and when you have all these which you think or imagine to have content in, presently troubles follow the heels thereof; and you see your self naked and are ashamed.

So that the selfish imaginary power within you is the power of darkness, the father of lies, the deceiver, the destroyer, and the serpent that twists about everything within your self, and so leads you astray from the right way of life and peace. And the whole world of mankind generally at this day, through all the nations of the world, is eating of this tree of knowledge of good and evil and are cast out of themselves, and know not the power that rules in them: and so are ignorant of their God. This is the fulness of the Beast's time, it is his last period; all places, persons and things stink with his imaginary power of darkness in teaching and ruling. Therefore it is that fulness of time in which the restorer of all things will come, to deliver the creation from that bondage and curse, and draw up all things to live in him, who is the true life, rest and light of all things.

For in the midst of this garden likewise there is the tree of life, who is this blessing or restoring power, called universal love, or pure knowledge; which when mankind by experience begins to eat thereof, or to delight himself herein, preferring this kingdom and law within, which is Christ, before the kingdom and law that lies in objects without, which is the devil:

Then man is drawn up into himself again; or new Jerusalem, which is the spirit of truth, comes down to earth, to fetch earth up to live in that life that is a life above objects; even to live in the enjoyment of Christ, the righteous spirit within himself, and to tread the earthly life, that lies in objects without, under foot. This is the life that will bring in true community, and destroy murdering property. Now mankind enters into the garden of God's rest, and lives for ever, he enjoys his kingdom, and the Word within himself, he knows sin and sorrow no more; for all tears now which blind imagination brought upon him are wiped away; and man is in peace.

This tree of life, I say, is universal love, which our age calls righteous conscience or pure reason; or the seed of life that lies under the clods of earth, which in his time is now rising up to bruise the serpent's head, and to cast that imaginary murderer out of the creation.

This seed is he that leads mankind into truth, making every one to seek the preservation and peace of others as of themselves. This teaches man inwardly to know the nature and necessity of every body, and to administer to every body accordingly. This was the Father in Jesus Christ, who let him see what was in man. This was that Godhead that dwelt bodily in Christ, reconciling the world to himself and so making peace. When this almighty power of life rules King of righteousness within, then Satan or outward objects shall find nothing in you to close with him when he tempts. This is the kingdom of heaven within, and the white stone with the new name written therein, which no man knows the glory, beauty, life, peace and largeness of, but they which have it.

This power is not a self-lover, but the universal lover. This will have all saved, that is, will have all live in peace and rest. This tree of life is full of humility, sincerity, patience, tenderness, moderation, reason, wisdom, truth, righteousness, chastity, joy, peace, liberty, yea full of the well-springs of sweet life.

This is the blessing of Abraham, the promised seed, that remains within as a servant for a time, times and dividing of time; then he is to arise and cast out the dragon, and to purge out that drossy, imaginary power, that is crept in to defile the creation. And so properly he is called the restorer, saviour, redeemer, yea and the true and faithful Leveller.

And when this tree of life is fed upon and delighted in (by the five senses, which is the creation, mankind, or the living soul), then these five rivers are called pure rivers of the waters of life; for the life of truth and peace is in them, and they are the sweet conveyors of the waters or breathings of life from one to another through the whole body: and so bringing all into a oneness, to be of one heart and one mind. And there is but one God and king in all and among all who is Michael our Prince of Peace.

And the whole creation now will laugh in righteousness, for there will be no murmuring or complaining heard in all the mountain of the Lord.

For this I can say, when this tree of life begins to rule within a particular heart, he casts out sorrow, fears, inward pressures; he subdues muttering, surmising, heart-rising; he kills envy, pride, vain-glory, unclean lust; in one word, he casts the wicked man out, and takes possession of his own house and temple himself (the heart) and sets it down in peace. So that the heart shall sit singing, 'Where are all my enemies become? They are sunk, they are gone, as if I never had any. All bondage within is gone, sighing and sorrowing is done away; my heart now indeed is a land of righteousness, full of life, light and fruit of peace and truth. Hallelujah, praise, honour and glory to him that sits upon the throne, and to the Lamb for evermore.'

And as there is this change and alteration wrought within a particular body; and all the power, authority and government of imagination is plucked up and cast out, and a new kingdom wherein dwells righteousness is set up:

Even so, as this restoring spirit spreads himself in variety of bodies, and he will spread; for he is the vine, teaching and ruling everyone, till at length the whole creation is brought into the unity of himself; so that that saying is fulfilled, 'You shall be all taught of God and I will be your God, I the one spirit of love; and you, the whole body of mankind, shall be my people':

Then that great reformation and restoration spoken of shall be made manifest in the nations of the world; then those pluckings up, shakings down, tearing to pieces of all rule, power and authority, shall be known what it is; that so Christ alone may be exalted in that day of his power.

For now mankind everywhere shall be made to speak and act purely, according to the life and necessity of everybody, and every business; and keep his dominion and lordship. And all inferior creatures shall stand in awe of and reverence and love man. And the wisdom and love in man shall preserve all others in safety and peace.

CHAP. II.

What the Tree of Knowledge of good and evil is.

But when imagination is fed upon and delighted in, as it is at this day amongst most people, this is he that puts all out of order; he corrupts the five senses and makes mankind walk disorderly and to tear and devour members of his own kind, just like the beast of the field, and to differ nothing from them. The beasts, they prey and devour one another; so does imaginary man, fights, makes wars, kills; robs, destroys and wastes one another. This is the reign of the Beast, and yet he would be called a god, though he be the murderer; well, thou art and still shalt be called a god. But thou art the god of the world, that runs round and when thou art brought to where thou beganst, then thy days are done, thou must die. And the voice is pronounced, 'It is done, time shall be to thee no more.' And thou shalt be destroyed without hand, that is, without sword or weapons, which is the rock of defence; for Christ will consume thee by the word of his mouth and by the brightness of his coming.

Well, this imaginary power is the dark side of the cloud; this is the son of the mother earth, mankind, which causes shame; this is the curse, the serpent, the devil, and his power hath filled the creation, and is the burden it groans under. This is the power of darkness.

And he would be as God, knowing good and evil; therefore the almighty power of life affords him a time, times and dividing of time to rule in mankind. And while he rules he fills all creatures with sorrow and slavery, and so in the end of his appointed time he is proved a devil and not the true God; the destroyer and murderer and not the saviour; the curse and not the blessing of the creation, the power of darkness and not the power of light.

This is the darkness that hath covered the earth, and the curse that destroys all things; this is he that calls light darkness, and darkness light, good evil, and evil good; and while this power rules in mankind, mankind is in prison and bondage within himself, and sees no light.

And under this power of imagination the whole government of the world amongst the sons of men is built; all nations are under this kingdom of darkness; the frame of this worldly government is the devil's proper kingdom. And the power of the sword, fighting and killing, cannot throw down his kingdom, but set it up in more power. But that power that must destroy the dark kingdom is a power contrary to him: and that is love and patience. Live in this life, and thou killst the devil and shakest his kingdom about his ears. This power of love and patience, acted with a cheerful life, kills imagination.

Indeed imagination is that god which generally everyone worships and owns; and in the matter they worship a lie, the devil and mere nothing. This is he that makes everyone wise in his own conceit; that makes men envy, censure and destroy one another; and to take pleasure in none but what pleases self. This imagination fears where no fear is; he rises up to destroy others, for fear lest others destroy him; he will oppress others, lest others oppress him; and fears he shall be in want hereafter: therefore he takes by violence that which others have laboured for. And so he beats the even ground before him, like a blind man, that imagines that [a] hill or block lies in his way.

And though this dark power be a god or mighty ruler in mankind; yet as soon as he appeared to rule, the true light appears to break his peace; as soon as imagination began to sit upon the throne (man's heart) the seed of life began to cast him out, and to take his kingdom from him. So that this is the great battle of God Almighty; light fights against darkness, universal love fights against selfish power; life against death; true knowledge against imaginary thoughts. These two powers are Michael and the dragon, and this battle is fought in heaven (that is in mankind, in the garden of Eden) where God principally resolves to set up his throne of righteous government. It is not fought in the spirit of beasts, but in heaven in the spirit of mankind, who is the lord. And this battle in our age of the world grows hotter and sharper than formerly; for we are under the dividing of time, which is the last period of the Beast's reign; and he will strive hardest now.

But it will be in vain, he must lose his kingdom; for the Lamb will cast the dragon out, and bring all into peace; then everything shall appear naked and bare before the lord of the whole earth, and all imaginary coverings shall be taken off everywhere.

Now the end of all societies of churches, preaching, praying, ordinances, should be to find out this darkness, and to cast it out; and to worship the Father in spirit and truth;

and so to advance the blessing, or the son in whom the Father is well pleased: that so mankind might cease speaking and acting from thoughts and imagination, and may come to speak and act purely, as the truth was in Jesus, he being the supreme lord of the earth.

This, you preachers and professors, is, or at least should be, the end of your profession. And if you come short of this, you lose all your pains, and will be ranked among imaginary hypocrites, that worship they know not what, but as their fancy tells them. And that is neither better nor worse, but the devil which you worship.

Therefore if man would live purely, to the honour of that spirit in him which is called the Seed; he is then to know what spirit is it, that rules in him, and to act from it; for that spirit that rules is the god, whether it be imagination, or whether it be the light of life, which is universal love.

This is the shame and misery of our age, that everyone professes Christ and the spirit, and they will preach of and pray to the spirit. And yet they know not inwardly by what spirit or inward power they are ruled. Everyone looks upon a god and a ruler without him, as the beast of the field does; few sees their ruler within. These have lost their dominion and lordship and they live under the curse, and are blind in their imagination, and are ignorant of the ways of truth.

These are cast out of the garden, they live out of themselves upon the earth; they live upon riches, honours, pleasures, ministers, lawyers, armies, wife, children, ordinances, customs and all outward forms of worship, or in that beastly community with women, nowadays cried up by the lust of the flesh; yea upon anything without them, which they imagine good. Take away these and they die, they know not how to govern themselves, nor others; these have lost their dominion and lordship; their kingdom is without, and their peace is placed upon perishing things, and as they vanish, so doth their peace and their kingdom.

For they have no peace nor kingdom within; God and they have no sweet communion together; the living soul and the creating spirit are not one but divided, the one looking after a kingdom without him; the other drawing him to look and wait for a kingdom within him, which moth and rust doth not corrupt, and thieves cannot break through and steal. This is a kingdom that will abide; the outward kingdom must be taken from you.

They that live upon outward objects are filled with inward trouble, and pierced through with many sorrows; slavish fear within them keeps the way of the tree of life; they dare not live in the life of free community or universal love, lest others jeer, hate and trouble them; or lest they come to want food and raiment; for imagination thinks, if they love and succour others, yet others will not love them again. These know not the spirit; they live without upon the earth, upon objects, under that dark power called unbelief.

But when man lives in the life of universal love, then God walks and delights himself in his garden, mankind; and man who is the living soul, consisting of hearing, seeing, tasting, smelling, feeling, hath sweet content and communion with that ruling spirit of love, righteousness and peace within, and this is Christ's kingdom or the day of the lord within.

While mankind lives out of himself, feeding his imaginary fancy upon outward perishing objects, then the creating spirit and the living soul are at variance and opposition. The spirit would have man live within himself, and take delight in love, humility, patience, chastity, wisdom, justice and all such sweet smelling spices that rules in the heart, leading forth the body to act accordingly; for this is the anointing in him, that teaches man all things, and leads him into all truth.

But imaginary man, he cannot live within himself; this is madness and foolishness to him, he must run abroad for delight, and content his senses altogether in outward objects, and strives with greediness after outward contents: and jeers, laughs, hates and persecutes the spirit, calling him madness, blasphemies, confusion, and that will destroy all government and order which imagination hath set up in the world. And this now is the hot time of the day: God, or the creating spirit, takes no delight to walk in his garden while it is so hot an opposition between him and dark flesh.

But when mankind begins to look within himself, and sees his pride, envy, covetousness, lust of the flesh, anger, hypocrisy and nothing but darkness and discontent; and begins to say with himself, 'O what have I done, how am I fallen? All outward content in objects flies away, and I am left naked and wants light, life, and rest within.

'O that I could see and feel love, humility, chastity, sincerity, truth, wisdom, contentedness and peace live and rule in power in me. Then I should rejoice abundantly in the enjoyment of myself, within myself; though all other outward contentments in objects were taken away. Though I were poor without, yet if I were rich within, I could rejoice: if I were in prison without, if I were in freedom within, I could rejoice; if all my outward friends and objects forsook me, yet if I had familiar friendship with that sweet spirit within, I should have peace enough. No life like to the life within; this kingdom within is excellent and full of glory; the outward kingdom and peace is a deceiver, it forsakes a man in his misery; but the inward kingdom never fails a man, in life nor death. O that I did enjoy this kingdom within!'

This now is the cool of the day, and the heat of opposition between flesh and spirit begins to decline; flesh sees his folly, and grows very weary thereof; the patience of the spirit is honoured by the flesh. And that righteous ruler (God), the seed and tree of life, begins to walk in this cool of the day, with delight, in the middle of the garden (man's heart); the sweet breathings of that pure spirit is now entertained, and fallen earth begins to see himself naked, and to acknowledge his nakedness before the spirit, and is ashamed;

And declares how he came by his nakedness: even by embracing objects and seeking a kingdom without himself. His covetous heart, closing with that imaginary conceit, promised him much delight; but like a subtle serpent, he hath deceived him. And now the seed begins to work, to bruise the serpent's head, and man begins to look upward, towards the life of the spirit within, which he sees now is a life above the life of earthly objects.

'Well', saith the spirit to this shattered earth: 'thou seest thy self naked, and thou seest the serpent that deceived thee; and thou art now separated from me; thou lookedst for peace and rest without, and thou art deceived. Thou art afraid to look within, because thy conscience, the light that is within thee, which is myself, condemns thee. And this fear is the fruit of thy imagination; thou fearst where there is no cause to fear. Thou lookedst for good to come from objects without; but behold sorrow; thou thoughtst, O that if thou hadst left outward objects, thou couldst have had no inward joy. But thou seest now how imagination, that serpent, hath deceived thee. O thou living soul, how art thou fallen?

'But the seed of all things, which is myself, will bruise that serpent's head, and I will restore thee again. I am thy redeemer, and besides me there is none.'

But yet the battle between Michael, that seed, and the dragon, that imaginary power, is not ended; it begins again to be fought in heaven, that is, within the garden, mankind; and the day grows hot again, flesh and spirit does begin afresh to oppose each other sharply.

For imagination begins to tell the soul, 'If thou enjoyst not fulness of all objects, thou wilt want and starve for food;' and so presently fear of poverty takes the throne and reigns; and fear bids thee. 'Go, get what thou canst, by hook or by crook, lest thou want, and perish, and die miserably.

'Thou seest how full of hardness of heart and deceit every man is, each one seeking to save himself; and if thou want food and raiment, love and life within will not preserve thy body from misery,

'Then thou seest the treachery of men beset thee, poverty threatening thee, thy body weak, thy mind distempered with fear and care what to do and how to live. Some laughs at thee, others cheats thee, yea, such as seem to profess the same spirit thou strivest for, are most bitter against thee; and they look after objects more than the inward life, for who more covetous and hard than they? And wilt thou be alone? Yea, thou art alone, where is any one that owns or tenders thee.'

'Well', saith the soul, 'this is an evil time'; and then saith imaginary fear, filling the soul with sorrow, 'O that this body had never been born. I would I had died in the womb; if this be the happiness of a man, I would I had been a bird, a beast or some other creature. While I had no care of doing rightly, I could live, I had friends, I had peace; but since I began to do as I would be done by, friends now stands afar off; everybody hates me, and I am open to all misery. Does righteousness bring thee to this, O miserable wretch?'

This now is a battle of another nature than the former was; for in the first battle the imaginary flesh was lofty and stout and full of presumption, self-conceit, scoffs, jeers, envy, vaporing and secret subtlety, laughing in his sleeve as we say at the ways of the spirit of life.

But now he is in another temper, he is furnished with the weapons of slavish fear, evil surmising, sense of misery, sometimes angry, sometimes ready to despair and to curse the day of his birth, his soul takes pleasure in nothing without, and yet hath no peace within.

And in this battle likewise, God and man, flesh and spirit, are separated, there is no sweet agreement. The selfish imagination would be a god still, and fight strongly to keep the tottering kingdom, and will not leave off till the spirit of burning, who is consuming fire, even God himself, come and fire imagination out of all his strongholds, and with a strong power redeem the imprisoned earth from his presumptuous and despairing bondage.

Though there was a parley before between flesh and spirit, the man and his righteous God, in the cool of the day, while the living earth saw himself a little naked, and was under a little sense of trouble and fear, yet the serpent (imagination) is not conquered by a slight parley but by a stronger contest. For after this parley within himself, man is cast out of himself, that is out of the garden, to seek content in outward objects, as in riches, friends, wife, children and the like; and then the battle grows hot again.

For if our true peace and rest lie in objects and in a law without, as imagination would have it, then the spirit is not within the creation but without. And if so, then there may be places found where the spirit is not, and then God is not everywhere; and so the words of Jesus Christ were not true when he said the kingdom of heaven is within you; and the word is nigh you, even in your mouth and in your heart; and as the apostle said, *God the Father is above all, and through all, and in you all*, Eph. 4.6.

But the spirit is within; for the creation is his clothing. God was in Christ, reconciling the world (or fallen earth) to himself; he was not without him in objects, offering peace, but he was within, drawing him from the deceitfulness of objects that fades away to look for rest and peace only within. Therefore it is said, Christ is our rest, that is, the anointing within is our rest, who teacheth us all things and leads us into all truth.

And by this relation you see here is the living soul, mankind; then here is the fall of mankind; then here is the rising or restoring of mankind.

And that which hath by imagination, or Judas's ministry, been held forth to us to be without us, as Adam, the serpent, the garden, the tree of knowledge of good and evil and the tree of life, and the Fall of man and promise of redemption, all to be without; yet all these are within the heart of man clearly.

And whether there was any such outward things or no, it matters not much; if thou seest all within, this will be thy life.

Therefore in this which follows I shall write of these three particulars.

The living soul, which is pure nature, that was called very good.

Then the serpent or curse, which is the imaginary power of darkness, or man's fall.

Then the seed of life, the blessing, called the restoring power, delivering mankind from that bondage and setting him down in rest and peace within himself.

CHAP. III.

What the Tree of Life is.

And when mankind begins to enter into himself again, and to enjoy rest and peace and life within, which is the resurrection of Christ: then woe, woe, woe, to the imaginary power that rules the world, he shall be shaken with terror and fall and burst asunder, for this is Judas and the Pharisees that have killed Christ all along.

But now Christ, or the anointing, is arising up in sons and daughters, they must die. Therefore whatsoever government is set up by imagination shall be thrown down; *For every plant which my heavenly Father hath not planted shall be rooted out.*

Surely then there is a fourfold power, much idolized and doted upon by covetous flesh, which must be shaken to pieces. And woe, woe, woe, to the inhabitants of the earth, to those that live in or are the upholders of those powers.

The first is the imaginary, teaching power, called hear-say, book-studying, university-divinity, which indeed is Judas's ministry, for this cries 'Hail Master' to the spirit, and seems to kiss him in love, in outward show, by preaching of him and by long prayers to him; but betrays him into the hand of the selfish power.

This power or ministry must destroy himself, as Judas did; and so he doth, for the divisions within the public ministry makes him burst asunder; and all his inward bowels, of covetousness, pride, self-seeking, evil surmisings, grudging, hypocrisy, seeking to please men more than the righteous power, and all their close envy, is discovered.

Then, secondly, the imaginary kingly power, who by the power of the sword and successive conquests do set up one part of mankind to rule over another; pretending to keep the creation in peace, but yet proves a self-upholder; by murder and theft, treading others under foot, this power takes ease, honour, fulness of the earth to himself by the sword, and rules over the labours and bodies of others at his will and prerogative.

This power must be shaken to pieces.

Therefore you kings and monarchs and state rulers, that upholds kingly authority in your hands, come in and kiss the Son betimes; it is not long before he will more gloriously appear, to shake terribly the nations, not England only, but all nations; for the dominion of Christ is to reach from east to west, from north to south; and of his kingdom there shall be no end.

Thirdly, the imaginary judicature called the law of justice, which indeed is but the declarative will of conquerors, how they will have their subjects [to] be ruled; and this pretends to keep all in peace, and yet it is the very support of envy, hardness of heart and unrighteous covetousness. Therefore woe to you lawyers, that binds heavy burdens upon men's shoulders, which you yourselves will not touch with the least of your fingers.

Fourthly, buying and selling of the earth, with the fruits of the earth. This is an imaginary art to fetch in content from without, and breeds discontent and divides the creation, and makes mankind to imprison, enslave and destroy one another.

These four imaginary selfish powers are to be shaken to pieces at the resurrection of Christ. For these are they that all the time, times and dividing of time of the Beast's reign put Christ to death. And these are they which Christ will destroy, by the brightness of his coming and by the word of his mouth.

Therefore woe, woe, woe, to the inhabitants of the earth whose delight, peace and life lies in and upon objects without them, and are strangers to the spirit within them.

These four powers are the four beasts, which Daniel saw rise up out of the sea: Dan. 7.3. etc.* And this sea is the bulk and body of mankind, which is that sea and waters upon which the spirit of God is said sometimes to move; for out of mankind arises all that darkness and tyranny that oppresses itself. And though these beasts appear diverse, one from another, yet they are all one in their power; for imaginary self ruling in man's heart is the father that created and bred them all.

The first beast which Daniel saw rise up out of the deceived heart of mankind was like a lion, and had eagles' wings: and this is kingly power, which takes the sword and makes way to rule over others thereby, dividing the creation, one part from another; setting up the conqueror to rule, making the conquered a slave; giving the earth to some, denying the earth to others. And his eagles' wings betokens his swiftness, to ride on horseback or march on foot quick, from place to place, conquering and to conquer.

The imaginary selfishness created this power, to burden and oppress the creation, which was the work of the righteous spirit.

Yet Daniel saw this beast lifted up from the earth, and made to stand upon the feet like a man, and a man's heart was given to it; that is, this power should be the image of true magistracy, and while the beastly power of self-love rules in the hearts of mankind this kingly power should be the preserver of the meek in spirit, and so help the woman.

And when the time comes for Christ to reign, this beast shall deliver up his crown, sceptre, authority and government unto Christ, and lay all down at his feet, Rev. 4.9. etc.

The second beast was like a bear; and this is the power of the selfish laws, which is full of covetousness and of a bear-

* The next eight pages draw heavily on Daniel and Revelation. See pp. 54–5 above.

like tearing and devouring nature; and he had three ribs in the mouth, which are these:

First, the power of prisons, whereby he kills and devours.

Secondly, the power of whipping, banishment and confiscation of goods, whereby he kills.

Thirdly, the power of hanging, pressing, burning, martyring, where he kills and devours much flesh; for take these three ribs out of the mouth of the law, or Inns of Court trade, and that beast hath no power, but dies.

The third beast was like a leopard, spotty; and this is the thieving art of buying and selling the earth with her fruits one to another. Imaginary selfish covetousness created this beast likewise. And this beast had four wings: policy, hypocrisy, self-love and hardness of heart; for this beast is a true self-lover, to get the earth to himself, to lock it up in chests and barns, though others starve for want.

And this beast had four heads, that guides him and upholds him in his ways.

The first is the power of the sword fighting for it.

Secondly, the power of the law, enslaving others to it.

Thirdly, the power of the covetous imaginary clergy, preaching it up and drawing the people to wander after him.

Fourthly, the power of a blind deceived heart, over-awed with fear of men, and a conceit that it is a righteous art; and this beast had dominion to rule.

The fourth beast is the imaginary clergy-power, which indeed is Judas; and this is more terrible and dreadful than the rest; and though he come last, yet indeed he is the father that begot the other. All these beasts, they differ in shape, and yet they agree all in one oppressing power, supporting one another; one cannot live without another; and yet they seem to persecute one another; and if one truly die, all dies.

What is the reason? Only this: they shew hereby that either alone or altogether they are the curse and plague upon the creation, and is the cause of all sorrows and tears amongst mankind; for they devour abundantly, and yet they rise out of the sea, even from the body of deceived, covetous, dark-powered mankind, in the night-time of that world.

These four beasts are all very fruitful; for from them, as from four fountains or monarchs, springs up divers heads and horns: that is, several spreadings forth of selfish tyrannical power, whereby the creation is oppressed and burdened; and these reign in power, while property rules as king. But when righteous community rises, which is the blessing, then they all fall and are shaken to pieces.

The creation will never be in quiet peace till these four beasts, with all their heads and horns, the variety of their branching powers, do run into the sea again, and be swallowed up in those waters; that is, into mankind, who shall be abundantly enlightened; and light, life and truth shall mightily overflow, as the waters of the seas over the earth; and all those beasts with their self-will powers shall sink like mud to the bottom, and their place shall be seen no more.

These are the herds of swine that must perish in the waters.

This work Christ will bring to pass, at his more glorious appearance; he will consume the mystery of iniquity by the brightness of his coming. You angels of the Lord, who are the lights of the earth, speak aloud, roar out and spare not, pour out the appointed plagues upon the Beast, in this her hypocritical dividing of time.

These are the four beasts or selfish beastly powers that rise up out of the sea to oppress, burden and destroy universal love, and their return back into the sea will be the rising up of love, who is the son of righteousness causing daylight.

The kingly power, he took the sword to kill and conquer and to lift up self to be the ruler; for all laws of the nations are laws made by the will of this murderer, kingly power.

And this beast shall be thrown down by his own power; for out of the serpent's root shall come forth a cocatrice that shall devour the body. I wonder not to see the Midianites destroy one another: he that takes the sword shall perish with the sword. This kingly power fighting is the army of the Midianites.

Therefore, where you see army against army, it is but the kingly power divided, tearing and devouring itself; for as he riseth by his own sword, so he shall fall by his own sword, as the Midianites did. They sheathed their swords one in another's bowels, while Israel looked on and at last took the spoil.

So shall kingly power do in his several governments by the sword; they shall dash one against another; time shall dash against times, and times shall dash against the dividing of time; and the divisions in the dividing of time shall destroy him, till the creation be cleansed of these plagues; and that curse which hath destroyed the earth shall now in the period of time destroy himself.

And this makes way for Christ, the universal love, to take the kingdom and the dominion of the whole earth.

Therefore, you soldiers, you may see the end of your trade; it is a destroyer and shall be destroyed by itself, and surely you shall find no true peace herein. No, no; there is no peace and rest but in Christ the saviour; your trade upholds the murderer or the devil.

Now the other three beasts, who are clergy, law and buying and selling, these rise up by craft, supported by the kingly power; and the chief beast is the clergy, he bred all the other. He is a king, understanding dark sayings, and he shall by craft deceive many; the other beasts are this beast's sons, he bred them.

For this teaching art first bids mankind to look abroad for a teacher and a ruler, and to look abroad for justice and content; and when he had deceived them, so to do, then he put mankind upon buying and selling of the earth and her fruits; and so by that means the creation is divided and mankind is put upon an art to cheat and burden himself; for the earth ought to remain a standing portion to them and their children successively, by the righteous law of creation.

Then this teaching art found out the law, calling it the law of justice; a very good name to cover his knavery. For he is a mighty beast with great teeth and is a mighty devourer of men; he eats up all that comes within his power; for this proverb is true, 'Go to law and none shall get but the lawyer.' The law is the fox, poor men are the geese; he pulls off their feathers and feeds upon them.

These four beasts are the fountains of tyranny to the creation, they are of a fruitful generation; one begetting divers beasts, that are of mighty devouring natures. But the most dreadful and terrible beast is the clergy power; for though the other three raised him up by action; yet this imaginary learned beast raised them up by policy, for self-ends.

For this stamped the other under foot, saith Daniel. And is not this true? Hath not the clergy ruled over kingly power, law and buying and selling, and brought all under his command? For at the first he was only a teaching power, and then it was a beast differing from the rest, yet he stamped them under foot, and all the other had their strength and succour from him by his teaching and imaginary instruction.

Out of this teaching beast rise up ten horns, or the branching forth of his strength in ten particulars: five fighting against the powers of the creation, hearing, seeing, tasting, smelling, feeling, which is called the body of the living soul, that is very good;

And five fighting against the powers of righteousness, which is understanding, will, affection, joy and peace, which is called the seed; and making war against him and so darkening heaven and earth.

This is he that restrains the liberty of the outward man, not suffering him to have a free enjoyment of his portion in the earth; making such actions to be sin which the righteous creating spirit made not a sin.

And he restrains thereby the liberty of the inward man, not suffering him to act in the liberty of himself; for he makes a man a sinner for a word, and so he sweeps the stars of heaven down with his tail, he darkens heaven and earth, and defiles body and mind.

For so long as I must not act according to the freedom of my own spirit and power within me, but must be guided by others without me, and punished for such actions which others in the ruling chair do in a higher nature than I do; I am then in bondage, and my eyes are put out.

And this is the covenant that the outward teaching power makes with the branches of mankind, to put out their own eyes, to see by others'; telling them none can see but scholars: so that this fourth beast is more dreadful than the other three; for it stamps the other three under foot, and rules over all.

And out of the ten horns of this beast rise up another little horn; and this is the dominion and rule which the teaching power takes up, called ecclesiastical power; and this little horn was raised by a power that was not his own: for the kingly power puts that dominion and rule into his hands. While he remained only a teaching power, he stamped the other under him, and over-awed others by his deceitful words.

But now he hath got a power to rule, called ecclesiastical power, which is the extract of selfish righteousness from the seeming righteousness of the four beasts into one ruling power; and by this, which was little in the beginning, there were three of the first horns plucked up; that is

Kingly power, law and buying and selling; for the little horn or ruling clergy lifted up himself above all these, and made these uncover and fall to him; he had dominion and power over all these, and these were in subjection and afraid, and bowed to him. He by his teaching lifted up these, and these by their acting lifted up him to rule; and he by his ruling treads these under his proud covetous feet.

And this is he who is said to be a king of a fierce countenance; understanding dark sayings, that is mighty but not by his own power, and he shall by craft and power destroy many; his rising was in the latter days, when transgressions were come to the full, when people were most blind by his outward teaching, then they easily receive him to be the outward ruler over their souls. For now the sea being bemuddied, that is, mankind being mightily deceived, he by his learned policy riseth up out of that deceived sea, for all the people wondered after him though he sore oppressed them. Dan. 8.23, Rev. 13.3

And as the sword, which is not his power, lifted him up and supports him by forcing the people to pay him tithes: for the law of the magistrate forces the people to pay them:

And he being lifted up, he made war with the saints, and overcame them for a time, times and dividing of time. But as he was lifted up by others' power through his own craft; even so he shall be destroyed again, without hand; the sword shall not destroy him, he shall be discovered in all his oppressing, hypocritical, bewitching knavery, by the light and wisdom of the spirit of truth, that shall rise up out of the sea of mankind likewise, appearing in sons and daughters of righteousness in the latter days.

As Paul said, Christ shall destroy him by the word of his mouth, and by the brightness of his coming, Dan. 7.26. etc., 2. Thess. 2.8.

When Christ the anointing spirit rises up and enlightens mankind, then in his light they shall see the deceit and falsehood of this beast that hath deceived all the world; and shall fall off from him, and leave him naked and bare; and if he will teach and rule, let him shew his power over the beasts; for the people will all look up to God, to be taught and governed by him.

The discovery of the fulness and foulness of this beast throws down all the rest likewise; for when mankind begins to fall off from one part of the beastly power, he will fall from all, for they all depend one upon another.

Kingly power depends upon the law, and upon buying and selling; and these three depend upon the clergy, to bewitch the people to conform; and all of them depend upon kingly power by his force, to compel subjection from those that will not be bewitched.

But when mankind once sees that his teacher and ruler is within him; then what need is there of a teacher and ruler without? They will easily cast off their burden.

Therefore woe, woe, woe, to the inhabitants of the earth when Christ rises in power and begins to come in glory with his saints. This discovery is coming on apace.

Therefore you soldiers, and you great powers of the earth, you need not fear that the Levellers will conquer you by the sword; I do not mean the fighting Levellers, for they be your selves; but I mean Christ levelling; who fights against you by the sword of love, patience and truth. For whosoever takes the iron sword to fight against you are your own sons that fights against you. For Christ came not to destroy but to save; but Antichrist, whose power you are, came not to save but to destroy.

Therefore, if there be any amongst you that count truth and peace precious, take the spirit's advice and come out of Babylon, dwell no longer in the courts and ways of imaginary confusion; come into truth, light and liberty, and be at peace.

When Christ comes and is glorified with thousand thousands attending upon him, they shall not be clothed with devouring instruments like dragons, but be clothed with love, righteousness and peace, like lambs. And at his appearing, said Daniel, the Beast was slain, and his body given to the burning flame; that is, all the imaginary selfish power, that made people run abroad for a teacher and a ruler, was all cast into the fire of pure light, and was consumed in that unquenchable flame: even destroyed by the brightness of Christ's coming, as darkness vanisheth when light comes in. Dan. 7.11.

He that hath ears to hear, let him hear what the Spirit speaks.

CHAP. IV.

What the Serpent is.

'If this be true, it will destroy all government and all our ministry and religion?'

I answer, it is very true; for all government and ministry that is lifted up by imagination is to be thrown down and plucked up, that Christ alone may be exalted in the day of his power. And you have Scripture for it: *Then cometh the end, when he shall have delivered up the kingdom of God, even the Father, when he shall have put down all rule and all authority and all power; for he must reign till he hath put all enemies under his feet,* 1 Cor. 15.24.

Look back into ages past, and see what overturnings and pluckings up there hath been of the authority, power and government of nations: every government standing his period, for when it was universally proved a devil, a destroyer and waster, then it was thrown down.

And this casting down, plucking up and wars in the nations shall be till Christ, the law of universal love, comes to reign; and then he shall settle all in peace, and be the true restorer.

You oppressing powers of the world, who think God hath blessed you because you sit down in that chair of government out of which the former tyrants are gone: do you remember this? Your overturning, overturning, overturning, is come on to you, as well as to your fellow break-promises that are gone before. You that pretend to be saviours of the people, and to seek the peace of the whole nation; and yet serve your selves upon the people's ruins, not regarding the cry of the poor: surely you must have your overturnings too.

For such a government as preserves part and destroys another part of the creation is not the power of Christ but of

Antichrist. That government that gives liberty to the gentry to have all the earth, and shuts out the poor commoners from enjoying any part: ruling by the tyrannical law of conquest over brethren; this is the government of imaginary, self-seeking Antichrist. And every plant which my heavenly Father hath not planted shall be rooted out.

'This man will have no government', some will say.

I answer, you run too fast. True government is that I long for to see, I wait till the power, authority and government of the King of righteousness rule over all, for as yet the power and dominion of the prince of darkness rules everywhere, and that is the government which must be thrown down.

'But government is called magistracy, and all magistracy is of God.'

I answer, magistracy is a good name, and the mystery of iniquity hath not only got this name, but many other excellent names, to be set upon the head of his blackness of darkness, that under a good name he may go undiscovered; and he puts bad names upon things that are excellent.

Therefore let us see whether imaginary government that divides part of mankind to enjoy the earth and the other part not to enjoy the earth, is worthy of the name, magistracy. No, no; such a dividing, self-loving power, is an enemy to magistracy.

For magistracy hath two excellent principles in his nature, which the dark selfish government is an enemy to:

First magistracy signifies a great light, as much as to say, greater light of love, greater light of humility, greater light of reason, greater light of truth, keeping promise and covenant; greater light of peace and tenderness of heart, greater light of boldness in a cause that is universally righteous.

And where this power, authority and government rules, this is pure magistracy, and it is the life and power of Christ.

Secondly, magistracy signifies the greatest bond, that ties the creation together in peace, and this bond is universal love; for this love streams out to preserve all and despises none. This is the unity of the spirit and the bond of peace;

this is pure majesty indeed, that ties people together in love; and this is the power, authority and government of Christ. The love of Christ in us constrains all men to do his will.

Now look and see, is the magistracy of the nations like this? Is it a light of pure excellency and universal love above others? Doth it tie the creation together in the unity of spirit and bond of peace? We cannot say it doth, or if any say it doth, then I'll answer:

What means then the lowing of the oxen and bleating of the sheep? What means such complaints that those that sit in the chair of magistracy are covenant-, promise- and oaths-breakers, and are self-lovers; lovers of honour, monies and ease, and regard not the cries of the oppressed? They favour the rich for reward and despise and slight the poor. They give the earth to some, and deny the earth others, by reason whereof murmurings and divisions multiply, and so uphold the slavish law of conquests.

Now judge: is such a magistracy as this the greatest light? Doth this tie the creation together in the unity of spirit and bond of peace? Surely as yet the mystery of iniquity sports himself uncontrolled under this excellent name or covering, called magistracy; but the babes and sucklings will draw off his veil, and shew all his nakedness and shame him.

If you would find true majesty indeed, go among the poor despised ones of the earth; for there Christ dwells and there you shall see light and love shine in majesty indeed, rising up to unite the creation indeed, into the unity of spirit and bond of peace; the blessing of the Lord is amongst the poor, and the covetous, scoffing, covenant-breaking thieves and murderers that crowd themselves under the name magistracy shall be sent empty away.

These great ones are too stately houses for Christ to dwell in; he takes up his abode in a manger, in and amongst the poor in spirit and despised ones of the earth.

Secondly, imaginary ministry and religion is to be plucked up, as unsavory salt; and this is the learned public ministry of the world; for this ministry is set up by craft and covetousness, how to draw the earth and the labours of men into the clergy's hands. These men make themselves ministers as a man teaches birds to speak. But they do not stay till Christ make them, for that will be too long for them to wait, the rich benefices will be all taken up.

This ministry, having learned other men's words by their long education in their university schools, takes upon them to interpret other men's words and writings, and this imaginary study of theirs they call pure doctrine; and tells the people it is pure religion to come and hear their sermon, and to give them tithes or a large maintenance for so doing.

But this is a false prophet, he runs before he be sent. Study and imagination was never appointed and sent of Christ to be a minister for him; this is Antichrist's ministry.

For when Christ sent out his disciples to preach, he saith, that which you have heard and seen, go preach; and saith Paul, we cannot but speak the things which we have heard and seen from the Father. But the university public ministry runs before he be sent; they take up another man's message, and carries abroad other men's words, or studies or imagines a meaning: and this is their ministry. This is not to preach the truth, as it was in Jesus, purely and experimentally, as they received it of the Father; but as they receive it from man and by man.

The Scriptures of the Bible were written by the experimental hand of shepherds, husbandmen, fishermen and such inferior men of the world. And the university learned ones have got these men's writings, and flourishes their plain language over with their dark interpretation and glosses, as if it were too hard for ordinary men now to understand them; and thereby they deceive the simple and makes a prey of the poor, and cozens them of the earth, and of the tenth of their labours.

And because those men's writings are taking with the world, therefore these learned ones shuts out the true penmen in whom the Spirit dwells, and saith now such mechanics must not meddle with spiritual things. And so by covetous policy, in opposition to the righteous spirit, they engross other men's experimental spiritual teachings to themselves, as if it were their own by university or school learning succession. Pope-like. Nay, just the Pope.

And by their blackness of darkness in their school learning, they have drawn a veil over the truth. And light by them is hid from the world; for the plain truth is, this imaginary ministry is neither better nor worse, but plain unmasked Judas. And the snappish bitter profession that cries it up, is the unmasked murdering scribes and Pharisees.

The one betrays Christ, the spirit of righteousness, with a kiss, pretending a great deal of love to the spirit, by preaching and praying to a God without, they know not where nor what he is.

The other kills him and will not suffer him to appear in the world; for these snappish professors calls everything blasphemy unless they approve of it, still tying the spirit to themselves; saying, 'Lo, here is Christ in this man, and lo, there is Christ in that man.'

But Christ is the light of life spread abroad, and he is now rising in husbandmen, shepherds, fishermen. And by these he first takes off the black interpretation that the imaginary learned scholars by their studies have defiled the Scriptures of old with, and restores them to their own genuine and pure light.

And then to discover his appearance in sons and daughters, in a fuller measure, the poor despised ones shall be honoured first in the work; and from this dust the blessing shall arise to cover the whole earth with peace, and with the knowledge of the Lord.

For this is the vine that shall overspread the earth, and shall be confined no longer within a college or private university chamber, or under a covetous, proud, black gown, that would always be speaking words, but fall off when people begins to act their words.

When Jesus Christ the Son of Man was upon earth, in that one person, he could very seldom speak but the hypocritical snappish Pharisees were either silent and watched to trap him in his speech, to bring him into bondage; or else with open mouth they cried out, 'He is a blasphemer, a devil and a friend of publicans and sinners', condemning him because he was no scholar. 'How knows this man letters seeing he never learned?'

And have not the Pharisees of our age, who are the imaginary bitter professors, the same subtlety and language? And as they of old sought to kill Christ, so these endeavour to suppress him, and will not suffer him to arise in sons and daughters; though the Scripture declare it, which they make such a strict profession of, as if they would not lose one letter.

These professors will still confine Christ to a private chamber and to particular bodies, and restrain him who is the universal power of love and peace. They own him in words, but they deny him in power; they worship God at a distance, not knowing where he is, nor what they worship. And they call this blasphemy, to say Christ is in you, though the Scriptures which they profess say the same. 'Know you not that Christ is in you; and the kingdom of heaven is in you; and they that worship the Father must worship him in spirit within, and in truth of action without, and fulfilling the law and the prophets.' Love your enemies, and do as you would be done by, in actions and not in words only.

CHAP. V.

What the living Soul (Man) is, that is called very good.

In the body of mankind, and indeed in every single body, there are three particulars necessary to be known, without which no man can know himself, let him say what he will.

The first is the creature or the living soul, which before

the curse defiles it, is very good; and this was the image of God (or of the righteous spirit) in flesh, or first Adam. And this living soul is the heaven in which the battle is fought between the curse and the blessing, Michael and the dragon. And this living soul is the wax fitted to receive either the impression of the curse, and so prove disobedient to righteousness, or the impression of the blessing, and so prove obedient to righteousness.

Secondly, there is the mystery of iniquity or the power of deceit, and this is the god of the world, or prince of darkness, that deceives the living soul first, and takes possession; and this in one man is the image or rather nature of that one power of darkness or devil, that is spread abroad through the creation, to cover over or keep down the blessing or seed of life from rising.

Thirdly, the life of God, or of the righteous spirit rising up in the living soul and casting the curse or power of darkness out, and bringing mankind into peace; and this is the second Adam, or the Lord from heaven.

Now this living soul mankind is a beast, and the king of beasts; for the life of the five senses only is the life of the beast. And this beast in everyone, as well as in the whole, is to reign for a time, times and dividing of time, before mankind can be united to the life of the righteous God, and made one with that one spirit of universal love. As Jesus Christ prayed, 'Father, I pray that they may be one in us, as thou O Father art one in me, and I in thee,' they were not united yet.

The image of God in flesh died, and was put out by darkness; but the seed, or spirit of true life rising up from under that darkness, dies no more, but lives for ever. This spirit is the tree of life.

Therefore, you that say you know but one power, be not deceived; for if this one power of righteousness, which is the tree of life, rule in you, then you are new creatures indeed, you are one with the Father and the son. And then you shall know death no more: that is, you shall not live in opposition to the spirit of righteousness no more, neither in thought, word nor deed. And then all sorrow and tears shall fly away likewise, and you shall be at rest, which is the day of the lord, or the light or day-time of mankind. Darkness is now swallowed up and gone.

But if selfish actions and selfish principles live in their strength in you still; if imagination be ruler, truly then that one power is but the power of darkness to whom you are in bondage, and you are not yet past the combat, the dragon is not yet cast out, and you must know a fuller resurrection before you can sit down in peace.

Some of you have got a speech, that those that see two powers within themselves, of darkness and light, love and envy, sorrow and comfort striving together, sees with two eyes: but you may say, you see every thing and power with a single eye * and nothing you see evil, but all things and actions are good, and as they must be.

Surely this is well, if you become, all of you that speak these words, to eat of that tree of life; for my part I'll not condemn you, I can rejoice to see the resurrection of Christ in any; but I must watch some of you, to see if your conversations be so universally filled with love as shall make the dark world startle; and then I can say of a truth, Christ is risen indeed in you.

If your own eye be dark, that is, if darkness rule your whole body; then all the actions of your body towards others are in darkness and builders up of selfishness, which is the one power you yet live in.

But if your eye be truly single and full of light, then the light power wholly rules in you, and actions of your outward man will be full of light and life and love towards every single branch of the whole creation.

---

* This must refer to the Ranter Lawrence Clarkson, though his *A Single Eye, all Light, no Darkness* was apparently not published till October 1650, more than six months after *Fire in the Bush*. But Clarkson had almost certainly been preaching on the same theme. See p. 32 above.

But some may say, explain these three particulars in mankind, that we may know them distinctly one from another. I answer, I shall readily do it.

The first particular is the living soul, or that estate of simple plain-heartedness which hath the life of the five senses only, and by that life preserves that single body or properties.

But the life of the spirit in sound reason lives not yet in the senses; for pure reason lives like a corn or wheat, under the clods of earth or beast, and is not yet risen up to rule as king.

This plain-hearted state is set in the midst of many objects, tempting him like the serpent; and it is open to many crosses and tears, like the tender grass, that is soon bruised by the foot of the ox. It hath not the true rest of Christ in it, though there be much rest and peace in it; for it is changeable.

This is such a state, that though there be self-love, yet there is no hatred towards others in it, but a quiet content to let others live too. As a child, though he love himself (the property of a beast so to do) yet he envies not others; for envy, pride, covetousness, hypocrisy, rash murdering, anger, hath not yet defiled the earth. The man is plain, honest-hearted, even innocent Adam.

Like Nathanael, in whom there was no guile, and yet Nathanael knew not Christ, that anointing spirit as yet ruled not as king in him; for he was open to temptation and change and many tears.

Like Peter, a man of the same plain-hearted temper, full of love to Christ and others; yet selfish, he was without guile and was loving, without knowledge, therefore open to temptation and change and tears.

Now though Christ commended Nathanael and prayed for Peter, that his faith or strength might not fail him, yet they were both strangers to the spirit, which was given them afterwards.

And as Christ told his disciples, 'I have chosen you twelve, and one of you is a devil;' that is, eleven of you are plain, honest, simple hearts, in whom there is no guile; you have sincerely in love to me forsaken all your friends and riches to follow me: so that covetousness doth not reign, imagination doth not frighten you, with 'What shall we eat, and what shall we drink, and wherewith shall be clothed hereafter?' As they themselves said, 'Master, we have forsaken all to follow thee, and what shall we have?' etc.

So that here is no subtlety but downright simplicity without guile, and these are like wax, prepared for any stamp.

But now Judas the twelfth man was a devil, he was defiled and fallen by temptation; that is, he was one that followed Christ for self-ends; not simply, like most preachers and covetous, bitter-hearted professors, that will covenant beforehand what they must have before they follow Christ; and when they hear they must part with all to follow Christ, then they are sorrowful. This is Judas, a devil, the power of covetousness, the curse that hath defiled mankind, and he strives to spread himself, that he may defile all. But Christ who is the blessing appears to destroy this curse.

And when plain-hearted Peter told Christ that though all forsook him, yet he would not; 'alas,' saith Christ, 'Peter, thou art plain-hearted and thou know'st not the wiles of the tempter; thou wilt be overcome and made to deny me, I know thy strength; for I that am the light and life of the world do not yet live in thee; thou art a downright living soul, a plain innocent harmless man; but thou art not yet anointed, nor cannot be till I be gone from you; and then I'll send you the comforter, that shall lead you into all truth, and abide with you for ever.

'Therefore, when I am taken from you, stay you quiet at Jerusalem, till you receive power from on high, which is the Father's promise to you, and that power ruling in you shall keep you from being overcome by temptation.'

And you see Peter's strength proved weakness, though there was simple-hearted innocence in Peter's love to Christ's body; yet his love was changeable: for when the trial came, Peter denied Christ.

And this plain-heartedness is the first time of the beast or self, which is full of peace while a man is in it; but it is a state like wax, flexible and easy to take any impression.

Therefore the two powers of light and darkness, Christ and the devil, strives who shall rule in this living soul first. And these two powers are Jacob and Esau, flesh and spirit, struggling within the womb of the living earth, who shall rule first. And darkness first prevails and rules within, enslaves and causes sorrow, and through his deceit draws the man to seek content in objects without. But then follows Christ the restoring power, and delivers the living soul again from that bondage, and sets him down in himself, which is the rest and strength of love unchangeable, who doth cast out all fear.

Now while the dark power rules, the man is as Judas, a devil, a betrayer of Christ; therefore when Christ begins to redeem he kills that darkness and brings mankind back to that plain-hearted estate of simplicity, in which the devil found the man when he deceived him; and makes him meek, humble, flexible, loving, plain-hearted, without guile, free from envy, like the state of a little child. *Except a man be born again and become as a little child, he cannot enter into heaven*, that is, into peace. The power of the devil must first be cast out before Christ will appear to sit down in rest.

This plain-hearted estate is that which Paul spake of: a man must first become a fool, that he may be wise – that is, void of guile or hypocritical deceit, which the power of darkness is full of; and these are the foolish things of the world, whereby God will destroy the imaginary wise.

This plain-heartedness without envy or guile is the virgin state of mankind; and this virgin is she that must bear a son, and call his name Emanuel, God with us.

This chaste virgin state, that hath no outward lover and that is not defiled but cleansed from deformity, is this virgin chaste state in whom the son of righteousness will arise and take the man into union with himself; he rules as king, and mankind, the living soul, is freely subject with delight.

So that this innocence or plain-heartedness in man was not an estate 6000 years ago only; but every branch of mankind passes through it; and first is defiled by imaginary covetousness, and thereby is made a devil; and then he is delivered from that darkness by Christ the restorer, and by him made one with the Father and the Son.

In one word, then, the innocence of mankind, which is the image of God, is plain-heartedness without guile, quiet, patient, chaste, loving, without envy: yet through weakness is flexible and open to temptation and change. This is the living soul which God breathed the breath of life into. This is the garden of Eden, it is the spirit's house or mansion, and in the body of mankind the spirit hath many mansions or dwelling places. This is the field or heaven wherein Michael and the dragon fights the great battle of God Almighty.

Many men live in their innocence longer than others, some are tempted sooner than others, but all must be tempted and tried by the evil one; that so way may be made for Christ to shew his power, for the office of Christ, the blessing, is to restore and deliver from death and bondage, and to set man down in life and unchangeable rest.

Therefore temptations and falling from innocence must be, that so man may be drawn up into the life and strength of the righteous God or ruler, from whom he shall never fall again; and this is the mystery of God, God manifest in the flesh, or righteousness ruling king in man.

So that this innocent estate is the image of God, but not the strength and life of God. It is wise, but not wisdom itself; it is just but not justice; it is loving, but not love itself. It rejoices, but it is not joy itself; it is patient, but not patience itself; it is chaste, yet not chastity; it is plain-hearted without guile, yet not sincerity itself. It is filled with rest and peace, while he enjoys himself within and doth not make a league with Satan or outward objects; for then he falls and meets with sorrow.

Therefore he is said to be made in the image of God, because this innocence is an estate very good, and there is no evil in it; yet it is changeable, subject to be overcome by temptation.

But now God or the righteous spirit is unchangeable; for he is wisdom, justice, love, patience, sincerity, chastity, joy and peace itself, nor cannot be overcome by any temptation.

And this is the mystery and wisdom of God, to let that innocent nature of man fall and be defiled by his own invention; that so he may declare his power in redeeming him from that defilement, and in taking him up into unity of the Godhead, to remain in that fountain of life and rest and never to be deceived again; and this is a redemption indeed: not only to deliver from bondage, but likewise to destroy the tempter, that he shall never appear to draw man into bondage again. This is the work of the Lamb, and the mystery of God. This work is that which makes us to have fellowship with the Father, and his Son Jesus Christ; this work puts those songs of praise and hallelujahs into our mouths and hearts, to him that sits upon the throne, and to the Lamb for evermore.

This is the first estate of mankind or the living soul in his innocence, and you need not look back six thousand years to find it; for every single man and woman passes through it; and when the restorer rises up, they shall be able to say, 'This is truth.'

The second estate of mankind is the time of the curse, while he reigns which is the power of darkness or dragon, that deceives the plain-hearted, simple man; making him to covet after content in objects without him, and to look for a god without, and so fills him with anger, envy, hypocrisy, vexation, grief; and brings him into bondage within himself. Now this curse reigns in these three particulars:

In the lust of the eye, in the lust of the flesh, and in pride of life.

The lust of the eye is covetousness after any object the man sees, thinking within himself that if he can obtain such and such objects he shall be at rest and filled with delight. And this is an unsatisfied roving lust, and is a self-lover, hurting others; for this lust of the eye would draw all to itself, and leave all others naked; and when he cannot enjoy those objects, then envy and anger arises, vexes, frets and torments the man mightily. But if he obtains, he rejoices; but his joy is the joy of envy, which doth perish again and ends in vexation.

The second is the lust of the flesh; and this is an excessive or immoderate degree of covetousness, which doth waste and consume the objects that his eye lusted after; not to preserve mankind or his body, but to satisfy excessive beastly desire. He eats and drinks excessively; clothes himself vain-gloriously, or runs into the immoderate use of women. And so those objects which are for the preservation and delight of mankind he immoderately uses, and by his excess destroys himself and them too.

The third is the pride of life; and this is the very height of covetousness, called vain-glory, or secret pride of heart, lifting up himself above others, making others bow to him; looking upon himself as a god above others, who indeed are his equals, vexing and fretting and ready to kill them if any refuse to give him that honour he would have. Haman's proud heart is mightily troubled if Mordecai will not bow. This is the pride of life.

As Nebuchadnezzar said, 'Is not this great Babel which I have built for the glory of my majesty?' So lifting up himself above others: this is the power of pride. But now humility stays, and lets others lift him up.

Look through the whole body of darkness, and every branch of him may be applied to one of these heads.

And while these lusts rule, the whole body of darkness reigns as king in the man: as envy, pride, covetousness, evil surmisings, hypocrisy, unclean lust of the flesh, gluttony, drunkenness. And the man hath lost his innocence and is become a devil; he is a prisoner to his lusts, and is in bondage within himself; he enjoys nothing with sweet content.

For let him have what he would have, still he is unsatisfied, and discontent dwells in his heart upon every cross; he lives without God in the world, and feeds upon husks like the swine: that is, his delight reaches to outward things only; to riches, honours, pleasures and women, they are the husks he feeds on, which dies and rots; take these away, and he hath lost his kingdom. And in this deceived estate, mankind is a complete devil, and is become a very decree of himself and others, as experience makes it appear.

The third estate of mankind is the day of Christ, or the rising up and reign of the blessing, which is the restoring power, delivering mankind from this bondage of lust and subduing this power of darkness, and drawing mankind into union with the Father, making all things new and so making peace.

And this he doth, first by bringing mankind back again to his estate of innocence and plain-heartedness, and so in the eye of the world is a fool, before he be made wise;

Then secondly he rises up in power and glory, and makes man one with himself, and sets him down in rest, never to fall again.

CHAP. VI.

What the Curse is, that doth defile the man.

Every branch of mankind is under one of these three estates: first either in his innocence, or secondly under the power of the curse, or thirdly under grace, or the power of the blessing. Now no man hath or can have true peace, till he be able to see this clear distinction within himself; he that sees nothing but one power, nor never saw any other but one power in him, that man as yet is a slave to the devil. But he that hath seen the two powers to oppose each other within him, and then at last the blessing prevails and casts the

other murderer out, and sits down and rules king of righteousness and prince of peace: this is heaven, and he that sees
this one power of righteousness and peace rule, and sees the
other quite fallen, this man now is come to eat of the tree of
life and shall live for ever; and is truly entered into the one
power or new Jerusalem.

Whosoever lives in this life, his actions will be actions of
peace, preservation, love and life to all. But if there appear
actions of darkness in any, whereby any part of the creation
is capable of destruction by those actions; truly then, that
one power in that man is but the curse, which may be called
the power likewise: but it is but the one power of darkness.

When a man sees the darkness rule in others, and in himself, he sees himself in bondage, and is troubled. Now the
seed begins to arise, to bruise the serpent's head.

Lot's righteous soul or the pure creation, man as he is
more or less restored from bondage, he is grieved to see the
bad conversation of the wicked power, as he rules in himself
and others. And there are many Lots at this day, whose
righteous soul is grieved to see how the devil and curse rules
and destroys the earth. The devil rules the world; imaginary self-loving covetousness rules the king in the earth. It
is seen plain, and he goes on boldly without fear; hardness
of heart riseth apace, proud murdering flesh grows secure,
though his judgment be near at hand.

Stand still, and you shall see the downfall of Pharaoh and
his company. As there are time, times and dividing of times
allotted to the reign of the Beast in outward government:
which is first the power of magistracy, meddling with matters
of conscience in restraining or punishing, before the universal bishop was raised: this is the first time.

Then the time of universal bishop, till reformed episcopacy came in, this is the second time. Then the time of reformed episcopacy, till the variety of Independent and Presbyterian churches or state-government came in, is the third
time, and these two latter are called times.

And now England is under the dividing of time, and it is

a fore-runner to the rest of the nations, and this is the image of the Beast; and this is the variety of churches and differences in religion that is amongst men, every one pleading his privilege. Or else it is called the dividing of time in regard the government of the land is taken out of the hands of one man and put into the hands of many; this is the dividing of time, or the half day of the Beast, in respect of outward government.

Even so there are time, times and dividing of time within the heart of man, which is the occasion of that outward division of times.

The first time is the state of simple plain-heartedness or innocence, when the five senses acts in their own light, which is the pure light of a beast, but knows not the power of the seed or of the creating spirit; but is a stranger to the spirit, and yet this state is the image of the spirit. For this is wise and loving and just; but not wisdom, love and justice it self; and being tempted, it breaks out into folly, envy and injustice, and this is the first time of the Beast's reign within a man.

Then the pleasure of sin enters, or a league is made between that living earth and outward objects; and the man, being deceived, looks altogether without him for good, for pleasure and for content, and follows all the pleasures of his five senses with greediness; and here he would be a ruler, and somebody over others; and in this estate man doth what he will, and his heart never smites him for it. He can lie and cheat and whore and oppress others, and thinks all is good, for nothing troubles him: this is the state of prodigality or presumption. And this is Esau, the hairy man's kingdom; and this is the first step of his fall, eating the apple.*

Then there follows a time of trouble of mind, arising for that pleasure of self-seeking delight; and this is called trouble for mis-spent time, whereby he meets with many

* This again probably refers to the Ranters, in particular to Clarkson.

rubs in his good name, in his health of body and in his outward livelihood amongst fellow-creatures; and now he begins to rebate of his wildness and follow; and the beast or sensitive power begins to be a little tamer and more moderate. Yet covetousness (that beast) reigns still, and that with more force within; yet this is a cooler time of the day than the former was, for he begins to consider what he doth. Yet here is no rest, and this is the third time and so these two latter degrees makes times; this is the second step of his fall.

Then comes in the dividing of time within a man, and this is when the law in the members fights against the law of the mind; when a man sees his folly and the bondage of his nature, he sees himself a prisoner to his lusts, and this light in him strives against darkness in him. He sees pride striving against humility, envy against love, contentedness against anger, uncleanness of flesh against chastity, sorrow against comfort, and so cries out, *Oh wretched man that I am, who shall deliver me from this body of death* or bondage to which I am a slave? This is the third step of man's darkness.

Well, this is the dividing of time within thee; this is the time of the battle within thee, between Michael, the Prince of Peace, and the red dragon, the selfish, imaginary, covetous, murdering power. There is no quiet rest in this estate neither; nay, this dividing of time is the sharpest and hottest time.

And now one step further in the first degree of time, and then the man enters into rest. And this is when the seed or blessing in thee kills that serpent and casts him out, and takes possession of thee and rules in righteousness in thee. For now all enemies are subdued under the anointing's feet, and he now delivers up the kingdom to his Father, who is the one spirit of righteousness and peace, in whom there is no sorrow. And this God or almighty ruler becomes all in all, the alone king in that living soul or earth, or the five living senses.

Now this spirit of freedom, being rising up in some already in part, assures the creation and gives those bodies as pledges that he will rise up in the whole, and restore all mankind to himself.

And thus those three particulars in mankind is considered: first, the pure creation of the living soul, the single life of the five senses, which is called the earth. *O earth, earth, earth,* etc.

Secondly, the curse that hath taken mankind, or this living earth, prisoner; and this is the power of darkness called sin or bondage, and this is called likewise flesh or carnal man. *If you by the spirit mortify the deeds of the flesh you shall live.*

Now the created flesh is not to be mortified or killed by us, but preserved; therefore the curse therein is called flesh and deeds of the flesh, because it is a mere selfish power, that would have ease and honour, and would be counted a god, and would rule over all, to the enslaving of all to himself; this is the reprobate, that shall have no peace, for all peace shall be taken from this flesh.

Thirdly, the blessing, who is the seed of life or Christ, the righteous and rational spirit arising up to rule and treading unreasonableness under his feet: this is the restorer or saviour of the captived or the imprisoned earth, which sets mankind free from bondage within himself.

And when this power riseth up to rule, he doth not rule to enslave others to him by the murdering sword, but he draws all men in love to him; and the union and communion of love by him is established in and among the creation.

And thus you see there are time, times and dividing of time within the heart; and though you be come to the dividing of time, yet you are not come to the mount of God, to true rest, till dividing of time run his course likewise.

But yet here is great comfort to burdened souls, that lies groaning under the darkness of this dividing of time within them, and that are mightily oppressed by men that rules in darkness and oppression over them. To you I say rejoice, your redeemer is come, he rides upon the clouds and he will speedily appear for your deliverance, as he hath done for some of your brethren already, who are witnesses that he is rising and spreading himself in the earth, casting out death, hell and bondage, and establishing life, peace and liberty in mankind and in the whole creation.

Therefore whatsoever your condition is, murmur not at it, but wait; he that is come to others will come to you, and not tarry. His power and name is love, and he will conquer all by love and patience. And the sons of strangers and enemies shall come and fall down to him, and say, 'Thou art the alone righteous power; take thee our crowns, sceptres, swords, do thou rule, for thou art worthy'.

This is the day of Sion's glory; this is the everlasting fire, that is unquenchable; this is the powerful day of the Lord; this is the Lamb that was slain, and is now risen again; this is the well-beloved son of the Father, in whom he delights; this is the promised seed, the blessing of the whole earth, who hath been hinted at and pointed at by prophecy, but never fully manifested in the whole creation.

But now he begins to appear, to draw all men after him, to cast out the curse, and to set the creation in peace; therefore, thou weeping soul, cast off this sackcloth and mourning weeds; thy redeemer is come, and he calls thee to follow him, acting love and patience.

This power of Christ takes away all peace from the flesh, and will not suffer any part of the creation to lie under a false peace any longer. And we see that while he appears but weakly, how the peace of covetous flesh is disturbed, and filled with much murmuring against the light.

'O,' say men, 'if this power of universal love be advanced, this will destroy all property and all trading, and bring every thing into confusion.' It is true, he shall be advanced for that end, to confound the wisdom and power and peace of the flesh, that the creation may be no longer deceived, but now at length may come into him and rest quiet for ever.

'O,' saith imaginary, covetous, proud, self-seeking flesh,

'If I take not the sword, to restrain the unruliness of mankind, we shall not live one by another.' But his intent is not in love to peace, but that he may rule over all himself, and beat down others under him. And indeed this power is the cause of all wars; for if this murdering self-honouring power were once cast out, love would live in peace, and know war, division and sorrow no more.

CHAP. VII.

What the blessing is that restores him again.

'But how came man's fall in at the first?' I answer, the outward objects of riches, honours, being set before the living soul, imaginary covetousness, which is the absence of the true light, moves the man to close with those objects, and to seek content without him; and through this dark night power, wars, divisions and discontent arises in mankind, to tear and devour itself; and so it is said to mankind, that his destruction is of himself. And the misery of mankind came in by these degrees:

First, when whole mankind walked in singleness and simplicity each to other, some bodies were more strong than others, as the elder brother was stronger than the younger, and the stronger did work for the weaker, and the whole earth was common to all without exception. But this singleness and simplicity was subject to corruption and change; and the change came in thus:

The stronger or elder brother, seeing the outward objects before him, thereupon imagines and saith, 'Why should I that do all the work be such a servant to these that do least work, and be equal with them? It is fit I should have some larger part of the earth than they, and be in some more esteem than others; and that they should acknowledge me in some degree above them.'

This imagination is the serpent that deceives the man; and as lust is thus conceived within, and the heart or the living soul consenting to these imaginary inventions, presently death is brought forth, and mankind falls from single simplicity to be full of divisions; and one member of mankind is separated from another, which before were all one, and looked upon each other as all one.

This is the first step of the fall, consent within being moved by outward objects of pleasure, riches and honour for one to be above another; whereas it was the honour of the elder to help the younger, and not to tread him down.

Secondly, it breaks forth into outward action; for this imaginary invention in the elder brother moves him to set about to enclose parcels of the earth into several divisions, and calls those enclosures proper or peculiar to himself, and that the younger or weaker brother should lay no claim to it, and the younger brother lets it go so; and presently their nakedness appears, that is, the imaginary covetousness of the heart is uncovered and laid open to the view hereby.

This dividing of the earth into parcels was long before it grew a strong settled custom; for plain-heartedness did much oppose the growth of this imaginary covetousness or serpent. For when contention began to arise amongst Abraham's servants and Lot's, about the earth: one side would have so much, and the other side so much; 'Well,' said single-hearted Abraham, 'let there be no strife between us, for we are brethren; let us spread farther'. And so the one went east and the other west, and gave more room in the earth each to other, and then they were quiet; this is the first breaking forth into action, to make division.

Then next to this, mankind began to buy and sell these enclosures of land, one of another, which the creating spirit of righteousness gave them no command to do. For by reason of this bargaining, the younger or weaker brother is more forcibly shut out of the earth; and so here is a foundation laid to steal the earth by craft, and to murder one another by the sword.

'For now,' saith the buyer, 'this parcel of land is mine; I have paid the fruit of my labours for it, to be properly my own'. But the younger brother comes in and saith, 'The land is our portion by creation as well as yours, and we give no consent to be shut out; therefore what authority had you to buy, or the other to sell? By thus doing you cheat us and cast us out of the earth'. And from hence now divisions and wars begins to arise between the brothers.

And so the elder brother Cain kills the younger brother Abel. Cain was subtle and covetous, and Abel single-hearted, and molested Cain and opposed him in his self-seeking principle or imaginary invention, to raise himself to be above others; thereupon anger ariseth in Cain, and he kills his brother, and removes him out of the way, though conscience tormented him afterwards for it.

And by this murdering power, over-aweing one another, the cheating art of buying and selling and of dividing the land into parcels prevails amongst mankind; till at last Moses was raised, who was the perfectest man in his time, and he, seeing mankind was run into this division,

He endeavours to keep peace; and to prevent war and bloodshed he makes a law, wherein there was much equity between man and man, called ten commandments, wherein every man is limited in his own property: so that if another coveted his neighbour's wife, land, house or servant, it was his sin, and was to be accursed or punished by a general consent of all the people. And they all said Amen to this law, and said they would observe it, and do it.

'Yes', saith Moses, 'though this be a law settling peace for the present; yet I am not he that shall restore you to your first singleness and innocence; for a prophet shall the Lord your God raise up like me, that shall do that restoring work; and him shall you hear; and he shall deliver Jacob from his sin and Israel from his transgression.'

And here he points out Christ, who is the power of universal love; and tells them that whosoever will not hear the voice of that restoring prophet shall be cut off from amongst the people.

And yet this buying and selling, and Moses's law of equity to preserve peace, was part of the fall, for it could not keep them in peace together; but still mankind did molest one another and rise higher in divisions, and fell to further contention, covetousness and pride amongst themselves.

The stronger brother goes further in his imaginary ambitious invention, and makes war against the younger or weaker brother, and takes their enclosures by force from them; and either kills them or turns them out of the land which they had bestowed labour upon; and so did break Moses's law, which said, thou shall not kill, thou shalt not steal.

And now divisions and enmity is risen to the height, and the power of the sword is the very strength of the curse, and is the murderer; for this takes not away property from others by labour or by buying and selling; but by cruel violence and force, casting down one, setting up another by force; and now mankind is in the extremity of division.

And they that enjoy the land, they or their fathers got it by the sword, and they keep possession by the sword, and no man regards the law of righteous creation, or of Moses's law of equity; for every man seeks himself, and thinks it equity for others to regard him, and is offended at those that do not regard him; and the whole earth is filled with this devouring self-righteousness.

Therefore high time for the great prophet which Moses spake of to arise, to restore fallen man, or else no flesh shall be saved; for one is bent to destroy another: and all is for the earth, who shall enjoy it.

And doth not the nakedness of man appear very manifest, that some parties are truly like Dives, that fares deliciously every day, goes in rich apparel, silk and gold upon their clothes, chests full of silver, houses full of corn and other fruits of the earth; and yet sees others starve for want before their faces. And these very rich men notwithstanding makes a profession of Christ, as though they were his servants. O doth not these men openly declare their hypocrisy, and discovers their own nakedness, that all the world may see that they are proud, covetous, envious and the power of darkness itself, and so open enemies and traitors to Christ! All the title they have to their land is by the power of the sword. Did Jesus Christ do so? O no, no; he was universal love, and bids everyone do as they would be done by.

This power of the sword doth not only kill and rob; but by his laws, made and upheld by his power, he hedges the weak out of the earth, and either starves them or else forces them through poverty to take from others, and then hangs them for so doing.

They that have the greatest power of the sword in their hands do kill and take away the labours of others, and say it is righteous; but if a weaker hand doth but take from others to supply necessaries, the other calls this unrighteous, and hangs them for it. Surely the King of righteousness is not so partial a God as to call one and the same action good in his hand that is the stronger, and bad in his hand that is the weaker brother.

No, no; this is the righteousness of the Man of Sin: this is the righteousness of the scribes, Pharisees and Judas, that counts every thing righteous that pleases them, and every thing unrighteous that displeases them. This is the extremity of the curse; and yet this is the law that everyone nowadays dotes upon; when the plain truth is the law of property is the shameful nakedness of mankind, and as far from the law of Christ as light from darkness.

And yet soldiers and lawyers and all that cry up this power of property, which is both brought in and upheld by the murdering sword, would be called saints and members of Christ.

Truly you are all deceived, you are members and actors of the curse, which is the destruction and bondage of the creation; you are that power that hedges some into the earth and hedges others out; and takes to yourselves, by the power of the killing sword, a liberty to rule over the labours and persons of the your fellow-creatures, who are flesh of your flesh and bone of your bone. And you do the very same things, in a higher degree and nature, for which you hang other men for, punishing others for such actions as you call sin; and yet you live in the daily action yourselves, taking the earth from the weaker brother, and so killing him by poverty or prison all day long.

Now this enmity that brought in this division, first of enclosing, then of buying and selling, then of killing one another for the earth, is the curse within of imaginary covetousness; and it was bred by the presentment of outward objects, tempting the five senses or the living soul.

And all the strivings that is in mankind is for the earth, who shall have it; whether some particular persons shall have it and the rest have none, or whether the earth shall be a common treasury to all without respect of persons.

And this is the battle that is fought between the two powers, which is property on the one hand, called the devil or covetousness, or community on the other hand, called Christ or universal love. And as Christ doth cast covetousness out of the heart, so property is cast out from amongst men, and mankind will not only become single-hearted again, but will walk in the light of pure reason and love, and never fall again into divisions, but shall be so acquainted with the wiles of Satan that he shall utterly reject and abhor his imaginary enticement, as Jesus Christ rejected the temptation of objects. And that Satan or tempter without prevailed not, because the anointing was in him, that was stronger than flesh.

Now this same power in man, that causes divisions and war, is called by some men the state of nature, which every man brings into the world with him.

But this law of darkness in the members is not the state of nature; for nature or the living soul is in bondage to it, and groans under it, waiting to be delivered from it, and is glad to hear of a saviour.

Look upon a child that is new born, or till he grows up to some few years: he is innocent, harmless, humble, patient, gentle, easy to be entreated, not envious; and this is Adam, or mankind in his innocence; and this continues till outward objects entice him to pleasure or seek content without him. And when he consents, or suffers the imaginary covetousness within to close with the objects, then he falls and is taken captive, and falls lower and lower.

First into the slavery of that power of lusts within, leading him forth to act all manner of selfishness, with greediness to the destruction of others;

And then falls from this delight into trouble of mind and touch of conscience and inward torment, and so falls deeper and deeper into hell, till the seed or blessing rise up in him to work deliverance and then carry him back again, and lead him into the ways of truth.

And thus we see how mankind came to fall from his innocence; and that was by closing to outward objects for content with inward imaginary covetousness, to find life in those objects without him.

And man's recovery will be to reject outward objects, and to close with the spirit of truth, life and peace within, preferring this kingdom within before the outward kingdom.

It is said that Christ was tempted in all things, like as we are tempted. Now how are we tempted? but by presentment of outward objects before us, and when the life of the five senses closes therewith, thinking to find content therefrom, we are deceived, and so fall from innocence.

As for example, if objects of riches be laid before me, and my inward covetousness close therewith, I fall; or if the beauty of the female sex be set before me, if my inward lust close therewith excessively, running after variety of strange flesh, I fall.

But if covetousness and lust be killed or doth not breathe

in me, then, though those objects be tendered to me, I reject them; and so I fall not. And now Satan or the tempter, which are the outward objects, finds nothing in me.

And thus it was said of Jesus Christ, that when the tempter came to him he found nothing in him; that is, Jesus Christ had not an imaginary covetous power in him, to seek a kingdom or happiness without himself, in those objects of pleasure, riches and honours of the world, but preferred the kingdom within him before that without him.

And so he was said to have no sin, because there was nothing in him that consented to the temptation without; he made use of outward objects in moderation, for the safety and peace of his body, but desired nothing in excess or immoderately.

The power of darkness which is covetousness, and imagination which is the devouring dragon, had no place in heaven, that is, in him; for the dragon was cast out, and the Godhead did dwell bodily in him, in the fulness of righteousness and peace.

Now I desire any man to shew by experience any other devil or dark power than these two, that is, the objects without and the powers of the curse within, joining in consent together to enslave the earth or the living soul, which is the innocence of the five senses.

While these two join together and meet in consent, mankind enters into sorrow, and hath [no] true rest.

But when the power of lust is killed within, by the blessing or the seed rising up, then outward objects troubles not nor enslaves the man. For then a man is content with his present condition, and seeks for a kingdom within, which moth and rust cannot corrupt, nor thieves break through and steal. If he have riches, he dotes not upon them, he knows not how to use them. If he be poor, he is quiet and content; if he be at liberty he is content, if in prison he is content.

So then kill covetousness or that imaginary darkness within, and the devil is killed; when the tempter comes, he shall find nothing in you. He that is free within is moved to excess or unrational action by no outward object; but he that is not free within, is moved by every object.

And this is the reason why many people are so angry and bitter, and flies upon their neighbours with reviling and reproachful words or envious actions, because they are slaves to their flesh; they are in bondage within, they know not liberty. It is the night-time with them, the son of love, righteousness and peace is not yet risen up in them.

Therefore they that are at liberty within, in whom the seed is risen to rule, do conquer all enemies by love and patience, and make use of any outward object with moderation and knows no excess.

The powers of the curse, he subdues others by the murdering sword, and thereby enslaves others to him; as we see the government of all nations is this, and the dark power in every man's heart is this; which indeed is the devil's kingdom that yet rules.

But now the blessing, he subdues his enemies by love, and saves and gives life and freedom to his enemies; he first brings mankind back to pure creation, and then rises up and rules King of righteousness within, and so keeps the man, that the curse never enslaves him again; and so he puts the man into a better condition than he was in before.

This seed or Christ then is to be seen within, to save you from the curse within, to free you from bondage within; he is no saviour that stands at a distance: therefore your public ministers bewitches you by telling you of a saviour at a distance.

The enmity which burdens you is within, even the law of your members that wars against the law of your mind; so that the members are the creature, and that curse wars within them, and so troubles and enslaves the members.

Therefore your saviour must be a power within you, to deliver you from that bondage within; the outward Christ or the outward god are but men saviours, such as Moses, Joshua and judges were, and such as kings are, and these gods sometimes proves devils. Surely such preachers as tells you your god and saviour is without, they know not the spirit, they are servants to the curse, their kingdom is all without, and therefore would have you to seek for a kingdom without that lies in objects; for that kingdom of Christ within they know not.

And here I shall end with this question, What are the greatest sins in the world? I answer, these two: first for a man to lock up the treasuries of the earth in chests and houses, and suffer it to rust or moulder while others starve for want to whom it belongs – and it belongs to all. This is the greatest sin against universal love; this is the destroying sin, this is Achan's sin; this is the action of covetousness.

The second sin is like to this, and is the same in nature with the other; and this is for any man or men first to take the earth by the power of the murdering sword from others, and then by the laws of their own making do hang or put to death any who takes the fruits of the earth to supply his necessaries, from places or persons where there is more than can be made use of by that particular family where it is hoarded up.

And he said, son of man, seest thou what they do? Thou shalt see greater abominations. Ezekiel. 8.6

FINIS.

THE
Law of Freedom
IN A
PLATFORM:
Or, True
Magistracy Restored.

Humbly presented to Oliver Cromwell, General of the Common-wealth's Army in England, Scotland, and Ireland. And to all English-men my brethren whether in Church-fellowship, or not in Church-fellowship, both sorts walking as they conceive according to the Order of the Gospel: and from them to all the Nations in the World.

Wherein is Declared, What is Kingly Government, and what is Commonwealth's Government.

By *Gerrard Winstanley.*

In thee, O England, is the Law arising up to shine,
If thou receive and practise it, the crown it will be thine.
If thou reject, and still remain a froward Son to be,
Another Land will it receive, and take the crown from thee. Revel. 11.15, Dan. 7.27.

To His Excellency

OLIVER CROMWELL,

General of the

Commonwealth's Army

in *England, Scotland* and *Ireland*.

Sir,

God hath honoured you with the highest honour of any man since Moses's time, to be the head of a people who have cast out an oppressing Pharaoh. For when the Norman power had conquered our forefathers, he took the free use of our English ground from them, and made them his servants. And God hath made you a successful instrument to cast out that conqueror, and to recover our land and liberties again, by your victories, out of that Norman hand.

That which is yet wanting on your part to be done is this, to see the oppressor's power to be cast out with his person; and to see that the free possession of the land and liberties be put into the hands of the oppressed commoners of England.

For the crown of honour cannot be yours, neither can those victories be called victories on your part, till the land and freedoms won be possessed by them who adventured person and purse for them.

Now you know, Sir, that the kingly conqueror was not beaten by you only as you are a single man, nor by the officers of the Army joined to you; but by the hand and assistance of the commoners, whereof some came in person and adventured their lives with you; others stayed at home and planted the earth and paid taxes and free-quarter to maintain you that went to war.

So that whatsoever is recovered from the conqueror is recovered by a joint consent of the commoners: therefore it is all equity, that all the commoners who assisted you should be set free from the conqueror's power with you: as David's law was, *The spoil shall be divided between them who went to war, and them who stayed at home.*

And now you have the power of the land in your hand, you must do one of these two things: first, either set the land free to the oppressed commoners who assisted you and paid the Army their wages; and then you will fulfil the Scriptures and your own engagements, and so take possession of your deserved honour:

Or secondly, you must only remove the conqueror's power out of the King's hand into other men's, maintaining the old laws still; and then your wisdom and honour is blasted for ever, and you will either lose yourself, or lay the foundation of greater slavery to posterity than you ever knew.

You know that while the King was in the height of his oppressing power, the people only whispered in private chambers against him: but afterwards it was preached upon the house-tops that he was a tyrant and a traitor to England's peace; and he had his overturn.

The righteous power in the creation is the same still. If you and those in power with you should be found walking in the King's steps, can you secure yourselves or posterities from an overturn? Surely no.

The spirit of the whole creation (who is God) is about the reformation of the world, and he will go forward in his work. For if he would not spare kings who have sat so long at his right hand governing the world, neither will he regard you, unless your ways be found more righteous than the King's.

You have the eyes of the people all the land over, nay I think I may say all neighbouring nations over, waiting to see what you will do. And the eyes of your oppressed friends who lie yet under kingly power are waiting to have the possession given them of that freedom in the land which was promised by you, if in case you prevailed. Lose not your crown; take it up and wear it. But know that it is no crown of honour, till promises and engagements made by you be performed to your friends. *He that continues to the end shall receive the crown.* Now you do not see the end of your work unless the kingly law and power be removed as well as his person.

Jonah's gourd is a remembrancer to men in high places.

The worm in the earth gnawed the root and the gourd died, and Jonah was offended.

Sir, I pray bear with me; my spirit is upon such a lock that I must speak plain to you, lest it tell me another day, 'If thou hadst spoke plain, things might have been amended'.

The earth wherein your gourd grows is the commoners of England.

The gourd is that power which covers you, which will be established to you by giving the people their true freedoms, and not otherwise.

The root of your gourd is the heart of the people, groaning under kingly bondage and desiring a commonwealth's freedom in their English earth.

The worm in the earth, now gnawing at the root of your gourd, is discontents, because engagements and promises made to them by such as have power are not kept.

And this worm hath three heads. The first is a spirit waiting opportunities till a blasting wind arise to cause your gourd to wither; and yet pretends fair to you, etc.

Another spirit shelters under your gourd for a livelihood, and will say as you say in all things; and these are called honest, yet no good friends to you nor the commonwealth, but to their own bellies.

There is a third spirit, which is faithful indeed and plain-dealing, and many times for speaking truth plainly he is cashiered, imprisoned and crushed: and the oppressions laid upon this spirit kindles the fire which the two former waits to warm themselves at.

Would you have your gourd stand for ever? Then cherish the root in the earth, that is the heart of your friends, the oppressed commoners of England, by killing the worm. And nothing will kill this worm but performance of professions, words and promises, that they may be made free men from tyranny.

It may be you will say to me, 'What shall I do?' I answer, 'You are in place and power to see all burdens taken off from your friends, the commoners of England.' You will say, 'What are those burdens?'

I will instance in some, both which I know in my own experience and which I hear the people daily complaining of and groaning under, looking upon you and waiting for deliverance.

Most people cry, 'We have paid taxes, given free-quarter, wasted our estates and lost our friends in the wars, and the task-masters multiply over us more than formerly.' I have asked divers this question, 'Why do you say so?'

Some have answered me that promises, oaths and engagements have been made as a motive to draw us to assist in the wars; that privileges of Parliament and liberties of subjects should be preserved, and that all popery and episcopacy and tyranny should be rooted out; and these promises are not performed. Now there is an opportunity to perform them.

For first, say they, 'The current of succeeding Parliaments is stopped, which is one of the great privileges (and people's liberties) for safety and peace; and if that continue stopped, we shall be more offended by an hereditary Parliment than we were oppressed by an hereditary king'.

And for the commoners, who were called subjects while the kingly conqueror was in power, have not as yet their liberties granted them: I will instance them in order, according as the common whisperings are among the people.

For, they say, the burdens of the clergy remains still upon us, in a threefold nature.

First, if any man declare his judgment in the things of God contrary to the clergy's report or the mind of some high officers, they are cashiered, imprisoned, crushed and undone, and made sinners for a word, as they were in the pope's and bishops' days; so that though their names be cast out, yet their High Commission Court's power remains still, persecuting men for conscience' sake when their actions are unblameable.

Secondly, in many parishes there are old formal ignorant episcopal priests established; and some ministers who are bitter enemies to commonwealth's freedom and friends to monarchy are established preachers, and are continually buzzing their subtle principles into the minds of the people, to undermine the peace of our declared commonwealth, causing a disaffection of spirit among neighbours, who otherwise would live in peace.

Thirdly, the burden of tithes remains still upon our estates, which was taken from us by the kings and given to the clergy to maintain them by our labours; so that though their preaching fill the minds of many with madness, contention and unsatisfied doubting, because their imaginary and ungrounded doctrines cannot be understood by them, yet we must pay them large tithes for so doing. This is oppression.

Fourthly, if we go to the lawyer, we find him to sit in the conqueror's chair though the kings be removed, maintaining the kings' power to the height; for in many courts and cases of law the will of a judge and lawyer rules above the letter of the law, and many cases and suits are lengthened to the great vexation of the clients and to the lodging of their estates in the purse of the unbounded lawyer. So that we see, though other men be under a sharp law, yet many of the great lawyers are not, but still do act their will as the conqueror did; as I have heard some belonging to the law say, 'What cannot we do?'

Fifthly, say they, if we look upon the customs of the law

itself, it is the same it was in the kings' days, only the name is altered; as if the commoners of England had paid their taxes, free-quarter and shed their blood not to reform but to baptize the law into a new name, from kingly law to state law; by reason whereof the spirit of discontent is strengthened, to increase more suits of law than formerly was known to be. And so, as the sword pulls down kingly power with one hand, the kings' old law builds up monarchy again with the other.

And indeed the main work of reformation lies in this, to reform the clergy, lawyers and law; for all the complaints of the land are wrapped up within them three, not in the person of a king.

Shall men of other nations say that notwithstanding all those rare wits in the Parliament and Army of England, yet they could not reform the clergy, lawyer and law, but must needs establish all as the kings left them?

Will not this blast all our honour, and make all monarchical members laugh in their sleeves, to see the government of our commonwealth to be built upon the kingly laws and principles?

I have asked divers soldiers what they fought for; they answered, they could not tell; and it is very true, they cannot tell indeed, if the monarchical law be established without reformation. But I wait to see what will be done; and I doubt not but to see our commonwealth's government to be built upon his own foundation.

Sixthly, if we look into parishes, the burdens there are many.

First, for the power of lords of manors remains still over their brethren, requiring fines and heriots; beating them off the free use of the common land, unless their brethren will pay them rent; exacting obedience as much as they did, and more, when the King was in power.

Now saith the people, 'By what power do these maintain their title over us!' Formerly they held title from the King, as he was the conqueror's successor. But have not the commoners cast out the King, and broke the bond of that conquest? Therefore in equity they are free from the slavery of that lordly power.

Secondly, in parishes where commons lie, the rich Norman freeholders, or the new (more covetous) gentry, over-stock the commons with sheep and cattle; so that inferior tenants and poor labourers can hardly keep a cow, but half starve her. So that the poor are kept poor still, and the common freedom of the earth is kept from them, and the poor have no more relief than they had when the king (or conqueror) was in power.

Thirdly, in many parishes two or three of the great ones bears all the sway in making assessments, over-awing constables and other officers; and when time was to quarter soldiers, they would have a hand in that, to ease themselves and over-burden the weaker sort; and many times make large sums of money over and above the justice's warrant in assessments, and would give no account why, neither durst the inferior people demand an account, for he that spake should be sure to be crushed the next opportunity; and if any have complained to committees or justices, they have been either wearied out by delays and waiting, or else the offence hath been by them smothered up; so that we see one great man favoured another, and the poor oppressed have no relief.

Fourthly, there is another grievance which the people are much troubled at, and that is this: country people cannot sell any corn or other fruits of the earth in a market town but they must either pay toll or be turned out of town. Now say they, 'This is a most shameful thing, that we must part with our estates in taxes and free-quarter to purchase the freedom of the land and the freedom of the towns, and yet this freedom must be still given from us into the hands of a covetous Norman toll-taker, according to the kings' old burdensome laws, and contrary to the liberty of a free commonwealth.'

'Now,' saith the whisperings of the people, 'the inferior

tenants and labourers bears all the burdens, in labouring the earth, in paying taxes and free-quarter beyond their strength, and in furnishing the armies with soldiers, who bear the greatest burden of the war; and yet the gentry, who oppress them and that live idle upon their labours, carry away all the comfortable livelihood of the earth.'

For is not this a common speech among the people? 'We have parted with our estates, we have lost our friends in the wars, which we willingly gave up, because freedom was promised us; and now in the end we have new task-masters, and our old burdens increased: and though all sorts of people have taken an Engagement to cast out kingly power, yet kingly power remains in power still in the hands of those who have no more right to the earth than ourselves.

'For,' say the people, 'if the lords of manors and our task-masters hold title to the earth over us from the old kingly power, behold that power is beaten and cast out.

'And two acts of Parliament are made: the one to cast out kingly power, backed by the Engagement against King and House of Lords, the other to make England a free commonwealth.

'And if lords of manors lay claim to the earth over us from the Army's victories over the King, then we have as much right to the land as they, because our labours and blood and death of friends were the purchasers of the earth's freedom as well as theirs.

'And is not this a slavery,' say the people, 'that though there be land enough in England to maintain ten times as many people as are in it, yet some must beg of their brethren, or work in hard drudgery for day wages for them, or starve or steal and so be hanged out of the way, as men not fit to live in the earth, before they must be suffered to plant the waste land for their livelihood, unless they will pay rent to their brethren for it?' Well, this is a burden the creation groans under; and the subjects (so called) have not their birthright freedoms granted them from their brethren, who hold it from them by club law, but not by righteousness.

'And who now must we be subject to, seeing the conqueror is gone?'

I answer, we must either be subject to a law, or to men's wills. If to a law, then all men in England are subjects, or ought to be, thereunto: but what law that is to which every one ought to be subject is not yet established in execution. If any say the old kings' laws are the rule, then it may be answered that those laws are so full of confusion that few knows when they obey and when not, because they were the laws of a conqueror to hold the people in subjection to the will of the conqueror; therefore that cannot be the rule for everyone. Besides, we daily see many actions done by state officers, which they have no law to justify them in but their prerogative will.

And again if we must be subject to men, then what men must we be subject to, seeing one man hath as much right to the earth as another, for no man now stands as a conqueror over his brethren by the law of righteousness?

You will say, 'We must be subject to the ruler'. It is true, but not to suffer the rulers to call the earth theirs and not ours, for by so doing they betray their trust and run into the line of tyranny; and we lose our freedom and from thence enmity and wars arise.

A ruler is worthy double honour when he rules well, that is, when he himself is subject to the law, and requires all others to be subject thereunto, and makes it his work to see the laws obeyed and not his own will; and such rulers are faithful, and they are to be subjected unto us therein, for all commonwealth's rulers are servants to, not lords and kings over, the people. But you will say, 'Is not the land your brother's? And you cannot take away another man's right by claiming a share therein with him.'

I answer, it is his either by creation right, or by right of conquest. If by creation right he call the earth his and not mine, then it is mine as well as his; for the spirit of the whole creation, who made us both, is no respecter of persons.

And if by conquest he call the earth his and not mine, it

must be either by the conquest of the kings over the commoners, or by the conquest of the commoners over the
kings.

If he claim the earth to be his from the kings' conquest,
the kings are beaten and cast out, and that title is undone.

If he claim title to the earth to be his from the conquest
of the commoners over the kings, then I have right to the
land as well as my brother, for my brother without me, nor
I without my brother, did not cast out the kings; but both
together assisting with person and purse we prevailed, so
that I have by this victory as equal a share in the earth which
is now redeemed as my brother by the law of righteousness.

If my brother still say he will be landlord (through his
covetous ambition) and I must pay him rent, or else I shall
not live in the land, then does he take my right from me,
which I have purchased by my money in taxes, free-quarter
and blood. And O thou spirit of the whole creation, who
hath this title to be called King of righteousness and Prince
of Peace: judge thou between my brother and me, whether
this be righteous, etc.

'And now', say the people, 'is not this a grievous thing that
our brethren that will be landlords, right or wrong, will
make laws and call for a law to be made to imprison, crush,
nay put to death, any that denies God, Christ and Scripture;
and yet they will not practise that golden rule, *Do to another
as thou wouldst have another do to thee*, which God, Christ
and Scriptures hath enacted for a law? Are not these men
guilty of death by their own law, which is the words of their
own mouth? Is it not a flat denial of God and Scripture?'

O the confusion and thick darkness that hath over-spread
our brethren is very great. I have no power to remove it, but
lament it in the secrets of my heart. When I see prayers,
sermons, fasts, thanksgiving, directed to this God in words
and shows, and when I come to look for actions of obedience
to the righteous law, suitable to such a profession, I find
them men of another nation, saying and not doing; like

an old courtier saying 'Your servant', when he was an enemy. I will say no more, but groan and wait for a restoration.

Thus, Sir, I have reckoned up some of those burdens which the people groan under.

And I being sensible hereof was moved in my self to present this platform of commonwealth's government unto you, wherein I have declared a full commonwealth's freedom, according to the rule of righteousness, which is God's Word. It was intended for your view above two years ago, but the disorder of the times caused me to lay it aside, with a thought never to bring it to light, etc. Likewise I hearing that Mr Peters and some others propounded this request, that the Word of God might be consulted with to find out a healing government,* which I liked well and waited to see such a rule come forth, for there are good rules in the Scripture if they were obeyed and practised. Thereupon

I laid aside this in silence, and said I would not make it public; but this word was like fire in my bones ever and anon, *Thou shalt not bury thy talent in the earth*; therefore I was stirred up to give it a resurrection, and to pick together as many of my scattered papers as I could find, and to compile them into this method, which I do here present to you, and do quiet my own spirit.

And now I have set the candle at your door, for you have power in your hand, in this other added opportunity, to act for common freedom if you will: I have no power.

It may be here are some things inserted which you may not like, yet other things you may like, therefore I pray you read it, and be as the industrious bee, suck out the honey and cast away the weeds.

Though this platform be like a piece of timber rough hewed, yet the discreet workmen may take it and frame a handsome building out of it.

* This probably refers to Hugh Peter's *Good Work for a Good Magistrate*, published 7 June 1651. In January 1652 Peter was put on a Parliamentary committee for the reform of the law.

It is like a poor man that comes clothed to your door in a torn country garment, who is unacquainted with the learned citizens' unsettled forms and fashions; take off the clownish language, for under that you may see beauty.

It may be you will say, 'If tithes be taken from the priests and impropriators, and copyhold services from lords of manors, how shall they be provided for again; for is it not unrighteous to take their estates from them?'

I answer, when tithes were first enacted, and lordly power drawn over the backs of the oppressed, the kings and conquerors made no scruple of conscience to take it, though the people lived in sore bondage of poverty for want of it; and can there be scruple of conscience to make restitution of this which hath been so long stolen goods? It is no scruple arising from the righteous law, but from covetousness, who goes away sorrowful to hear he must part with all to follow righteousness and peace.

But though you do take away tithes and the power of lords of manors, yet there will be no want to them, for they have the freedom of the common stock, they may send to the store-houses for what they want, and live more free than now they do; for now they are in care and vexation by servants, by casualties, by being cheated in buying and selling and many other encumbrances, but then they will be free from all, for the common store-houses is every man's riches, not any one's.

'Is it not buying and selling a righteous law?' No, it is the law of the conqueror, but not the righteous law of creation: how can that be righteous which is a cheat? For is not this a common practice, when he hath a bad horse or cow, or any bad commodity, he will send it to the market, to cheat some simple plain-hearted man or other; and when he comes home will laugh at his neighbour's hurt, and much more etc.

When mankind began to buy and sell, then did he fall from his innocence; for then they began to oppress and cozen one another of their creation birthright. As for example: if the land belong to three persons, and two of them buy and sell the earth and the third give no consent, his right is taken from him, and his posterity is engaged in a war.

When the earth was first bought and sold, many gave no consent: as when our crown lands and bishops' lands were sold, some foolish soldiers yielded, and covetous officers were active in it, to advance themselves above their brethren; but many who paid taxes and free-quarter for the purchase of it gave no consent but declared against it as an unrighteous thing, depriving posterity of their birthrights and freedoms.

Therefore this buying and selling did bring in, and still doth bring in, discontent and wars, which have plagued mankind sufficiently for so doing. And the nations of the world will never learn to beat their swords into ploughshares, and their spears into pruning hooks, and leave off warring, until this cheating device of buying and selling be cast out among the rubbish of kingly power.

'But shall not one man be richer than another?'

There is no need of that; for riches make men vain-glorious, proud, and to oppress their brethren; and are the occasion of wars.

No man can be rich, but he must be rich either by his own labours, or by the labours of other men helping him. If a man have no help from his neighbour, he shall never gather an estate of hundreds and thousands a year. If other men help him to work, then are those riches his neighbours' as well as his; for they may be the fruit of other men's labours as well as his own.

But all rich men live at ease, feeding and clothing themselves by the labours of other men, not by their own; which is their shame, and not their nobility; for it is a more blessed thing to give than to receive. But rich men receive all they have from the labourer's hand, and what they give, they give away other men's labours, not their own. Therefore they are not righteous actors in the earth.

'But shall not one man have more titles of honour than another?'

Yes. As a man goes through offices, he rises to titles of honour till he comes to the highest nobility, to be a faithful commonwealth's man in a Parliament House. Likewise he who finds out any secret in nature shall have a title of honour given him, though he be a young man. But no man shall have any title of honour till he win it by industry, or come to it by age or office-bearing. Every man that is above sixty years of age shall have respect as a man of honour by all others that are younger, as is shewed hereafter.

'Shall every man count his neighbour's house as his own, and live together as one family?'

No. Though the earth and storehouses be common to every family, yet every family shall live apart as they do; and every man's house, wife, children and furniture for ornament of his house, or anything which he hath fetched in from the store-houses, or provided for the necessary use of his family, is all a property to that family, for the peace thereof. And if any man offer to take away a man's wife, children or furniture of his house, without his consent, or disturb the peace of his dwelling, he shall suffer punishment as an enemy to the commonwealth's government, as is mentioned in the platform following.

'Shall we have no lawyers?'

There is no need of them, for there is to be no buying and selling; neither any need to expound laws, for the bare letter of the law shall be both judge and lawyer, trying every man's actions. And seeing we shall have successive Parliaments every year, there will be rules made for every action a man can do.

But there is to be officers chosen yearly in every parish, to see the laws executed according to the letter of the laws; so that there will be no long work in trying of offences, as it is under kingly government, to get the lawyers money and to enslave the commoners to the conqueror's prerogative law or will. The sons of contention, Simeon and Levi, must not bear rule in a free commonwealth.

At the first view you may say, 'This is a strange government'. But I pray judge nothing before trial. Lay this platform of commonwealth's government in one scale, and lay monarchy or kingly government in the other scale, and see which give true weight to righteous freedom and peace. There is no middle path between these two, for a man must either be a free and true commonwealth's man, or a monarchical tyrannical royalist.

If any say, 'This will bring poverty'; surely they mistake. For there will be plenty of all earthly commodities, with less labour and trouble than now it is under monarchy. There will be no want, for every man may keep as plentiful a house as he will, and never run into debt, for common stock pays for all.

If you say, 'Some will live idle': I answer, No. It will make idle persons to become workers, as is declared in the platform: there shall be neither beggar nor idle person.

If you say, 'This will make men quarrel and fight':

I answer, No. It will turn swords into ploughshares, and settle such a peace in the earth, as nations shall learn war no more. Indeed the government of kings is a breeder of wars, because men being put into the straits of poverty are moved to fight for liberty, and to take one another's estates from them, and to obtain mastery. Look into all armies, and see what they do more, but make some poor, some rich; put some into freedom, and others into bondage. And is not this a plague among mankind?

Well, I question not but what objections can be raised against this commonwealth's government, they shall find an answer in this platform following. I have been something large, because I could not contract my self into a lesser volume, having so many things to speak of.

I do not say, nor desire, that every one shall be compelled to practise this commonwealth's government; for the spirits of some will be enemies at first, though afterwards will prove the most cordial and true friends thereunto.

Yet I desire that the commonwealth's land, which is the ancient commons and waste land, and the lands newly got in by the Army's victories out of the oppressors' hands, as parks, forests, chases and the like, may be set free to all that have lent assistance, either of person or purse, to obtain it; and to all that are willing to come in to the practice of this government and be obedient to the laws thereof. And for others who are not willing, let them stay in the way of buying and selling, which is the law of the conqueror, till they be willing.

And so I leave this in your hand, humbly prostrating my self and it before you; and remain

Novemb. 5,   A true lover of commonwealth's

1651.
                    government, peace and freedom,

                    Gerrard Winstanley.

To the Friendly and Unbiased READER

Reader,

It was the apostle's advice formerly, to try all things, and to hold fast that which is best. This platform of government which I offer is the original righteousness and peace in the earth, though he hath been buried under the clods of kingly covetousness, pride and oppression a long time.

Now he begins to have his resurrection, despise it not while it is small; though thou understand it not at the first sight, yet open the door and look into the house, for thou mayst see that which will satisfy thy heart in quiet rest.

To prevent thy hasty rashness, I have given thee a short compendium of the whole.

First, thou knowest that the earth in all nations is governed by buying and selling, for all the laws of kings hath relation thereunto.

Now this platform following declares to thee the government of the earth without buying and selling, and the laws are the laws of a free and peaceable commonwealth, which casts out everything that offends; for there is no pricking briar in all this holy mountain of the righteous law or peaceable ruler.

Every family shall live apart, as now they do; every man shall enjoy his own wife, and every woman her own husband, as now they do; every trade shall be improved to more excellency than now it is; all children shall be educated, and be trained up in subjection to parents and elder people more than now they are. The earth shall be planted, and the fruits reaped and carried into store-houses, by common assistance of every family. The riches of the store-houses shall be the common stock to every family. There shall be no idle person nor beggar in the land.

And because offences may arise from the spirit of unreasonable ignorance, therefore was the law added.

For if any man abuse his neighbour by provoking words, by striking his person, by offering offence to his neighbour's wife or children, or to his house or furniture therein, or to live idle upon other men's labours, here are laws to punish them sharply, and officers to see those laws executed, according to the right order of commonwealth's government, for the peace of every family in the land.

This commonwealth's government unites all people in a land into one heart and mind. And it was this government which made Moses to call Abraham's seed one house of Israel, though they were many tribes and many families. And it may be said, 'Blessed is the people whose earthly government is the law of common righteousness'.

While Israel was under this commonwealth's government, they were a terror to all oppressing kings in all nations of the world; and so will England be, if this righteous law become our governor. But when the officers of Israel began to be covetous and proud, they made a breach, or, as Isaiah said, The rulers of the people caused them to err; *and then the government was altered and fell into the hand of kings like other nations, and then they fled before their enemies and were scattered.*

The government of kings is the government of the scribes and Pharisees, who count it no freedom unless they be lords of the earth and of their brethren. But commonwealth's government is the government of righteousness and peace, who is no respecter of persons.

Therefore Reader, here is a trial for thy sincerity. Thou shalt have no want of food, raiment or freedom among brethren in this way propounded. See now if thou canst be content, as the Scriptures say, having food and raiment, therewith be content, and grudge not to let thy brother have the same with thee.

Dost thou pray and fast for freedom, and give God thanks again for it? Why know that God is not partial; for if thou pray, it must be for freedom to all; and if thou give thanks, it must be because freedom covers all people, for this will prove a lasting peace.

Everyone is ready to say, they fight for their country; and what they do, they do it for the good of their country. Well, let it appear now that thou hast fought and acted for thy country's freedom. But if, when thou hast power to settle freedom in thy country, thou takest the possession of the earth into thy own particular hands, and makest thy brother work for thee as the kings did, thou has fought and acted for thyself, not for thy country; and here thy inside hypocrisy is discovered.

But here take notice that common freedom, which is the rule I would have practised and not talked on, was thy pretence; but particular freedom to thyself was thy intent. Amend, or else thou wilt be shamed, when knowledge doth spread to cover the earth, even as the waters cover the seas. And so farewell.

G.W.

THE

Law of Freedom in a Platform;

OR,

True Magistracy Restored.

CHAP. I.

The great searching of heart in these days is to find out where true freedom lies, that the commonwealth of England might be established in peace.

Some say, 'It lies in the free use of trading, and to have all patents, licences and restraints removed'. But this is a freedom under the will of a conqueror.

Others say, 'It is true freedom to have ministers to preach, and for people to hear whom they will, without being restrained or compelled from or to any form of worship'. But this is an unsettled freedom.

Others say, 'It is true freedom to have community with all women, and to have liberty to satisfy their lusts and greedy appetites'. But this is the freedom of wanton unreasonable beasts, and tends to destruction.

Others say, 'It is true freedom that the elder brother shall be landlord of the earth, and the younger brother a servant'. And this is but a half freedom, and begets murmurings, wars and quarrels.

All these and such like are freedoms: but they lead to bondage, and are not the true foundation-freedom which settles a commonwealth in peace.

True commonwealth's freedom lies in the free enjoyment of the earth.

True freedom lies where a man receives his nourishment and preservation, and that is in the use of the earth. For as man is compounded of the four materials of the creation, fire, water, earth and air; so is he preserved by the compounded bodies of these four, which are the fruits of the earth; and he cannot live without them. For take away the free use of these and the body languishes, the spirit is brought into bondage and at length departs, and ceaseth his motional action in the body.

All that a man labours for, saith Solomon, is this, That he may enjoy the free use of the earth, with the fruits thereof. Eccles. 2.24.

Do not the ministers preach for maintenance in the earth? the lawyers plead causes to get the possessions of the earth? Doth not the soldier fight for the earth? And doth not the landlord require rent, that he may live in the fulness of the earth by the labour of his tenants?

And so, from the thief upon the highway to the king who sits upon the throne, do not everyone strive, either by force of arms or secret cheats, to get the possessions of the earth one from another, because they see their freedom lies in plenty, and their bondage lies in poverty?

Surely then, oppressing lords of manors, exacting land-lords and tithe-takers, may as well say their brethren shall not breathe in the air, nor enjoy warmth in their bodies, nor have the moist waters to fall upon them in showers, unless they will pay them rent for it: as to say their brethren shall not work upon earth, nor eat the fruits thereof, unless they will hire that liberty of them. For he that takes upon him to restrain his brother from the liberty of the one, may upon the same ground restrain him from the liberty of all four, viz. fire, water, earth and air,

A man had better to have had no body than to have no food for it; therefore this restraining of the earth from brethren by brethren is oppression and bondage; but the free enjoyment thereof is true freedom.

I speak now in relation between the oppressor and the oppressed; the inward bondages I meddle not with in this place, though I am assured that, if it be rightly searched into, the inward bondages of the mind, as covetousness, pride, hypocrisy, envy, sorrow, fears, desperation and madness, are all occasioned by the outward bondage that one sort of people lay upon another.

And thus far natural experience makes it good, that true freedom lies in the free enjoyment of the earth.

If we look into the old Scriptures,

We find that when Israel had conquered the nations he took possession of the enemies' land, and divided it by lot among the tribes, counting the enjoyment of the earth their perfect freedom.

In the beginning of their wars they first sent spies to view the land of Canaan (Numb. 13.23 to 33), for the enjoyment of that was the freedom they aimed at; for being so long in the barren wilderness, and children multiplying upon them, they wanted land to live upon, Deut. 1.28.

And when the spies returned and shewed them the fruits of the land, and had declared what a fruitful land it was, they were encouraged and restless till they were come thither; and when they heard bad tidings of the land, their hearts fell and they were discouraged.

And when the spirit of wisdom, courage and providence in them had subdued those giants, and had given the house of Israel the land of Canaan, the rulers and chief officers of Israel's army did not divide the land among themselves; but, being faithful-spirited men, they forthwith divided the land by lot, to every tribe his portion without exception.

And when Israel entreated the King of Sihon to suffer him to pass through his land, he would not suffer him, but gathered all his people together and fought with Israel; and the Lord gave Sihon into Israel's hand: and he took possession of his land.

So that we see by Scripture proof likewise, the land is that which every one place their freedom in.

If we look into the practice of kings and conquerors,

Since the Scriptures of Moses were writ, we find they placed their freedom in the enjoyment of the free use of the earth.

When William Duke of Normandy had conquered England, he took possession of the earth for his freedom and disposed of our English ground to his friends as he pleased, and made the conquered English his servants, to plant the earth for him and his friends.

And all kings, from his time to King Charles, were successors of that conquest; and all laws were made to confirm that conquest.

For there are his old laws and statutes yet to be read, that do shew how he allowed the conquered English but three pence and four pence a day for their work, to buy them bread of their task-masters; but the freedom of the earth he and his friends kept in their own hands.

And as kings, so the old gentry and the new gentry likewise, walking in the same steps, are but the successors of the Norman victory.

But are not the Normans and their power conquered by the commoners of England? And why then should we not recover the freedom of our land again, from under that yoke and power?

Then further, the Norman conqueror made laws whereby this English earth should be governed, and appointed two national officers to see those laws performed.

The first officer was the lawyer; and his work is conversant about nothing but the disposing of the earth, and all courts of judicature and suits of law is about the ordering of the earth, according to his law made by him and his party.

The next officer was the national clergy; and their work

was to persuade the multitude of people to let William the Conqueror alone with a quiet possession and government of the earth, and to call it his and not theirs, and so not to rebel against him.

And they were to tell the people that if they would acknowledge William Duke of Normandy and his successors to be their lord, king and ruler, and would be obedient to his government: then they should live in the haven, that is, in peace; and they should quietly enjoy their land which they rented, their houses and fruits of their labours without disturbance.

But if they would not acknowledge him to be their lord, king and ruler, nor submit to his government, then they should be cast into hell; that is, into the sorrows of prisons, poverty, whips and death: and their houses and riches should be taken from them, etc.

And this was a true prophetical and experimental doctrine. For do we not see that the laws of a king, while a king, had the power of life and death in them? And he who fell under the power of this lord * must pay the uttermost farthing before he was released.

And for their pains for thus preaching, the king established by his laws that they should have the tenth of the increase of all profits from the earth (1 Sam. 8.15), placing their freedom where he placed his own, and that is in the use of the earth brought into their hands by the labours of the enslaved men.

But in after times, when this national ministry appeared to the people to be but hirelings, and as the people grew in knowledge, they discovered their hypocrisy more and more, as they do in these days: then this clergy (the spirit of the old Pharisees) began to divine and to deceive the people by a shew of holiness or spiritual doctrine, as they call it, difficult to be understood by any but themselves: persuading the people to believe or fancy that true freedom lay in hearing them preach, and to enjoy that heaven which, they say,

* Law?

every man who believes their doctrine shall enjoy after he is dead: and so tell us of a heaven and hell after death, which neither they nor we know what will be. So that the whole world is at a loss in the true knowledge thereof, as Solomon said, *Who shall bring him to see what shall be after he is dead?* Eccles. 3.22 and 6.11.

The former hell of prisons, whips and gallows they preached to keep the people in subjection to the king; but by this divined hell after death they preach to keep both king and people in awe to them, to uphold their trade of tithes and new-raised maintenance. And so having blinded both king and people they become the god that rules. This subtle divining spirit is the Whore that sits upon many waters; this is Nahash the Ammonite, that would not make peace with Israel, unless Israel would suffer him to put out their right eyes and to see by his, 1 Sam. 11.2.

For so long as the people call that a truth which they call a truth, and believe what they preach, and are willing to let the clergy be the keepers of their eyes and knowledge (that is as much as Nahash did, put out their eyes to see by theirs); then all is well, and they tell the people they shall go to heaven.

But if the eyes of the people begin to open, and they seek to find knowledge in their own hearts and to question the ministers' doctrine, and become like unto wise-hearted Thomas, to believe nothing but what they see reason for:

Then do the minsters prepare war against that man or men, and will make no covenant of peace with him till they consent to have their right eyes put out, that is, to have their reason blinded, so as to believe every doctrine they preach and never question any thing, saying, 'The doctrine of faith must not be tried by reason.' No, for if it be, their mystery of iniquity will be discovered, and they would lose their tithes.

Therefore no marvel though the national clergy of England and Scotland, who are the tithing priests and lords of blinded men's spirits, stuck so close to their master the King and to his monarchical oppressing government; for say they, 'If the people must not work for us and give us tithes, but we must work for ourselves as they do, our freedom is lost'. Aye, but this is but the cry of an Egyptian task-master, who counts other men's freedom his bondage.

Now if the earth could be enjoyed in such a manner as every one might have provision, as it may by this platform I have offered, then will the peace of the commonwealth be preserved, and men need not act so hypocritically as the clergy do, and others likewise, to get a living. But when some shall enjoy great possessions, and others who have done as much or more for to purchase freedom shall have none at all, and be made slaves to their brethren, this begets offences.

The glory of Israel's commonwealth is this, They had no beggar among them.

As you read, when they had conquered the Canaanites and won that land by the purchase of the blood and labour, and by a joint assistance throughout the whole tribes of Israel; the officers and leaders of the people did not sell the land again to the remainder of their enemies, nor buy and sell it among themselves, and so by cheating the people set up a new oppression upon a new account. Neither did they fall a-parting the land before the crowning victory was gotten: but they forbore the disposing of the land till the war was over, and all the tribes stuck close together till all the fighting work was done.

And when they saw the enemies' heart was broke, and that now they were the masters of the field, then they quietly took possession of the land as a free reward for all their hazards and labour.

The officers and leaders were careful to keep promise and engagements to the people, and there was no treachery found in them, as to enrich themselves with the commonwealth's land, and to deprive others of the price of their blood and free-quarter and taxes.

But they made canon * with all the crown lands therein, and all other forfeited lands which was gotten by a joint assistance of person and purse of all the tribes. The Scriptures say, they made this canon land * a common treasury of livelihood to the whole commonwealth of Israel, and so disposed of it as they made provision for every tribe and for every family in a tribe, nay for every particular man in a family; every one had enough, no man was in want, there was no beggary among them.

They did not divide this land only to particular men who went out to war, but they who stayed at home had an equal share; they did not make one brother a lord of manor and landlord, and other brothers to be servants to them. But seeing the enemies were beaten not by the counsellors only, not by the leaders of the army only, but by the common soldiers also; and not only by them, but by the labourers who stayed at home to provide victuals and free-quarter: therefore did the counsellors and chief officers of the army agree to make provision for every one that assisted, either by person or purse; and this was pure righteousness.

And to those families in a tribe which had many persons in it, to them they allotted more land; and to those families which had less number of persons, they allotted less land. So that not only the tribes in general but every family and person in a tribe, younger brother as well as elder brother, he who wrought at home to provide food as well as he that went to war, all had sufficient, there was no want, the oppression of beggary was not known among them. All burdens were taken off, and Israel in all his tribes and families was made a free commonwealth in power, as well as in name, 1 Sam. 30.24, Josh. 16, 17 and 18 Chapters.

And thus the land was divided, and the whole land was the common stock, every one had a brotherly freedom therein. For the freedom of the one was the freedom of the other,

---

* 'Canon' might be a misprint for 'common'. But it is a legal term meaning 'quit rent'. 'Canon land' here probably means land subject to some form of customary rent.

there was no difference in that, they were men of true, faithful and public spirits, not false-hearted.

And so likewise when Esther prevailed with King Ahasuerus for freedom, she did not seek her own freedom and interest, but the freedom of all her kindred and friends; for common freedom was that which men of righteous spirits always sought after.

All that I shall say is this, O that those who pretend to set up a gospel-commonwealth in England, Scotland and Ireland would not be worse than Moses, but rather exceed Moses, knowing that if this our English commonwealth's government carry perfect freedom in his hand, then shall the law go forth from England to all the nations of the world.

This foundation being laid from the example of Israel's commonwealth and testimony of God's Word, I shall proceed how the earth shall be governed for the peace of a commonwealth. But by the way, to prevent mistake, I shall insert

A short declaration to take off prejudice.

Some, hearing of this common freedom, think there must be a community of all the fruits of the earth whether they work or no, therefore strive to live idle upon other men's labours.

Others, through the same unreasonable beastly ignorance, think there must be a community of all men and women for copulation, and so strive to live a bestial life.

Others think there will be no law, but that everything will run into confusion for want of government; but this platform proves the contrary.

Therefore, because that transgression doth and may arise from ignorant and rude fancy in man, is the law added.

That which true righteousness in my judgment calls community is this, to have the earth set free from all kingly bondage of lords of manors and oppressing landlords, which came in by conquest as a thief takes a true man's purse upon the highway, being stronger than he.

And that neither the earth, nor any fruits thereof, should be bought or sold by the inhabitants one among another, which is slavery the kingly conquerors have brought in; therefore he set his stamp upon silver, that every one should buy and sell in his name.

And though this be, yet shall not men live idle; for the earth shall be planted and reaped, and the fruits carried into barns and store-houses by the assistance of every family, according as is shewed hereafter in order.

Every man shall be brought up in trades and labours, and all trades shall be maintained with more improvement, to the enriching of the commonwealth, more than now they be under kingly power.

Every tradesman shall fetch materials, as leather, wool, flax, corn and the like, from the public store-houses, to work upon without buying and selling; and when particular works are made, as cloth, shoes, hats and the like, the tradesmen shall bring these particular works to particular shops, as it is now in practice, without buying and selling. And every family as they want such things as they cannot make, they shall go to these shops and fetch without money, even as now they fetch with money, as hereafter is shewed how in order.

If any say, 'This will nurse idleness'; I answer, this platform proves the contrary, for idle persons and beggars will be made to work.

If any say, 'This will make some men to take goods from others by violence and call it theirs, because the earth and fruits are a common stock'; I answer, the laws or rules following prevents that ignorance. For though the store-houses and public shops be commonly furnished by every family's assistance, and for every family's use, as is shewed hereafter how: yet every man's house is proper to himself, and all the furniture therein, and provision which he hath fetched from the store-houses is proper to himself; every man's wife and every woman's husband proper to themselves, and so are their children at their dispose till they come to age.

And if any other man endeavour to take away his house, furniture, food, wife or children, saying every thing is common, and so abusing the law of peace, such a one is a transgressor, and shall suffer punishment, as by the government and laws following is expressed.

For though the public store-houses be a common treasury, yet every man's particular dwelling is not common but by his consent, and the commonwealth's laws are to preserve a man's peace in his person and in his private dwelling, against the rudeness and ignorance that may arise in mankind.

If any man do force or abuse women in folly, pleading community, the laws following do punish such ignorant and unrational practice; for the laws of a commonwealth are laws of moderate diligence and purity of manners.

Therefore I desire a patient reading of what hereafter follows; and when you have heard the extent of commonwealth's government or freedom, then weigh it in the balance with kingly government or bondage; and see whether [i.e. which] brings most peace to the land, and establish that for government.

For you must either establish commonwealth's freedom in power, making provision for every one's peace, which is righteousness; or else you must set up monarchy again.

Monarchy is twofold; either for one king to rule, or for many to rule by kingly principles; for the king's power lies in his laws, not in the name. And if either one king rule, or many rule by king's principles, much murmuring, grudges, troubles and quarrels may and will arise among the oppressed people upon every gained opportunity.

But if common freedom be found out and ease the oppressed, it prevents murmurings and quarrels, and establishes universal peace in the earth.

Therefore seeing the power of government is in the hands of such as have professed to the world a godly righteousness, more purely than that of oppressing kings, without doubt their faithfulness and wisdom is required to be manifested in action as well as in words.

But if they who profess more righteousness and freedom in words than the kings' government was, and yet can find out no government to ease the people but must establish the kings' old laws though they give it a new name; I will leave the sentence, worthy such a profession and such a people, to be given by the heart of every rational man. And so I shall proceed how the earth should be governed for the peace of a commonwealth.

CHAP. II.

What is Government in general.

Government is a wise and free ordering of the earth and the manners of mankind by observation of particular laws or rules, so that all the inhabitants may live peaceably in plenty and freedom in the land where they are born and bred.

In the government of a land there are three parts, viz. laws, fit officers and a faithful execution of those laws.

First, there must be suitable laws for every occasion, and almost for every action that men do; for one law cannot serve in all seasons, but every season and every action have their particular laws attending thereupon for the preservation of right order. As for example,

There is a time to plough, and the laws of right understanding attends upon that work; and there is a time to reap the fruits of the earth, and the laws of right observation attending thereupon.

So that true government is a right ordering of all actions, giving to every action and thing its due weight and measure, and this prevents confusion. As Solomon speaks, *There is a time for all things*; a time to make promises and engagements and a time to see them performed; a right order in times of war, and a right order in times of peace; every season and time having its law or rule suitable; and this makes a healthful government, because it preserves peace in a right order.

Secondly, there must be fit officers, whose spirits are so humble, wise and free from covetousness, as they can make the established laws of the land their will; and not through pride and vain-glory make their wills to rule above the rules of freedom, pleading prerogative.

For when the right ordered laws do rule, the government is healthful; but when the will of officers rule above law, that government is diseased with a mortal disease.

Thirdly, there must be a faithful execution of those laws; and herein lies the very life of government. For a right order in government lies not in the will of officers without laws, nor in laws without officers, nor in neither of them without execution. But when these three go hand in hand the government is healthful; but if any one of these be wanting the government is diseased.

There is a twofold government, a kingly government and a commonwealth's government.

What is kingly government or monarchy?

Kingly government governs the earth by that cheating art of buying and selling, and thereby becomes a man of contention, his hand is against every man, and every man's hand against him; and take this government at the best, it is a diseased government, and the very city Babylon, full of confusion. And if it had not a club law to support it, there would be no order in it, because it is the covetous and proud will of a conqueror, enslaving a conquered people.

This kingly government is he who beats pruning hooks and ploughs into spears, guns, swords and instruments of war, that he might take his younger brother's creation birthright from him, calling the earth his and not his brother's, unless his brother will hire the earth of him, so that he may live idle and at ease by his brother's labours.

Indeed this government may well be called the government

of highwaymen, who hath stolen the earth from the younger brethren by force, and holds it from them by force. He sheds blood not to free the people from oppression, but that he may be king and ruler over an oppressed people.

The situation of this monarchical government

Lies in the will of kings, alias conquerors, setting up lords of manors, exacting landlords, tithing priests and covetous lawyers, with all those pricking briars attending thereupon, to be task-masters to oppress the people, lest they should rise up in riches and power to disthrone him, and so to share the earth with him, redeeming their own creation rights again, which this kingly government withholds from mankind in all nations. For he is the great Man of Sin who is now revealed, who sits in the temple of God, ruling above all that is called God, and both by force and cheating policy takes the people's freedoms from them, Exod. 1.8, 2 Thes. 2.8, 9.

This kingly government is he that makes the elder brethren freemen in the earth, and the younger brethren slaves in the earth, before they have lost their freedom by transgression to the law.

Nay, he makes one brother a lord and another a servant while they are in their mother's womb, before they have done either good or evil. This is the mighty ruler that hath made the election and rejection of brethren from their birth to their death, or from eternity to eternity.

He calls himself the Lord God of the whole creation, for he makes one brother to pay rent to another brother for the use of the water, earth and air, or else he will not suffer him by his laws and lawyers to live above ground, but in beggary; and yet he will be called righteous.

And whereas the Scriptures say that the creator of all things (God) is no respecter of persons, yet this kingly power doth nothing else but respect persons, preferring the rich and the proud; therefore he denies the Scriptures and the true God of righteousness, though he pray and preach of the

Scriptures, and keep fasts and thanksgiving-days to God, to be a cloak to hide his oppression from the people, whereby he shews himself to be the great Antichrist and mystery of iniquity, that makes war with Christ and his saints under pretence of owning him.

The great law-giver of this kingly government

Is covetousness ruling in the heart of mankind, making one brother to covet a full possession of the earth and a lordly rule over another brother, which he will have or else he will enslave or kill his brother; for this is Cain who killed Abel: and because of this, he is called *the great red dragon, the god of this world, the oppressor, under which the whole creation hath groaned a long time, waiting to be delivered from him.*

The rise of kingly government is twofold.

First, by a politic wit, in drawing the people out of common freedom into a way of common bondage; for so long as the earth is a common treasury to all men, kingly covetousness can never reign as king. Therefore his first device was to put the people to buy and sell the earth and the fruits one to another; for this would beget discontents and muddy the waters.

And when this spirit of monarchy hath drawn the people into the way of buying and selling, and the people begin to vex one another, then began his opportunity to reign.

For in that man wherein this kingly spirit seats himself, he tells the people that are wronged, 'Well, I'll ease you, and I'll set things to rights'. And then he went about to establish buying and selling by law, whereby the people had some ease for a time, but the cunning Machiavellian spirit got strength thereby to settle himself king in the earth.

For after some time the people through ignorance began to multiply suits of law one against another, and to quarrel and fight. Now saith this subtle spirit, 'Come follow me' to one sort of people that are oppressed, 'and stick to me, and we will fight with those who wrong you; and if we conquer them, then we will govern the earth as we please, and they shall be our servants, and we will make them work for us'.

Thereupon one sort of people followed one head, and another sort of people followed another head, and so wars began in the earth, and mankind fell a-fighting, one part conquering and enslaving another. And now man is fallen from his innocence, and from the glory of the spirit of common freedom, love and peace, into enmity; everyone striving to be king one over another; everyone striving to be a landlord of the earth, and to make his brother his servant to work for him.

But still here is disorder, therefore this subtle spirit of darkness goes further and tells the people, 'You must make one man king over you all, and let him make laws, and let every one be obedient thereunto'. And when the people consented thereunto, they gave away their freedom, and they set up oppression over themselves.

And this was the rise of kingly power: first by policy, drawing the people from a common enjoyment of the earth to the crafty art of buying and selling; secondly, to advance himself by the power of the sword, when that art of buying and selling had made them quarrel among themselves.

So that this spirit of monarchy it is the spirit of subtlety and covetousness, filling the heart of mankind with enmity and ignorance, pride and vain-glory, because the strong destroys the weak; and so one Scripture calls this *the power and government of the Beast*, another Scripture calls it *the god of this world or the devil*. For indeed the monarchical spirit is the power of darkness, for it is the great thick cloud that hath hid the light of the sun of righteousness from shining in his full strength a long time.

And though this kingly spirit doth call buying and selling a righteous thing, thereby to put the simple younger brother upon it, yet he will destroy it as he pleaseth, by patents, licences or monopolizing.

Or else he will at his pleasure take away the riches which

his younger brother hath got by trading, and so still lift up himself above his brother.

And as he rise to the throne by the crafty art of buying and selling and by the sword, so he is maintained upon the throne by the same means.

And the people now see that kingly power is the oppressor, and the maintainers thereof are called oppressors by the ancient writers of the Bible.

This kingly power is the old heaven and the old earth that must pass away, wherein unrighteousness, oppression and partiality dwells.

For indeed we never read that the people began to complain of oppression till kingly government rose up, which is the power of covetousness and pride; and which Samuel sets forth to be a plague and a curse upon the people in the first rise of it.

He will take your sons and your daughters to be his servants and to run before his chariots, to plant his ground and to reap his harvest. He will take your fields, your vineyards and oliveyards, even the best of them, and give to his servants as pleaseth him. He will take the tenth of your seed and of your vineyards and give to his officers or ministers. 1 Sam. 8.

And this was that god who appointed the people to pay tithes to the clergy.

And many other oppressions did the kingly government bring upon the people, as you may read at large in Samuel.

Read 1 Sam. 8. from Vers. 10. to 19.

The winter's past, the spring time now appears,
Begone thou kingly tyrant, with all thy Cavaliers.
Thy day is past, and sure thou dost appear
To be the bond-man's son, and not the free-born heir.
Matt. 15.13.

What is commonwealth's government?

Commonwealth's government governs the earth without buying and selling; and thereby becomes a man of peace, and the restorer of ancient peace and freedom. He makes provision for the oppressed, the weak and the simple, as well as for the rich, the wise and the strong. He beats swords and spears into pruning hooks and ploughs; he makes both elder and younger brother freemen in the earth. Micah 4.3, 4, Isai. 33.1. and 65.17 to 25.

All slaveries and oppressions which have been brought upon mankind by kings, lords of manors, lawyers and landlords and the divining clergy, are all cast out again by this government, if it be right in power as well as in name.

For this government is the true restorer of all long-lost freedoms, and so becomes the joy of all nations, and the blessing of the whole earth: for this takes off the kingly curse, and makes Jerusalem a praise in the earth. Therefore all you who profess religion and spiritual things, now look to it, and see what spirit you do profess, for your profession is brought to trial.

If once commonwealth's government be set upon the throne, then no tyranny or oppression can look him in the face and live.

For where oppression lies upon brethren by brethren, that is no commonwealth's government, but the kingly government still; and the mystery of iniquity hath taken that peace-maker's name to be a cloak to hide his subtle covetousness, pride and oppression under.

O England, England, wouldst thou have thy government sound and healthful? Then cast about and see and search diligently to find out all those burdens that came in by kings, and remove them; and then will thy commonwealth's government arise from under the clods, under which as yet it is buried and covered with deformity.

If true commonwealth's freedom lie in the free enjoyment of the earth, as it doth, then whatsoever law or custom doth deprive brethren of their freedom in the earth, it is to be cast out as unsavory salt.

The situation of commonwealth's government

Is within the laws of common freedom, whereby there is a provision for livelihood in the earth both for elder and younger brother; and not the one enslaving the other, but both living in plenty and freedom.

The officers, laws and customs hereafter mentioned, or such like, according to such a method, may be the foundation and pillars of commonwealth's government.

This government depends not upon the will of any particular man or men; for it is seated in the spirit of mankind, and it is called the *light,* or *son of righteousness and peace.* The tyrants in all ages have made use of this man's name, while he hath lain buried, to cover their cheating mystery of iniquity: for if common freedom were not pretended, the commoners of a land would never dance after the pipe of self-seeking wits.

This commonwealth's government may well be called the *ancient of days*; for it was before any other oppressing government crept in.

It is the moderator of all oppression; and so is like Moses and Joseph in Pharaoh's court, and in time will be the restorer of long lost freedoms to the creation, and delights to plant righteousness over the face of the whole earth.

The great lawgiver in commonwealth's government

Is the spirit of universal righteousness dwelling in mankind, now rising up to teach every one to do to another as he would have another do to him, and is no respecter of persons: and this spirit hath been killed in the Pharisaical kingly spirit of self-love, and been buried in the dunghill of that enmity for many years past.

And if these be the days of his resurrection to power, as we may hope, because the name of commonwealth is risen and established in England by a law, then we or our posterity shall see comfortable effects.

In that nation where this commonwealth's government shall be first established, there shall be abundance of peace and plenty, and all nations of the earth shall come flocking thither to see his beauty, and to learn the ways thereof; and the law shall go forth from that Sion, and that Word of the Lord from that Jerusalem, which shall govern the whole earth. Micah 4.1, 2.

There shall be no tyrant kings, lords of manors, tithing priests, oppressing lawyers, exacting landlords, nor any such like pricking briar in all this holy mountain of the Lord God our righteousness and peace; for the righteous law shall be the rule for everyone, and the judge of all men's actions.

David desired rather to be a door-keeper in this house of God, or commonwealth's government, than to live in the tents of wickedness, which was the kingly oppressing courts.

If any go about to build up commonwealth's government upon kingly principles, they will both shame and lose themselves; for there is a plain difference between the two governments.

And if you do not run in the right channel of freedom, you must, nay you will, as you do, face about and turn back again to Egyptian monarchy: and so your names in the days of posterity shall stink and be blasted with abhorred infamy for your unfaithfulness to common freedom; and the evil effects will be sharp upon the backs of posterity.

Therefore seeing England is declared to be a free commonwealth, and the name thereof established by a law; surely then the greatest work is now to be done, and that is to escape all kingly cheats in setting up a commonwealth's government, that the power and the name may agree together; so that all the inhabitants may live in peace, plenty and freedom, otherwise we shall shew our government to be gone no further but to the half day of the Beast, or to the dividing of time, of which there must be an overturn. Dan. 7.25, Rev. 12.14.

For oppression was always the occasion why the spirit of freedom in the people desired change of government.

When Samuel's sons took bribes and grew rich upon the common purse, and forgot to relieve the oppressed, that made the people forsake the government by judges, and to desire a kingly government. 1 Sam. 8.34.

And the oppressions of the kingly government have made this age of the world to desire a commonwealth's government and the removal of the kings; for the spirit of light in man loves freedom and hates bondage.

And because the spirit in mankind is various within itself, for some are wise, some are foolish, some idle, some laborious, some rash, some mild, some loving and free to others, some envious and covetous, some of an inclination to do as they would have others do to them, but others seek to save themselves and to live in fulness, though others perish for want:

Therefore because of this was the law added, which was to be a rule and judge for all men's actions, to preserve common peace and freedom; and Paul writ, *The law was added because of transgression*, one against another.

The haven gates are now set ope for English man to enter:
The freedoms of the earth's his due, if he will make
adventure.

CHAP. III.

Where began the first original of Government in the Earth among Mankind?

The original root of magistracy is common preservation, and it rose up first in a private family: for suppose there were but one family in the world, as is conceived, father Adam's family, wherein were many persons:

Therein Adam was the first governor or officer in the earth, because as he was the first father, so he was the most wise in contriving and the most strong for labour, and so the fittest to be the chief governor. For this is the golden rule,

Let the wise help the foolish, and let the strong help the weak. Psa. 35.10, Rom. 15.1,2.

But some may say here that Adam was under no law, but his will was a law to him and his household; therefore, from the root from whence magistracy first rose, it is clear that officers are to be under no law but their own wills, and the people are to be subject thereunto.* I answer:

The law of necessity, that the earth should be planted for the common preservation and peace of his household, was the righteous rule and law to Adam, and this law was so clearly written in the hearts of his people that they all consented quietly to any counsel he gave them for that end.

Therefore not Adam's will only, but the will of his people likewise, and the law of common preservation, peace and freedom, was the righteous law that governed both Adam and his household.

But yet observe, that from the father in a family was the first rise of magisterial government, because children wanting experience of their own preservation, therefore such as are experienced are to propound the law of government to them: and therefore from Adam to this day, the law of common preservation is the rule and foundation of true magistracy: and it is the work of all magistrates to help the weak and the foolish.

There are two root[s] from whence laws do spring.

The first root you see is common preservation, when there is a principle in everyone to seek the good of others as himself, without respecting persons: and this is the root of the tree magistracy, and the law of righteousness and peace: and all particular laws found out by experience, necessary

---

* This theory had been put forward by Sir Robert Filmer in *The Anarchy of a Limited or Mixed Monarchy* (1648).

to be practised for common preservation, are the boughs and branches of that tree.

And because, among the variety of mankind, ignorance may grow up; therefore this original law is written in the heart of every man, to be his guide or leader: so that if an officer be blinded by covetousness and pride, and that ignorance rule in him, yet an inferior man may tell him where he goes astray; for common preservation and peace is the foundation rule of all government. And therefore if any will preach or practise fundamental truths or doctrine, here you may see where the foundation thereof lies.

The second root is self-preservation: when particular officers seek their own preservation, ease, honour, riches and freedom in the earth, and do respect persons that are in power and riches with them and regard not the peace, freedom and preservation of the weak and foolish among brethren.

And this is the root of the tree tyranny, and the law of unrighteousness; and all particular kingly laws found out by covetous policy to enslave one brother to another, whereby bondage, tears, sorrows and poverty are brought upon many men, are all but the boughs and branches of that tree, tyranny; and such officers as these are fallen from true magistracy, and are no members thereof, but the members of tyranny, who is the devil and Satan.

And indeed this tyranny is the cause of all wars and troubles, and of the removal of the government of the earth out of one hand into another, so often as it is, in all nations.

For if magistrates had a care to cherish the peace and liberties of the common people, and see them set free from oppression, they might sit in the chair of government and never be disturbed.

But when their sitting is altogether to advance their own interest, and to forget the afflictions of Joseph or their brethren that are under bondage: this is a forerunner of their own downfall, and oftentime proves the plague to the whole land.

Therefore the work of all true magistrates is to maintain the common law, which is the root of right government and preservation and peace to everyone; and to cast out all self-ended principles and interests, which is tyranny and oppression, and which breaks common peace.

For surely the disorderly actings of officers break the peace of the commonwealth more than any men whatsoever.

All officers in a true magistracy of a commonwealth are to be chosen officers.

In the first family, which is the foundation from whence all families sprang, there was the father; he is the first link of the chain magistracy. The necessity of the children that sprang from him doth say,

'Father, do thou teach us how to plant the earth, that we may live, and we will obey'. By this choice they make him not only a father, but a master and ruler. And out of this root springs up all magistrates and officers, to see the law executed and to preserve peace in the earth, by seeing that right government is observed.

For here take notice, that though the children might not speak, yet their weakness and simplicity did speak and chose their father to be their overseer.

So that he who is a true commonwealth's officer is not to step into the place of magistracy by policy or violent force, as all kings and conquerors do; and so become oppressing tyrants, by promoting their self-ended interests or Machiavellian cheats, that they may live in plenty and rule as lords over their brethren.

But a true commonwealth's officer is to be a chosen one, by them who are in necessity and who judge him fit for that work.

And thus a father in a family is a commonwealth's officer, because the necessity of the young children chose him by a joint consent, and not otherwise.

Secondly, in a bigger family called a parish, the body of the people are confused and disordered, because some are wise, some foolish, some subtle and cunning to deceive, others plain-hearted, some strong, some weak, some rash, angry, some mild and quiet-spirited. By reason whereof offences do arise among brethren, and their common peace is broken.

Therefore as necessity hath added a law to limit men's manners, because of transgressions one against another,

So likewise doth the necessity of common peace move the whole body of the parish to choose two, three or more, within that circuit, to be their overseers, to cause the unruly ones, for whom only the law was added, to be subject to the law or rule, that so peace may be preserved among them in the planting of the earth, reaping the fruits, and quiet enjoyment.

Thirdly, in every county, shire or land, wherein the families are increased to a larger commonwealth, the necessity of the people moves them still to choose more overseers and officers to preserve common peace.

And when the people have chose[n] all officers, to preserve a right order in government of [the] earth among them, then doth the same necessity of common peace move the people to say to their overseers and officers:

'Do you see our laws observed for our preservation and peace, and we will assist and protect you.' And this word 'assist' and 'protect' implies:

The rising up of the people by force of arms to defend their laws and officers against any invasion, rebellion or resistance, yea to beat down the turbulence of any foolish or self-ended spirit that endeavours to break their common peace.

So that all true officers are chosen officers, and when they act to satisfy the necessity of them who chose them, then they are faithful and righteous servants to that commonwealth, and then there is a rejoicing in the city.

But when officers do take the possessions of the earth into their own hands, lifting themselves up thereby to be lords over their masters, the people who chose them, and will not suffer the people to plant the earth and reap the fruits for their livelihood, unless they will hire the land of them or work for day-wages for them, that they may live in ease and plenty and not work:

These officers are fallen from true magistracy of a commonwealth, and they do not act righteously; and because of this, sorrows and tears, poverty and bondages, are known among mankind; and now that city mourns.

And surely if it be carefully looked into, the necessity of the people never chose such officers, but they were either voluntary soldiers or officers chosen by them who ran before they were called; and so by policy and force they sat down in the chair of government, strengthening one sort of people to take the free use of the earth from another sort; and these are sons of bondage, and they act in darkness: by reason whereof the prophet Isaiah cries out, *Darkness hath covered the earth, and thick darkness the people; for the leaders of the people have caused them to err*: I fear so, O England, etc.

All officers in a commonwealth are to be chosen new ones every year.

When public officers remain long in place of judicature, they will degenerate from the bounds of humility, honesty and tender care of brethren, in regard the heart of man is so subject to be overspread with the clouds of covetousness, pride and vain-glory: for though at the first entrance into places of rule they be of public spirits, seeking the freedom of others as their own; yet continuing long in such a place where honours and greatness is coming in, they become selfish, seeking themselves and not common freedom; as experience proves it true in these days, according to this common proverb,

Great offices in a land and army have changed the disposition of many sweet-spirited men.

And nature tells us that if water stand long, it corrupts; whereas running water keeps sweet and is fit for common use.

Therefore as the necessity of common preservation moves the people to frame a law and to choose officers to see the law obeyed, that they may live in peace:

So doth the same necessity bid the people, and cries aloud in the ears and eyes of England to choose new officers and to remove the old ones, and to choose state-officers every year; and that for these reasons:

First, to prevent their own evils; for when pride and fulness take hold of an officer, his eyes are so blinded therewith that he forgets he is a servant to the commonwealth, and strives to lift up himself high above his brethren, and oftentimes his fall proves very great: witness the fall of oppressing kings, bishops and other state officers.

Secondly, to prevent the creeping in of oppression into the commonwealth again: for when officers grow proud and full, they will maintain their greatness, though it be in the poverty, ruin and hardship of their brethren: witness the practice of kings and their laws, that have crushed the commoners of England a long time.

And have we not experience in these days that some officers of the commonwealth are grown so mossy for want of removing that they will hardly speak to an old acquaintance, if he be an inferior man, though they were very familiar before these wars began? Etc.

And what hath occasioned this distance among friends and brethren but long continuance in places of honour, greatness and riches?

Thirdly, let officers be chosen new every year in love to our posterity; for if burdens and oppressions should grow up in our laws and in our officers for want of removing, as moss and weeds grow in some land for want of stirring, surely it will be a foundation of misery, not easily to be removed by our posterity; and then will they curse the time that ever we their fore-fathers had opportunities to set things to rights for their ease, and would not do it.

Fourthly, to remove officers of state every year will make them truly faithful, knowing that others are coming after who will look into their ways; and if they do not do things justly, they must be ashamed when the next officers succeed. And when officers deal faithfully in the government of the commonwealth, they will not be unwilling to remove. The peace of London is much preserved by removing their officers yearly.

Fifthly, it is good to remove officers every year, that whereas many have their portions to obey, so many may have their turns to rule; and this will encourage all men to advance righteousness and good manners in hopes of honour; but when money and riches bears all the sway in the rulers' hearts, there is nothing but tyranny in such ways.

Sixthly, the commonwealth hereby will be furnished with able and experienced men, fit to govern, which will mightily advance the honour and peace of our land, occasion the more watchful care in the education of children, and in time will make our commonwealth of England the lily among the nations of the earth.

Who are fit to choose, and fit to be chosen, officers in a commonwealth?

All uncivil livers, as drunkards, quarrellers, fearful ignorant men, who dare not speak truth lest they anger other men; likewise all who are wholly given to pleasure and sports, or men who are full of talk; all these are empty of substance, and cannot be experienced men, therefore not fit to be chosen officers in a commonwealth; yet they may have a voice in the choosing.

Secondly, all those who are interested in the monarchical power and government ought neither to choose nor be chosen officers to manage commonwealth's affairs, for these cannot be friends to common freedom. And these are of two sorts:

First, such as have either lent money to maintain the King's army, or in that army have been soldiers to fight against the recovering of common freedom; these are neither to choose nor be chosen officers in the commonwealth as yet, for they have lost their freedom; yet I do not say that they should be made servants, as the conquered usually are made servants, for they are our brethren, and what they did, no doubt, they did in a conscionable zeal, though in ignorance.

And seeing but few of the Parliament's friends understand their common freedoms, though they own the name commonwealth, therefore the Parliament's party ought to bear with the ignorance of the King's party, because they are brethren, and not make them servants, though for the present they be suffered neither to choose nor be chosen officers, lest that ignorant spirit of revenge break out in them to interrupt our common peace.

Secondly, all those who have been so hasty to buy and sell the commonwealth's land, and so to entangle it upon a new account, ought neither to choose nor be chosen officers, for hereby they declare themselves either to be for kingly interest, or else are ignorant of commonwealth's freedom, or both, therefore unfit to make laws to govern a free commonwealth, or to be overseers to see those laws executed.

What greater injury could be done to the commoners of England, than to sell away their land so hastily, before the people knew where they were, or what freedom they had got by such cost and bloodshed as they were at? And what greater ignorance could be declared by officers than to sell away the purchased land from the purchasers, or from part of them, into the hands of particular men to uphold monarchical principles?

But though this be a fault, let it be bore withal, it was ignorance of brethren; for England hath lain so long under kingly slavery that few knew what common freedom was; and let a restoration of this redeemed land be speedily made by them who have the possession of it.

For there is neither reason nor equity that a few men should go away with that land and freedom which the whole commoners have paid taxes, free-quarter and wasted their estates, healths and blood to purchase out of bondage, and many of them are in want of a comfortable livelihood.

Well, these are the men that take away other men's rights from them, and they are members of the covetous generation of self-seekers, therefore unfit to be chosen officers, or to choose.

Who then are fit to be chosen commonwealth's officers?

Why truly, choose such as have a long time given testimony by their actions to be promoters of common freedom, whether they be members in church fellowship or not in church fellowship, for all are one in Christ.

Choose such as are men of peaceable spirits, and of a peaceable conversation.

Choose such as have suffered under kingly oppression, for they will be fellow-feelers of others' bondages.

Choose such as have adventured the loss of their estates and lives to redeem the land from bondage, and who have remained constant.

Choose such as are understanding men, and who are experienced in the laws of peaceable and right-ordered government.

Choose men of courage, who are not afraid to speak the truth; for this is the shame of many in England at this day, they are drowned in the dung-hill mud of slavish fear of men; these are covetous men, not fearing God, and their portion is to be cast without the city of peace amongst the dogs.

Choose officers out of the number of those men that are above forty years of age, for these are most likely to be experienced men; and all these are likely to be men of courage, dealing truly and hating covetousness.

And if you choose men thus principled, who are poor men, as times go (for the conqueror's power hath made many a righteous man a poor man); then allow them a yearly maintenance from the common stock, until such time as a commonwealth's freedom is established, for then there will be no need of such allowances.

What is the reason that most people are so ignorant of their freedoms, and so few fit to be chosen commonwealth's officers?

Because the old kingly clergy, that are seated in parishes for lucre of tithes, are continually distilling their blind principles into the people, and do thereby nurse up ignorance in them; for they observe the bent of the people's minds, and make sermons to please the sickly minds of ignorant people, to preserve their own riches and esteem among a charmed, befooled and besotted people.

CHAP. IV.

What are the Officers' Names in a free Commonwealth?

In a private family, a father or master is an officer.

In a town, city or parish,
- a peace-maker.
- a four-fold office of overseers.
- a soldier.
- a task-master.
- an executioner.

In a county or shire,
- a judge.
- the peace-makers of every town within that circuit.
- the overseers and soldiers attending thereupon.

This is called either the judge's court, or the county senate.

In a whole land,
- a parliament.
- a commonwealth's ministry.
- a post-master.
- an army.

All these offices are like links of a chain, they arise from one and the same root, which is necessity of common peace, and all their works tend to preserve common peace; therefore they are to assist each other, and all others are to assist them, as need requires, upon pain of punishment by the breach of the laws. And the rule of right government being thus observed may make a whole land, nay the whole fabric of the earth, to become one family of mankind, and one well-governed commonwealth; as Israel was called *one house of Israel*, though it consisted of many tribes, nations and families.

The work of a father or master of a family.

A father is to cherish his children till they grow wise and strong, and then as a master he is to instruct them in reading, in learning languages, arts and sciences, or to bring them up to labour, or employ them in some trade or other, or cause them to be instructed therein, according as is shewed hereafter in the education of mankind.

A father is to have a care that as all his children do assist to plant the earth, or by other trades provide necessaries, so he shall see that everyone have a comfortable livelihood, not respecting one before another.

He is to command them their work and see they do it, and not suffer them to live idle; he is either to reprove by words or whip those who offend, for the rod is prepared to bring the unreasonable ones to experience and moderation:

That so children may not quarrel like beasts, but live in peace like rational men, experienced in yielding obedience to the laws and officers of the commonwealth, everyone doing to another as he would have another do to him.

The work of a peace-maker.

In a parish or town may be chosen three, four or six peace-makers, or more, according to the bigness of the place; and their work is twofold.

First, in general to sit in council to order the affairs of the parish, to prevent troubles and to preserve common peace, and here they may be called councillors.

Secondly, if there arise any matters of offence between man and man, by reason of any quarrels, disturbance or foolish actings, the offending parties shall be brought by the soldiers before any one or more of these peace-makers, who shall hear the matter and shall endeavour to reconcile the parties and make peace, and so put a stop to the rigour of the law, and go no further.

But if the peace-maker cannot persuade or reconcile the parties, then he shall command them to appear at the judge's court at the time appointed to receive the judgment of the law.

If any matters of public concernment fall out wherein the peace of the city, town or country in one county is concerned, then the peace-makers in every town thereabouts shall meet and consult about it; and from them, or from any six of them if need require, shall issue forth any order to inferior officers.

But if the matters concern only the limits of a town or city, then the peace-makers of that town shall from their court send forth orders to inferior officers for the performing of any public service within their limits.

Thirdly, if any proof be given that any officer neglects his duty, a peace-maker is to tell that officer between them two of his neglect; and if the officer continue negligent after this reproof, the peace-maker shall acquaint either the county senate or the national Parliament therewith, that from them the offender may receive condign punishment.

And it is all to this end, that the laws be obeyed; for a careful execution of laws is the life of government.

And while a peace-maker is careful to oversee the officers, all officers and others shall assist him, upon pain of forfeiture of freedom or other punishment, according to the rules following.

One thing remember, that when any offender is brought before any of these chief peace-makers, then this is to be noted, that the offender hath rejected mercy once before by refusing to yield obedience to the overseers, as is explained further hereafter.

The work of an overseer.

In a parish or town there is to be a fourfold degree of overseers, which are to be chosen yearly.

The first is an overseesr to preserve peace, in case of any quarrels that may fall out between man and man; for though the earth with her fruits be a common treasury, and is to be planted and reaped by common assistance of every family, yet every house and all the furniture for ornament therein is a property to the indwellers; and when any family hath fetched in from the store-houses or shops either clothes, food or any ornament necessary for their use, it is all a property to that family.

And if any other family or man come to disturb them, and endeavour to take away furniture, which is the ornament of his neighbour's house, or to burn, break or spoil wilfully any part of his neighbours' houses, or endeavour to take away either the food or clothing which his neighbour hath provided for his use, by reason whereof quarrels and provoking words may arise:

This office of overseers is to prevent disturbance, and is an assistance to the peace-maker; and at the hearing of any such offence, this overseer shall go and hear the matter, and endeavour to persuade the offender, and to keep peace; and if friendship be made, and subjection be yielded to the laws for the peace of the commonwealth, the offender is only to be reproved for his rashness by his overseer; and there is an end.

But if the offender be so violent that he will not refrain his offence to his neighbour at this overseer's persuasion, but remain stiff and stubborn, this overseer shall then give out an order to the soldier to carry the body of the offender before the council of the peace-makers, or before any one or more of them.

And if the offender will not yield obedience to the laws of

peace by the persuasion of the chief peace-makers neither, then this is to be noted to be the second time that this offender hath refused mercy.

Then shall the peace-maker appoint him a day, and command him to appear before the judge's court, either in the city or country where the offence is given, and there he shall receive sentence according to the rigour of the law.

And if an overseer should make peace, and do not send the offender to the peace-maker's court, yet this shall be noted the first time of such a one's disobedience to the laws.

And all this is to prevent quarrels and offences; and the chief peace-makers or councillors may not always be at hand at the beginning of such disturbance, therefore this overseer is an assistance thereunto, and is a member of that court.

One man shall not take away that commodity which another man hath first laid hands on, for any commodity for use belongs to him that first laid hands on it for his use; and if another come and say, 'I will have it', and so offences do arise, this overseer shall go to them, or give order to the soldier to bring the offender to him, and shall endeavour to make peace, either by giving the commodity to him who first laid hands on it, or else by taking the commodity from both, and bid them go to the store-houses and fetch more, seeing the store-houses are full and afford plenty of the same commodities, giving the offender a sharp reproof for offering to break the peace, noting this to be the first time that such a one offered violence to break the laws of peace.

And all persons whatsoever shall assist the overseers herein; and if any person strike or affront by words this overseer, he shall give order to the soldier to carry him before the peace-makers, and from them the offender shall receive a command to appear before the judge's court, where he shall receive the sentence of the law without mitigation.

For when a peace-maker or councillor doth appoint an offender to appear before the judge's court, such an offender hath refused mercy twice.

All this is to be done in case of small offences; but if any offence be offered by any which comes within compass of death, there shall be no peace-maker to be a mediator aforehand, but the offender shall be tried by the law.

The second office of overseership is for trades.

And this overseer is to see that young people be put to masters, to be instructed in some labour, trade, science, or to be waiters in store-houses, that none shall be idly brought up in any family within his circuit.

Likewise this overseer is to assist any master of a family by his advice and counsel in the secrets of his trades, that by the experience of the elders the young people may learn the inward knowledge of the things which are, and find out the secrets of nature.

And seeing there are variety of trades, there are to be chosen overseers for every trade, so many overseers as the largeness of the town and city requires; and the employment of this overseer is not to work (unless he will himself) but to go from house to house to view the works of the people of every house belonging to his trade and circuit, and to give directions as he sees cause, and see that no youth be trained up in idleness, as is said.

And if this overseer find any youth more capable and fit for another trade than his own, he shall speak to some overseers of another trade, who shall provide him a master, with the consent of his father, and appoint him what family to live in.

And if the father of a family be weak, sick or naturally foolish, wanting the power of wisdom and government, or should be dead before his children should be instructed; then the overseers of this trade wherein the father was brought up are to put those children into such families where they may be instructed according to the law of the commonwealth.

One man may be an overseer for twenty or thirty families of shoemakers; another for smiths, another for weavers of cloth, another for the keepers of store-houses or shops; for every trade is to have an overseer for that particular trade.

And truly the government of the halls and companies in London is a very rational and well-ordered government; and the overseers of trades may very well be called masters, wardens, and assistants of such and such a company, for such and such a particular trade. Only two things are to be practised to preserve peace:

The first is, that all these overseers shall be chosen new ones every year. And secondly, the old overseers shall not choose the new ones, to prevent the creeping in of lordly oppression; but all the masters of families and freemen of that trade shall be the choosers, and the old overseers shall give but their single voice among them.

And as there are to be overseers for trades in towns and cities:

So there are to be chosen overseers in the country parishes, to see the earth planted; and in every parish in the country may be chosen four or six overseers of husbandry, to see the ground planted within their circuits, and to see that the work of husbandry be done orderly and according to reason and skill.

Some overseers to look after the shepherds, and appoint out such men as are skilled in that work. Some overseers to look after the herdsmen. Some overseers of them who look to horses, and some for the dairies. And the work of these overseers is to see that every family send in their assistance to work, both in ploughing and dressing the earth in that season of the year, in seed time; and in reaping the fruits of the earth, and housing them in store-houses in time of harvest.

Likewise they are to see that all barns belonging to any family, or more public store-houses belonging to a parish, be kept in sufficient repair. Likewise they are to see that every family do keep sufficient working tools for common use, as ploughs, carts and furniture, according as every family is furnished with men to work therewith: likewise pickaxes, spades, pruning-hooks, and any such like necessary instrument.

Likewise it is the work of this overseership to see that schoolmasters, postmasters and ministers do their several offices according to the laws.

Likewise this overseership for trades shall see that no man shall be a house-keeper, and have servants under him, till he hath served under a master seven years and hath learned his trade; and the reason is that every family may be governed by staid and experienced masters, and not by wanton youth.

And this office of overseership keeps all people within a peaceable harmony of trades, sciences or works, that there be neither beggar nor idle person in the commonwealth.

The third office of overseership is to see particular tradesmen bring in their works to store-houses and shops, and to see the waiters in store-houses do their duty.

As there are particular trades requiring strength, and some men are strong to perform such works; so there are some weak in body, whose employment shall be to be keepers of store-houses and shops, both to receive in commodities, and deliver out again, as any particular family or man wants and comes for them.

As for example:

When leather is tanned, it shall be brought into the store-houses for leather; and from thence shoemakers and harness-makers and such like may fetch it as they need.

So for linen and woollen cloth, it is to be brought by the weavers into the store-houses or shops, from whence particular families of other trades may fetch as they need: and so for any commodity, as in the law for store-houses is declared.

Now the work of this overseership is of the same nature with the other trades; only this is to be employed only about the oversight of store-houses and shops.

And they are to see that particular tradesmen, as weavers

of linen and woollen cloth, spinners, smiths, hatters, glovers and such like, do bring in their works into the shops appointed; and they are to see that the shops and storehouses within their several circuits be kept still furnished:

That when families of other trades want such commodities as they cannot make, they may go to the shops and storehouses where such commodities are, and receive them for their use without buying or selling.

And as this officer sees the particular tradesmen to furnish the shops and store-houses, so they shall see that the keepers of the shops and store-houses be diligent to wait, both to receive in and deliver out again, according to the law, any commodity under their charge.

And if any keeper of a shop and store-house neglect his duty of his place, through idleness or vain conversation or pride, whereby just offence is given, the overseers shall admonish him and reprove him. If he amend, all is well; if he doth not, he shall give order to the soldiers to carry him before the peace-makers' court; and if he reform upon the reproof of that court, all is well: but if he doth not reform, he shall be sent unto by the officers to appear before the judge's court, and the judge shall pass sentence, that he shall be put out of that house and employment, and sent among the husbandmen to work in the earth; and some other shall have his place and house till he be reformed.

Likewise this overseer shall see to it that the keepers of shops and store-houses do keep their houses in sufficient repair; and when any house wants repair, the keepers thereof shall speak to any of the overseers for trades, and they shall appoint either brick-layers, masons, smiths or carpenters forthwith to take the work in hand and finish it.

Fourthly, all ancient men, above sixty years of age, are general overseers

And wheresoever they go and see things amiss in any officer or tradesman, they shall call any officer or others to account for their neglect of duty to the commonwealth's peace: and these are called elders.

And everyone shall give humble respect to these as to fathers, and as to men of the highest experience in the laws for the keeping of peace in the commonwealth.

And if these see things amiss and do speak, all officers and others shall assist and protect them, to see the laws carefully executed; and everyone that affronts or abuses these in words or deeds shall suffer punishment according to the sentence of the judge.

And all these shall be general assistances and encouragers of all officers in the doing the work of their places.

And the reason of all is this that many eyes being watchful, the laws may be obeyed, for to preserve peace.

But if any of these elders should vent their passion, or express envy against anyone and set up his own will above the law, and do things contrary to law, upon complaint the senators at the judge's court shall examine the matter. If he be faulty the judge shall reprove him the first time, but the second time he does so the judge shall pronounce that he shall lose his authority and never bear office nor general oversight more while he lives, only he shall have respect as a man of age.

What is the office of a soldier?

A soldier is a magistrate as well as any other officer, and indeed all state officers are soldiers, for they represent power; and if there were not power in the hand of officers, the spirit of rudeness would not be obedient to any law or government but their own wills.

Therefore every year shall be chosen a soldier, like unto a marshal of a city, and being the chief he shall have divers soldiers under him at his command, to assist in case of need.

The work of a soldier in times of peace is to fetch in offenders, and to bring them before either officer or courts, and to be a protection to the officers against all disturbances.

The soldier is not to do anything without order from the

officers; but when he hath an order, then he is to act accordingly; and he is to receive orders from the judge's court or from the peace-makers' court or from overseers, as need shall require.

If a soldier hath brought an offender before a peace-maker, and if the offender will not be subject to the law by his persuasion, and the peace-maker send him to the judge's court, if the offence be under matters of death, the offender shall not be imprisoned in the mean time: but the peace-maker shall command him to appear before the judge's court at the time appointed, and the offender shall promise to obey; and this shall be for two reasons:

First, to prevent cruelty of prisons. Secondly, in the time of his binding over he may remember himself and amend his ways, and by testimony of his own actions and neighbours' reports, his sentence may be mitigated by the judge; for it is amendment not destruction that commonwealth's law requires.

And if this offender run away from that country * to another, and so both disobey the peace-makers' command and break his own promise of appearance: then shall the soldiers be sent forth into all places to search for him, and if they catch him, they should bring him before the judge, who shall pronounce sentence of death upon him without mercy.

And if any protect him or shelter him, after hue and cry is made after him, all such protectors shall suffer the loss of freedom for twelve months' time, as is shewed hereafter what that is.

But if the offence should be matter of death, then the peace-maker shall take no promise from him for his appearance, but let the soldier carry him to prison till the next judge's court sits where he shall have his trial.

The work of a task-master.

The work or office of a task-master is to take those into his

---

* County.

over-sight as are sentenced by the judge to lose their freedom, and to appoint them their work and to see they do it.

If they do their tasks, he is to allow them sufficient victuals and clothing to preserve the health of their bodies.

But if they prove desperate, wanton or idle, and will not quietly submit to the law, the task-master is to feed them with short diet, and to whip them, *for a rod is prepared for the fool's back*, till such time as their proud hearts do bend to the law.

And when he finds them subject, he shall then carry a favourable hand towards them, as to offending brethren, and allow them sufficient diet and clothes in hopes of their amendment, but withal see they do their work till by the sentence of the law he be set free again.

The task-master shall appoint them any kind of work or labour as he pleases that is to be done by man.

And if any of these offenders run away, there shall be hue and cry sent after him, and he shall die by the sentence of the judge when taken again.

The work of an executioner.

If any have so highly broke the laws as they come within the compass of whipping, imprisoning and death, the executioner shall cut off the head, hang or shoot to death, or whip the offender according to the sentence of law. Thus you may see what the work of every officer in a town or city is.

What is the work of a judge?

The law itself is the judge of all men's actions, yet he who is chosen to pronounce the law is called judge, because he is the mouth of the law: for no single man ought to judge or interpret the law:

Because the law itself, as it is left us in the letter, is the mind and determination of the Parliament and of the people of the land, to be their rule to walk by and to be the touchstone of all actions.

And that man who takes upon him to interpret the law doth either darken the sense of the law, and so makes it confused and hard to be understood, or else puts another meaning upon it, and so lifts up himself above the Parliament, above the law, and above all people in the land.

Therefore the work of that man who is called judge is to hear any matter that is brought before him; and in all cases of difference between man and man, he shall see the parties on both sides before him, and shall hear each man speak for himself without a fee'd lawyer; likewise he is to examine any witness who is to prove a matter in trial before him.

And then he is to pronounce the bare letter of the law concerning such a thing, for he hath his name 'judge' not because his will and mind is to judge the actions of offenders before him, but because he is the mouth to pronounce the law, who indeed is the true judge. Therefore to this law and to this testimony let everyone have a regard who intends to live in peace in the commonwealth.

But from hence hath arose much misery in the nations under kingly government, in that the man called the judge hath been suffered to interpret the law; and when the mind of the law, the judgment of the Parliament and the government of the land, is resolved into the breast of the judges, this hath occasioned much complaining of injustice in judges, in courts of justice, in lawyers, and in the course of the law itself, as if it were an evil rule.

Because the law, which was a certain rule, was varied according to the will of a covetous, envious or proud judge, therefore no marvel though the kingly laws be so intricate, and though few know which way the course of the law goes, because the sentence lies many times in the breast of a judge, and not in the letter of the law.

And so the good laws made by an industrious Parliament are like good eggs laid by a silly goose, and as soon as she hath laid them, she goes her way and lets others take them, and never looks after them more, so that if you lay a stone in her nest, she will sit upon it as if it were an egg.

And so though the laws be good, yet if they be left to the will of a judge to interpret, the execution hath many times proved bad.

And truly as the laws and people of nations have been abused by suffering men (judges) to alter the sense by their interpretation:

So likewise hath the Scriptures of Moses, the prophets, Christ and his apostles been darkened and confounded by suffering ministers to put their inferences and interpretations upon them.

And surely both the judges for the law and the ministers for God's Word have been both unfaithful servants to man and to God, by taking upon them to expound and interpret that rule which they are bound to yield obedience to, without adding to or diminishing from.

What is the judge's court?

In a county or shire there is to be chosen
    a judge,
      the peace-makers of every town within that circuit,
      the overseers, and
      a band of soldiers attending thereupon.

And this is called the judge's court or the county senate. This court shall sit four times in the year (or oftener if need be) in the country, and four times in the year in great cities. In the first quarter of the year they shall sit in the east part of the county, and the second quarter of the year in the west, in the third in the south and in the fourth in the north.

And this court is to oversee and examine any officer within their county or limits; for their work is to see that everyone be faithful in his place; and if any officer hath done wrong to any, this court is to pass sentence of punishment upon the offender, according to his offence against the law.

If any grievance lie upon any man, wherein inferior officers cannot ease him, this court shall quietly hear his complaint, and ease him; for where a law is wanting, they may prepare a way of ease for the offender till the Parliament sit, who may either establish that conclusion for a law, if they approve of it, or frame another law to that effect; for it is possible that many things may fall out hereafter which the law-makers for the present may not foresee.

If any disorder break in among the people, this court shall set things to rights. If any be bound over to appear at this court, the judge shall hear the matter and pronounce the letter of the law, according to the nature of the offence.

So that the alone work of the judge is to pronounce the sentence and mind of the law; and all this is but to see the laws executed, that the peace of the commonwealth may be preserved.

What is the work of a commonwealth's Parliament in general?

A Parliament is the highest court of equity in a land, and it is to be chosen every year; and out of every city, town and certain limits of a country * through the land, two, three or more men are to be chosen to make up this court.

This court is to oversee all other courts, officers, persons and actions, and to have a full power, being the representative of the whole land, to remove all grievances and to ease the people that are oppressed.

A Parliament hath his rise from the lowest office in a commonwealth, viz. from the father in a family. For as a father's tender care is to remove all grievances from the oppressed children, not respecting one before another; so a Parliament are to remove all burdens from the people of the land, and are not to respect persons who are great before them who are weak; but their eye and care must be principally to relieve the oppressed ones, who groan under the tyrants' laws and power. The strong, or such as have the tyrant power to uphold them, need no help.

But though a Parliament be the father of a land, yet by the covetousness and cheats of kingly government the heart of this father hath been alienated from the children of the

* County.

land, or else so over-awed by the frowns of a kingly tyrant that they could not or durst not act for the weakest children's ease.

For hath not Parliaments sat and rose again and made laws to strengthen the tyrant in his throne, and to strengthen the rich and the strong by those laws, and left oppression upon the backs of the oppressed still?

But I'll not reap * up former weaknesses, but rather rejoice in hope of amendment, seeing our present Parliament hath declared England to be a free commonwealth, and to cast out kingly power; and upon this ground I rejoice in hope that succeeding Parliaments will be tender-hearted fathers to the oppressed children of the land;

And not only dandle us upon the knee with good words and promises till particular men's turns be served, but will fill our bellies and clothe our backs with good actions of freedom, and give to the oppressed children's children their birthright portion, which is freedom in the commonwealth's land, which the kingly law and power, our cruel step-fathers and step-mothers, have kept from us and our fathers for many years past.

The particular work of a Parliament is fourfold.

First, as a tender father, a Parliament is to empower officers and give out orders for the free planting and reaping of the commonwealth's land, that all who have been oppressed and kept from the free use thereof by conquerors, kings and their tyrant laws may now be set at liberty to plant in freedom for food and raiment; and are to be a protection to them who labour the earth, and a punisher of them who are idle. But some may say, 'What is that I call commonwealth's land?'

I answer, all that land which hath been withheld from the inhabitants by the conqueror or tyrant kings, and is now recovered out of the hands of that oppression by the joint assistance of the persons and purses of the commoners of

* Rip.

the land; for this land is the price of their blood. It is their birthright to them and their posterity, and ought not to be converted into particular hands again by the laws of a free commonwealth.

And in particular, this land is all abbey lands, formerly recovered out of the hands of the pope's power by the blood of the commoners of England, though the kings withheld their rights herein from them.

So likewise all crown lands, bishops' lands, with all parks, forests, chases, now of late recovered out of the hands of the kingly tyrants, who have set lords of manors and task-masters over the commoners to withhold the free use of the land from them.

So likewise all the commons and waste lands, which are called commons because the poor was to have part therein; but this is withheld from the commoners, either by lords of manors requiring quit rents and overseeing the poor so narrowly that none dares build him a house upon this common land, or plant thereupon without his leave, but must pay him rent, fines and heriots and homage, as unto a conqueror; or else the benefit of this common land is taken away from the younger brethren by rich landlords and freeholders, who overstock the commons with sheep and cattle, so that the poor in many places are not able to keep a cow unless they steal grass for her.

And this is the bondage the poor complain of, that they are kept poor by their brethren in a land where there is so much plenty for every one, if covetousness and pride did not rule as king in one brother over another, and kingly government occasions all this.

Now it is the work of a Parliament to break the tyrants' bonds, to abolish all their oppressing laws, and to give orders, encouragements and directions unto the poor oppressed people of the land, that they forthwith plant and manure this their own land for the free and comfortable livelihood of themselves and posterities;

And to declare to them, it is their own creation rights,

faithfully and courageously recovered by their diligence, purses and blood from under the kingly tyrants' and oppressors' power.

The work of a Parliament, secondly,

Is to abolish all old laws and customs which have been the strength of the oppressor, and to prepare and then to enact new laws for the ease and freedom of the people, but yet not without the people's knowledge.

For the work of a Parliament herein is threefold.

First, when old laws and customs of the kings do burden the people, and the people desire the remove of them and the establishment of more easy laws:

It is now the work of a Parliament to search into reason and equity, how relief may be found out for the people in such a case, and to preserve a common peace; and when they have found out a way by debate of counsel among themselves, whereby the people may be relieved, they are not presently to establish their conclusions for a law.

But in the next place, they are to make a public declaration thereof to the people of the land who choose them, for their approbation; and if no objection come in from the people within one month, they may then take the people's silence as a consent thereto.

And then in the third place they are to enact it for a law, to be a binding rule to the whole land. For as the remove of the old laws and customs are by the people's consent, which is proved by their frequent petitioning and requests of such a thing: so the enacting of new laws must be by the people's consent and knowledge likewise.

And here they are to require the consent, not of men interested in the old oppressing laws and customs, as kings used to do, but of them who have been oppressed. And the reason is this:

Because the people must be all subject to the law, under pain of punishment; therefore it is all reason they should know it before it be enacted, that if there be any thing of the counsel of oppression in it, it may be discovered and amended.

But you will say, 'If it must be so, then will men so differ in their judgments, that we shall never agree'. I answer:

There is but bondage and freedom, particular interest or common interest; and he who pleads to bring in particular interest into a free commonwealth will presently be seen and cast out, as one bringing in kingly slavery again.

And men in place and office, where greatness and honour is coming in, may sooner be corrupted to bring in particular interest than a whole land can be, who must either suffer sorrow under a burdensome law, or rejoice under a law of freedom.

And surely those men who are not willing to enslave the people will not be unwilling to consent hereunto.

The work of a Parliament, thirdly,

Is to see all those burdens removed actually, which have hindered or do hinder the oppressed people from the enjoyment of their birthrights.

If their common lands be under the oppression of lords of manors, they are to see the land freed from that slavery.

If the commonwealth's land be sold by the hasty counsel of subtle, covetous and ignorant officers, who act for their own particular interest, and so hath entangled the commoners' land again under colour of being bought and sold:

A Parliament is to examine what authority any had to sell or buy the commonwealth land without a general consent of the people; for it is not any one's but everyone's birthright. And if some through covetousness and self-interest gave consent privately, yet a Parliament, who is the father of a land, ought not to give consent to buy and sell that land which is all the children's birthright and the price of their labours, monies and blood.

They are to declare likewise that the bargain is unrighteous, and that the buyers and sellers are enemies to the peace and freedom of the commonwealth. For indeed the necessity of the people chose a Parliament to help them in their weakness; and where they see a danger like to impoverish or enslave one part of the people to another, they are to give warning and so prevent that danger; for they are the eyes of the land. And surely those are blind eyes that lead the people into bogs, to be entangled in mud again after they are once pulled out.

And when the land is once freed from the oppressors' power and laws, a Parliament is to keep it so, and not suffer it by their consent to have it bought or sold, and so entangled in bondage upon a new account.

And for their faithfulness herein to the people, the people are engaged by love and faithfulness to cleave close to them, in defence and protection. But when a Parliament have no care herein, the hearts of the people run away from them like sheep who have no shepherd.

All grievances are occasioned either by the covetous wills of state-officers, who neglect their obedience to the good laws, and then prefer their own ease, honour and riches before the ease and freedom of the oppressed people. And here a Parliament is to cashier and punish those officers, and place others who are men of public spirits in their rooms:

Or else the people's grievances arise from the practice and power that the kings' laws have given to lords of manors, covetous landlords, tithe-takers or unbounded lawyers, being all strengthened in their oppressions over the people by that kingly law. And when the people are burdened herewith and groan, waiting for deliverance, as the oppressed people of England do at this day; it is then the work of a Parliament to see the people delivered, and that they enjoy their creation freedoms in the earth. They are not to dally with them, but as a father is ready to help his children out of misery, when they either see them in misery or when the children cry for help; so should they do for the oppressed people.

And surely for this end, and no other, is a Parliament

chosen, as is cleared before: for the necessity of common preservation and peace is the fundamental law both to officers and people.

The work of a Parliament, fourthly, is this:

If there be an occasion to raise an army to wage war, either against an invasion of a foreign enemy or against an insurrection at home, it is the work of a Parliament to manage that business for to preserve common peace. And here their work is threefold:

First, to acquaint the people plainly with the cause of the war, and to shew them the danger of such an invasion or insurrection; and so from that cause require their assistance in person for the preservation of the laws, liberties and peace of the commonwealth, according to their engagement when they were chosen, which was this: do you maintain our laws and liberties, and we will protect and assist you.

Secondly, a Parliament is to make choice of understanding, able and public-spirited men to be leaders of an army in this case, and to give them commissions and power in the name of the commonwealth to manage the work of an army.

Thirdly, a Parliament's work in this case is either to send ambassadors to another nation which hath invaded our land, or that intends to invade, to agree upon terms of peace, or to proclaim war; or else to receive and hear ambassadors from other lands for the same business, or about any other business concerning the peace and honour of the land.

For a Parliament is the head of a commonwealth's power, or (as it may be said) it is the great council of an army, from whom originally all orders do issue forth to any officer or soldier.

For if so be a Parliament had not an army to protect them, the rudeness of the people would not obey their proceedings: and if a Parliament were not the representative of the people, who indeed is the body of all power, the army would not obey their orders.

So then, a Parliament is the head of power in a commonwealth, and it is their work to manage public affairs, in times of war and in times of peace; not to promote the interest of particular men, but for the peace and freedom of the whole body of the land, viz. of every particular man, that none be deprived of his creation rights unless he hath lost his freedom by transgression, as by the laws is expressed.

The work of a commonwealth's ministry, and why one day in seven may be a day of rest from labour.

If there were good laws, and the people be ignorant of them, it would be as bad for the commonwealth as if there were no laws at all.

Therefore according to one of the laws of Israel's commonwealth made by Moses, who was the ruler of the people at that time:

It is very rational and good that one day in seven be still set apart, for three reasons:

First, that the people in such a parish may generally meet together to see one another's faces, and beget or preserve fellowship in friendly love;

Secondly, to be a day of rest or cessation from labour, so that they have some bodily rest for themselves and cattle;

Thirdly, that he who is chosen minister (for that year) in that parish may read to the people three things:

First the affairs of the whole land, as it is brought in by the postmaster (as it is related in his office, hereafter following).

Secondly, to read the law of the commonwealth: not only to strengthen the memory of the ancients, but that the young people also, who are not grown up to ripeness of experience, may be instructed to know when they do well and when they do ill; for the laws of a land hath the power of freedom and bondage, life and death, in its hand, therefore the necessary knowledge to be known, and he is the best prophet that acquaints men therewith: that as men grow up in years, they may be able to defend the laws and government of the land. But these laws shall not be expounded by the reader, for to expound a plain law, as if a man would put a better meaning than the letter itself, produces two evils:

First the pure law and the minds of people will be thereby confounded, for multitude of words darken knowledge;

Secondly the reader will be puffed up in pride, to contemn the lawmakers, and in time that will prove the father and nurse of tyranny, as at this day is manifested by our ministry;

And thirdly because the minds of people generally love discourses, therefore that the wits of men both young and old may be exercised, there may be speeches made in a threefold nature.

First to declare the acts and passages of former ages and governments, setting forth the benefit of freedom by well-ordered governments, as in Israel's commonwealth, and the troubles and bondage which hath always attended oppression and oppressors; as the state of Pharaoh and other tyrant kings, who said the earth and people were theirs and only at their dispose.

Secondly speeches may be made of all arts and sciences, some one day, some another: as in physic, chirurgery,* astrology, astronomy, navigation, husbandry and such like. And in these speeches may be unfolded the nature of all herbs and plants from the hyssop to the cedar, as Solomon writ of.

Likewise men may come to see into the nature of the fixed and wandering stars, those great powers of God in the heavens above; and hereby men will come to know the secrets of nature and creation, within which all true knowledge is wrapped up, and the light in man must arise to search it out.

Thirdly speeches may be made sometimes of the nature of mankind, of his darkness and of his light, of his weakness and of his strength, of his love and of his envy, of his sorrow and of his joy, of his inward and outward bondages, and of his inward and outward freedoms, etc. And this is

* Surgery.

346

that which the ministry of churches generally aim [at], but only that they confound their knowledge by imaginary study, when anyone takes upon him to speak without experience.

Now this is the way

To attain to the true knowledge of God (who is the spirit of the whole creation) as he hath spread himself forth in every form, and more eminently in man; as Paul writ, *The creation in all the several bodies and forms are but the mansions or fulness of him who hath filled all things with himself.*

And if the earth were set free from kingly bondage, so that everyone were sure to have a free livelihood, and if this liberty were granted, then many secrets of God, and his works in nature, would be made public, which men nowadays keep secret to get a living by: so that this kingly bondage is the cause of the spreading of ignorance in the earth. But when commonwealth's freedom is established, and Pharisaical or kingly slavery cast out, then will *knowledge cover the earth, as the waters cover the seas*; and not till then.

He who is the chosen minister for that year to read shall not be the only man to make sermons or speeches; but everyone who hath any experience, and is able to speak of any art or language or of the nature of the heavens above or of the earth below, shall have free liberty to speak when they offer themselves, and in a civil manner desire an audience, and appoint his day. Yet he who is the reader may have his liberty to speak too, but not to assume all the power to himself, as the proud and ignorant clergy have done, who have bewitched all the world by their subtle covetousness and pride.

And everyone who speaks of any herb, plant, art or nature of mankind, is required to speak nothing by imagination, but what he hath found out by his own industry and observation in trial.

And because other nations are of several languages, therefore these speeches may be made sometimes in other languages, and sometimes in our mother tongue, that so the men of our English commonwealth may attain to all knowledges, arts and languages, and that everyone may be encouraged in his industry, and purchase the countenance and love of their neighbourhood for their wisdom and experimental knowledge in the things which are.

And thus to speak, or thus to read the law of nature (or God) as he hath written his name in every body, is to speak a pure language, and this is to speak the truth as Jesus Christ spake it, giving to everything its own weight and measure.

By this means in time men shall attain to the practical knowledge of God truly, that they may serve him in spirit and truth; and this knowledge will not deceive a man.

'Aye but,' saith the zealous but ignorant professor,

'This is a low and carnal ministry indeed, this leads men to know nothing but the knowledge of the earth and the secrets of nature, but we are to look after spiritual and heavenly things.' I answer:

To know the secrets of nature is to know the works of God; and to know the works of God within the creation is to know God himself, for God dwells in every visible work or body.

And indeed if you would know spiritual things, it is to know how the spirit or power of wisdom and life, causing motion or growth, dwells within and governs both the several bodies of the stars and planets in the heavens above, and the several bodies of the earth below, as grass, plants, fishes, beasts, birds and mankind; for to reach God beyond the creation, or to know what he will be to a man after the man is dead, if any otherwise than to scatter him into his essences of fire, water, earth and air of which he is compounded, is a knowledge beyond the line or capacity of man to attain to while he lives in his compounded body.

And if a man should go to imagine what God is beyond the creation, or what he will be in a spiritual demonstration after a man is dead, he doth (as the proverb saith) build castles in the air, or tells us of a world beyond the moon and beyond the sun, merely to blind the reason of man.

I'll appeal to your self in this question, what other knowledge have you of God but what you have within the circle of the creation?

For if the creation in all its dimensions be the fulness of him that fills all with himself, and if you yourself be part of this creation, where can you find God but in that line or station wherein you stand?

God manifests himself in actual knowledge, not in imagination; he is still in motion, either in bodies upon earth, or in the bodies in the heavens, or in both; in the night and in the day, in winter, in summer, in cold, in heat, in growth or not in growth.

But when a studying imagination comes into man, which is the devil, for it is the cause of all evil and sorrows in the world: that is he who puts out the eyes of man's knowledge, and tells him he must believe what others have writ or spoke, and must not trust to his own experience. And when this bewitching fancy sits in the chair of government, there is nothing but saying and unsaying, frowardness, covetousness, fears, confused thoughts and unsatisfied doubtings, all the days of that man's reign in the heart.

Or secondly, examine yourself, and look likewise into the ways of all professors, and you shall find that the enjoyment of the earth below, which you call a low and a carnal knowledge, is that which you and all professors (as well as the men of the world, as you call them) strive and seek after.

Wherefore are you so covetous after the world, in buying and selling? counting yourself a happy man if you be rich, and a miserable man if you be poor. And though you say, heaven after death is a place of glory, where you shall enjoy God face to face, yet you are loath to leave the earth to go thither.

Do not your ministers preach for to enjoy the earth? Do not professing lawyers, as well as others, buy and sell the conqueror's justice, that they may enjoy the earth? Do not professing soldiers fight for the earth, and seat themselves in that land which is the birthright of others as well as theirs, shutting others out? Do not all professors strive to get earth, that they may live in plenty by other men's labours?

Do you not make the earth your very rest? Doth not the enjoying of the earth please the spirit in you? And then you say, God is pleased with your ways and blesseth you. If you want earth and become poor, do you not say, God is angry with you and crosseth you?

Why do you heap up riches? Why do you eat and drink and wear clothes? Why do you take a woman and lie with her to beget children? Are not all these carnal and low things of the earth? And do you not live in them, and covet them as much as any? nay more than many which you call men of the world?

And it being thus with you, what other spiritual or heavenly things do you seek after more than others? And what is in you more than in others? If you say, 'There is'; then surely you ought to let these earthly things alone to the men of the world, as you call them, whose portions these are; and keep you within the compass of your own sphere, that others seeing you live a life above the world in peace and freedom, neither working yourself nor deceiving, nor compelling others to work for you, they may be drawn to embrace the same spiritual life by your single-hearted conversation. Well, I have done here.

Let us now examine your divinity,

Which you call heavenly and spiritual things, for herein speeches are made not to advance knowledge, but to destroy the true knowledge of God. For divinity does not speak the truth as it is hid in every body, but it leaves the motional knowledge of a thing as it is and imagines, studies or thinks what may be, and so runs the hazard, true or false. And this divinity is always speaking words to deceive the simple, that he may make them work for him and maintain him, but he never comes to action himself to do as he would be done by; for he is a monster who is all tongue and no hand.

This divining doctrine, which you call spiritual and heavenly things, is the thief and the robber. He comes to spoil the vineyard of a man's peace, and does not enter in at the door but he climbs up another way. And this doctrine is twofold.

First he takes upon him to tell you the meaning of other men's words and writing by his studying or imagining what another man's knowledge might be, and by thus doing darkens knowledge and wrongs the spirit of the authors who did write and speak those things which he takes upon him to interpret.

Secondly he takes upon him to foretell what shall befall a man after he is dead, and what that world is beyond the sun and beyond the moon, etc. And if any man tell him there is no reason for what you say, he answers, 'You must not judge of heavenly and spiritual things by reason, but you must believe what is told you, whether it be reason or no'. There is a threefold discovery of falsehood in this doctrine.

For first it is a doctrine of a sickly and weak spirit, who hath lost his understanding in the knowledge of the creation and of the temper of his own heart and nature, and so runs into fancies, either of joy or sorrow.

And if the passion of joy predominate, then he fancies to himself a personal God, personal angels and a local place of glory which, he saith, he and all who believes what he saith shall go to after they are dead.

And if sorrow predominate, then he fancies to himself a personal devil and a local place of torment, that he shall go to after he is dead, and this he speaks with great confidence.

Or secondly, this is the doctrine of a subtle running spirit, to make an ungrounded wise man mad: that he might be called the more excellent man in knowledge. For many times when a wise understanding heart is assaulted with this doctrine of a God, a devil, a heaven and a hell, salvation and damnation after a man is dead, his spirit being not strongly grounded in the knowledge of the creation, nor in the temper of his own heart, he strives and stretches his brains to find out the depth of that doctrine and cannot attain to it: for indeed it is not knowledge but imagination; and so, by poring and puzzling himself in it, loses that wisdom he had, and becomes distracted and mad. And if the passion of joy predominate, then he is merry and sings and laughs, and is ripe in the expressions of his words and will speak strange things: but all by imagination. But if the passion of sorrow predominate, then he is heavy and sad, crying out, He is damned, God hath forsaken him and he must go to hell when he dies, he cannot make his calling and election sure. And in that distemper many times a man doth hang, kill or drown himself; so that this divining doctrine, which you call 'spiritual and heavenly things' torments people always when they are weak, sickly and under any distemper; therefore it cannot be the doctrine of Christ the saviour.

For my own part, my spirit hath waded deep to find the bottom of this divining spiritual doctrine: and the more I searched, the more I was at a loss; and I never came to quiet rest, and to know God in my spirit, till I came to the knowledge of the things in this book. And let me tell you, they who preach this divining doctrine are the murderers of many a poor heart who is bashful and simple, and that cannot speak for himself but that keeps his thoughts to himself.

Or thirdly, this doctrine is made a cloak of policy by the subtle elder brother, to cheat his simple younger brother of the freedoms of the earth. For, saith the elder brother, 'The earth is mine and not yours, brother; and you must not work upon it unless you will hire it of me; and you must not take the fruits of it unless you will buy them of me, by that which I pay you for your labour. For if you should do otherwise, God will not love you, and you shall not go to heaven when you die, but the devil will have you and you must be damned in hell.'

If the younger reply and say, 'The earth is my birthright

as well as yours, and God who made us both is no respecter of persons: therefore there is no reason but I should enjoy the freedoms of the earth for my comfortable livelihood as well as you, brother.'

'Aye but', saith the elder brother, 'you must not trust to your own reason and understanding, but you must believe what is written and what is told you; and if you will not believe, your damnation will be the greater.'

'I cannot believe', saith the younger brother, 'that our righteous creator should be so partial in his dispensations of the earth, seeing our bodies cannot live upon earth without the use of the earth.'

The elder brother replies, 'What, will you be an atheist and a factious man? Will you not believe God?'

'Yes,' saith the younger brother, 'if I knew God said so I should believe, for I desire to serve him.'

'Why', saith the elder brother, 'this is his Word, and if you will not believe it, you must be damned; but if you will believe it, you must go to heaven.'

Well, the younger brother, being weak in spirit and having not a grounded knowledge of the creation nor of himself, is terrified and lets go his hold in the earth, and submits himself to be a slave to his brother for fear of damnation in hell after death, and in hopes to get heaven thereby after he is dead; and so his eyes are put out, and his reason is blinded.

So that this divining spiritual doctrine is a cheat; for while men are gazing up to heaven, imagining after a happiness or fearing a hell after they are dead, their eyes are put out, that they see not what is their birthrights, and what is to be done by them here on earth while they are living. This is the filthy dreamer, and the cloud without rain.

And indeed the subtle clergy do know that if they can but charm the people, by this their divining doctrine, to look after riches, heaven and glory when they are dead, that then they shall easily be the inheritors of the earth, and have the deceived people to be their servants.

This divining doctrine, which you call spiritual and heavenly, was not the doctrine of Christ; for his words were pure knowledge, they were words of life. For he said, *He spoke what he had seen with his Father*; for he had the knowledge of the creation, and spake as everything was.

And this divinity came in after Christ to darken his knowledge; and it is the language of the mystery of iniquity and Antichrist, whereby the covetous, ambitious and serpentine spirit cozens the plain-hearted of his portions in the earth.

And divinity cozens a plain heart two ways. First, if a man have an estate, according to the kings' laws, he is made by this charm to give it or bazle * it away to the priests or to religious uses, in hopes to get heaven when he is dead.

Or secondly, a man by running to hear divinity sermons, and dancing after his charming pipe, neglects his labour and so runs into debt, and then his fellow professors will cast him into prison and starve him there, and their divinity will call him a hypocrite and wicked man, and become a devil to torment him in that hell.

But surely light is so broke out that it will cover the earth, so that the divinity charmers shall say, *The people will not hear the voice of our charming, charm we never so wisely*. And all the priests and clergy and preachers of these spiritual and heavenly things, as they call them, shall take up the lamentation, which is their portion, *Alas, alas, that great city Babylon, that mighty city divinity, which hath filled the whole earth with her sorcery and deceived all people, so that the whole world wondered after this Beast; how is it fallen, and how is her judgment come upon her in one hour?* And further, as you may read, Rev. 18.10.

The officer of the postmaster.

In every parish throughout the commonwealth shall be chosen two men (at the time when other officers are chosen), and these shall be called postmasters. And whereas there are

* Waste or squander. This spelling of the word 'bezzle' is not in the *Oxford English Dictionary*.

four parts of the land, east, west, north, south, there shall be chosen in the chief city two men to receive in what the postmaster of the east country brings in, and two men to receive in what the postmaster of the west brings in, and two for the north, and so two for the south.

Now the work of the country postmaster shall be this: they shall every month bring up or send by tidings from their respective parishes to the chief city, of what accidents or passages fall out which is either to the honour or dishonour, hurt or profit, of the commonwealth; and if nothing have fallen out in that month worth observation, then they shall write down peace or good order in such a parish.

And when these respective postmasters have brought up their bills or certificates from all parts of the land, the receivers of those bills shall write down everything in order from parish to parish in the nature of a weekly bill of observation.

And those eight receivers shall cause the affairs of the four quarters of the land to be printed in one book with what speed may be, and deliver to every postmaster a book, that as they bring up the affairs of one parish in writing, they may carry down in print the affairs of the whole land.

The benefit lies here, that if any part of the land be visited with plague, famine, invasion or insurrection, or any casualties, the other parts of the land may have speedy knowledge, and send relief.

And if any accident fall out through unreasonable action or careless neglect, other parts of the land may thereby be made watchful to prevent like danger.

Or if any through industry or ripeness of understanding have found out any secret in nature, or new invention in any art or trade or in the tillage of the earth, or such like, whereby the commonwealth may more flourish in peace and plenty, for which virtues those persons received honour in the places where they dwelt:

When other parts of the land hear of it, many thereby will be encouraged to employ their reason and industry to do the like, that so in time there will not be any secret in nature which now lies hid (by reason of the iron age of kingly oppressing government) but by some or other will be brought to light, to the beauty of our commonwealth.

The rise of a commonwealth's army.

After that the necessity of the people in a parish, in a county and in a land, hath moved the people to choose officers to preserve common peace, the same necessity causeth the people to say to their officers,

'Do you see our laws observed for our common preservation, and we will assist and protect you.'

This word 'assist' and 'protect' implies the rising of the people by force of arms to defend their laws and officers, who rule well, against any invasion, insurrection or rebellion of selfish officers or rude people; yea to beat down the turbulency of any foolish spirit that shall arise to break our common peace.

So that the same law of necessity of common peace, which moved the people to choose officers and to compose a law for to be a rule of government, the same law of necessity of protection doth raise an army; so that an army, as well as other officers in a commonwealth, spring from one and the same root, viz. from the necessity of common preservation.

An army is twofold, viz. a ruling army or a fighting army.

A ruling army is called magistracy in times of peace, keeping that land and government in peace by execution of the laws, which the fighting army did purchase in the field by their blood out of the hands of oppression.

And here all officers, from the father in a family to the parliament in a land, are but the heads and leaders of an army; and all people arising to protect and assist their officers, in defence of a right-ordered government, are but the body of an army.

And this magistracy is called the rejoicing of all nations, when the foundation thereof are laws of common equity, whereby every single man may enjoy the fruit of his labour in the free use of the earth, without being restrained or oppressed by the hands of others.

Secondly, a fighting army, called soldiers in the field, when the necessity of preservation, by reason of a foreign invasion or inbred oppression, do move the people to arise in an army to cut and tear to pieces either degenerated officers, or rude people who seek their own interest and not common freedom, and through treachery do endeavour to destroy the laws of common freedom, and to enslave both the land and people of the commonwealth to their particular wills and lusts.

And this war is called a plague, because that cursed enmity of covetousness, pride and vain-glory and envy in the heart of mankind did occasion the rise of it, because he will not be under the moderate observation of any free and right order unless he himself be king and lord over other persons and their labours.

For now the people do arise to defend their faithful officers against such officers as are unfaithful, and to defend their laws and common peace.

The use or work of a fighting army in a commonwealth

Is to beat down all that arise to endeavour to destroy the liberties of the commonwealth. For as, in the days of monarchy, an army was used to subdue all who rebelled against kingly property, so in the days of a free commonwealth an army is to be made use of to resist and destroy all who endeavour to keep up or bring in kingly bondage again.

The work of this fighting army is twofold.

The first is to withstand the invasion or coming in of a foreign enemy, whose invasion is for no other end but to take away our land and earth from us, to deny us the free use thereof, to become kings and landlords over us and to make us their slaves.

As William the Conqueror when he had conquered England, he gave not only the land in parcels to his soldiers, but he gave all men, their wives and children within such a lordship to his lords of manors, to do with them as they pleased. And for this cause now doth an army arise to keep out an invasion of a foreigner, that by the defence of our army, who is part of ourselves, the rest of our brethren in the commonwealth may plough, sow and reap, and enjoy the fruits of their labours, and so live in peace in their own land.

Or secondly, if a land be conquered and so enslaved as England was under the kings and conquering laws, then an army is to be raised with as much secrecy as may be, to restore the land again and set it free, that the earth may become a common treasury to all her children, without respecting persons, as it was before kingly bondage came in, as you may read, 1 Sam. 8.

This latter is called civil wars, and this is the wars of the commoners of England against King Charles now cast out, for he and his laws were the successive power of that Norman conquest over England.

And now the commoners of England in this age of the world are rise up in an army, and have cast out that invasion of the Duke of Normandy and have won their land and liberties again by the sword, if they do not suffer their counsels to befool them into slavery again upon a new account.

Therefore you army of England's commonwealth, look to it! The enemy could not beat you in the field, but they may be too hard for you by policy in counsel, if you do not stick close to see common freedom established.

For if so be that kingly authority be set up in your laws again, King Charles hath conquered you and your posterity by policy and won the field of you, though you seemingly have cut off his head.

For the strength of a king lies not in the visible appearance of his body, but in his will, laws and authority, which is called monarchical government.

But if you remove kingly government and set up true and free commonwealth's government, then you gain your crown, and keep it, and leave peace to your posterity, otherwise not.

And thus doing makes a war either lawful or unlawful.

An army may be murderers and unlawful.

If an army be raised to cast out kingly oppression, and if the heads of that army promise a commonwealth's freedom to the oppressed people if in case they will assist with person and purse, and if the people do assist, and prevail over the tyrant, those officers are bound by the law of justice (who is God) to make good their engagements. And if they do not set the land free from the branches of the kingly oppression, but reserve some part of the kingly power to advance their own particular interest, whereby some of their friends are left under as great slavery to them as they were under the kings, those officers are not faithful commonwealth's soldiers, they are worse thieves and tyrants than the kings they cast out; and that honour they seemed to get by their victories over the commonwealth's oppressor they lose again by breaking promise and engagement to their oppressed friends who did assist them.

For what difference is there between a professed tyrant, that declares himself a tyrant in words, laws and deeds, as all conquerors do, and him who promises to free me from the power of the tyrant if I'll assist him; and when I have spent my estate and blood and the health of my body, and expect my bargain by his engagements to me, he sits himself down in the tyrant's chair and takes the possession of the land to himself, and calls it his and none of mine, and tells me he cannot in conscience let me enjoy the freedom of the earth with him, because it is another man's right?

And now my health and estate is decayed, and I grow in age, I must either beg or work for day wages, which I was never brought up to, for another; whenas the earth is as freely my inheritance and birthright as his whom I must work for; and if I cannot live by my weak labours but take where I need, as Christ sent and took the ass's colt in his need, there is no dispute but by the kings and * laws he will hang me for a thief.

But hear, O thou righteous spirit of the whole creation, and judge who is the thief: him who takes away the freedom of the common earth from me, which is my creation rights and which I have helped to purchase out of the hands of the kingly oppressor by my purse and person, and which he hath taken for wages of me;

Or I, who takes the common earth to plant upon for my free livelihood, endeavouring to live as a free commoner in a free commonwealth, in righteousness and peace.

Such a soldier as this engagement-breaker is neither a friend to the creation nor to a particular commonwealth, but a self-lover and a hypocrite, for he did not fight to set the earth free from the bondage of the oppressor as he pretended by his engagements: but to remove that power out of the other's hand into his own. And this is just like the beasts who fight for mastery and keeps it, not relieving but still lording and kinging over the weak. These are monarchical soldiers not commonwealth's soldiers; and such a soldier is a murderer and his warfare is unlawful.

But soldiers of true noble spirits will help the weak and set the oppressed free, and delight to see the commonwealth flourish in freedom, as well as their own gardens. There is none of this true nobility in the monarchical army, for they are all self-lovers; the best is as a briar, and the most upright amongst them is as a thorn held. Speak you prophets of old if this be not true.

A monarchical army lifts up mountains and makes valleys, viz. advances tyrants and treads the oppressed in the barren lanes of poverty.

But a commonwealth's army is like John Baptist, who levels the mountains to the valleys, pulls down the tyrant and lifts up the oppressed: and so makes way for the spirit of peace and freedom to come in to rule and inherit the earth.

* Old?

And by this which hath been spoken, an army may see wherein they may do well, and wherein they may do hurt.

CHAP. V.

Education of mankind, in Schools and Trades.

Mankind in the days of his youth is like a young colt, wanton and foolish, till he be broke by education and correction; and the neglect of this care, or the want of wisdom in the performance of it, hath been and is the cause of much division and trouble in the world.

Therefore the law of a commonwealth does require that not only a father but that all overseers and officers should make it their work to educate children in good manners, and to see them brought up in some trade or other, and to suffer no children in any parish to live in idleness and youthful pleasure all their days, as many have been; but that they be brought up like men and not like beasts: that so the commonwealth may be planted with laborious and wise experienced men, and not with idle fools.

Mankind may be considered in a fourfold degree, his childhood, youth, manhood and old age. His childhood and his youth may be considered from his birth till forty years of age; and within this compass of time, after he is weaned from his mother, who shall be the nurse herself if there be no defect in nature, his parents shall teach him a civil and humble behaviour toward all men. Then send him to school, to learn to read the laws of the commonwealth, to ripen his wits from his childhood, and so to proceed in his learning till he be acquainted with all arts and languages. And the reason is threefold:

First, by being acquainted with the knowledge of the affairs of the world, by this traditional knowledge they may be the better able to govern themselves like rational men;

Secondly, they may become thereby good commonwealth's

men, in supporting the government thereof, by being acquainted with the nature of government;

Thirdly, if England have occasion to send ambassadors to any other land, we may have such as are acquainted with their language; or if any ambassador come from other lands, we may have such as can understand their speech.

But one sort of children shall not be trained up only to book learning and no other employment, called scholars, as they are in the government of monarchy; for then through idleness and exercised wit therein they spend their time to find out policies to advance themselves to be lords and masters above their labouring brethren, as Simeon and Levi do, which occasions all the trouble in the world.

Therefore, to prevent the dangerous events of idleness in scholars, it is reason, and safe for common peace, that after children have been brought up at schools to ripen their wits, they shall then be set to such trades, arts and sciences as their bodies and wits are capable of; and therein continue till they come to forty years of age.

For all the work of the earth, or in trades, is to be managed by youth, and by such as have lost their freedoms.

Then from forty years of age till fourscore, if he live so long, which is the degree of manhood and old age, they shall be freed from all labour and work, unless they will themselves.

And from among this degree of mankind shall be chosen all officers and overseers, to see the laws of the commonwealth observed.

For as all men shall be workers or waiters in store-houses till they be forty years of age, so none shall be chosen a public officer till he be full forty years of age: for by this time man hath learned experience to govern himself and others: for when young wits are set to govern, they wax wanton, etc.

What trades should mankind be brought up in?

In every trade, art and science, whereby they may find

out the secrets of the creation, and that they may know how to govern the earth in right order.

There are five fountains from whence all arts and sciences have their influences: he that is an actor in any or in all the five parts is a profitable son of mankind; he that only contemplates and talks of what he reads and hears, and doth not employ his talent in some bodily action for the increase of fruitfulness, freedom and peace in the earth, is an unprofitable son.

The first fountain is the right planting of the earth to make it fruitful, and this is called husbandry. And there are two branches of it:

As first, planting, digging, dunging, liming, burning, grubbing and right ordering of land, to make it fit to receive seed, that it may bring forth a plentiful crop. And under this head all millers, maltsters, bakers, harness-makers for ploughs and carts, rope-makers, spinners and weavers of linen and such like, are all but good husbandry.

The second branch of husbandry is gardening, how to plant, graft and set all sort of fruit trees, and how to order the ground for flowers, herbs and roots for pleasure, food or medicinal. And here all physicians, chirurgeons,* distillers of all sorts of waters, gatherers of drugs, makers of wines and oil, and preservers of fruits and such like, may learn by observation what is good for all bodies, both man and beasts.

The second fountain is mineral employment, and that is to search into the earth to find out mines of gold and silver, brass, iron, tin, lead, cannel,† coal and stone of all sorts, saltpetre, salt and alum-springs and such like. And here all chemists, gunpowder-makers, masons, smiths and such like, as would find out the strength and power of the earth, may learn how to order these for the use and profit of mankind.

The third fountain is the right ordering of cattle, whether by shepherds or herdsmen; and such may learn here how to breed and train up cows for the dairies, bulls and horses for the saddle or yoke. And here all tanners, hatters, shoemakers,

* Surgeons.   † 'Cannel' is a bituminous coal.

glovers, spinners of wool, clothiers, tailors, dyers and such like, may learn how to order and look to these.

The fourth fountain is the right ordering of woods and timber trees, for planting, dressing, felling, framing of timber for all uses, for building houses or ships. And here all carpenters, joiners, throsters,* plough-makers, instrument-makers for music, and all who work in wood and timber, may find out the secret[s] of nature, to make trees more plentiful and thriving in their growth and profitable for use.

The fifth fountain, from whence reason is exercised to find out the secrets of nature, is [to] observe the rising and setting of the sun, moon and the powers of the heavens above; and the motion of the tides and seas, and their several effects, powers and operations upon the bodies of man and beast. And here may be learned astrology, astronomy and navigation, and the motions of the winds and the causes of several appearances of the face of heaven, either in storms or in fairness.

And in all these five fountains here is knowledge in the practice, and it is good.

But there is traditional knowledge, which is attained by reading or by the instruction of others, and not practical but leads to an idle life; and this is not good.

The first is a laborious knowledge, and a preserver of common peace, which we find God himself acting; for he put forth his own wisdom in practice when he set his strength to work to make the creation: for God is an active power, not an imaginary fancy.

The latter is an idle, lazy contemplation the scholars would call knowledge; but it is no knowledge but a show of knowledge, like a parrot who speaks words but he knows not what he saith. This same show of knowledge rests in reading or contemplating or hearing others speak, and speaks so too, but will not set his hand to work. And from this traditional knowledge and learning rise up both clergy and lawyer, who by their cunning insinuations live merely

* Turners (probably).

upon the labour of other men, and teach laws which they themselves will not do, and lays burdens upon others which they themselves will not touch with the least of their fingers. And from hence arises all oppressions, wars and troubles in the world; the one is the son of contention, the other the son of darkness, but both the supporters of bondage, which the creation groans under.

Therefore to prevent idleness and the danger of Machiavellian cheats, it is profitable for the commonwealth that children be trained up in trades and some bodily employment, as well as in learning languages or the histories of former ages.

And as boys are trained up in learning and in trades, so all maids shall be trained up in reading, sewing, knitting, spinning of linen and woollen, music, and all other easy neat works, either for to furnish store-houses with linen and woollen cloth, or for the ornament of particular houses with needle-work.

And if this course were taken, there would be no idle person nor beggars in the land, and much work would be done by that now lazy generation for the enlarging of the common treasuries.

And in the managing of any trade, let no young wit be crushed in his invention; for if any man desire to make a new trial of his skill in any trade or science, the overseers shall not hinder him, but encourage him therein: that so the spirit of knowledge may have his full growth in man, to find out the secret in every art.

And let everyone who finds out a new invention have a deserved honour given him; and certainly, when men are sure of food and raiment, their reason will be ripe and ready to dive into the secrets of the creation, that they may learn to see and know God (the spirit of the whole creation) in all his works; for fear of want, and care to pay rent to task-masters, hath hindered many rare inventions.

So that kingly power hath crushed the spirit of knowledge, and would not suffer it to rise up in its beauty and fulness, but by his club law hath preferred the spirit of imagination, which is a deceiver, before it.

There shall be no buying and selling of the earth, nor of the fruits thereof.

For by the government under kings, the cheaters hereby have cozened the plain-hearted of their creation birthrights, and have possessed themselves in the earth and calls it theirs and not the others' and so have brought in that poverty and misery which lies upon many men.

And whereas the wise should help the foolish, and the strong help the weak, the wise and the strong destroys the weak and the simple.

And are not all children generally simple and weak, and know not the things that belong to their peace till they come to ripe age? But before they come to that understanding, the cunning ones who have more strength and policy have by this hypocritical, lying, unrighteous and cheating art of buying and selling wrung the freedoms of the earth out of their hands, and cozened them of their birthrights.

So that when they come to understanding, they see themselves beggars in the midst of a fruitful land, and so the proverb is true, 'Plain dealing is a jewel, but he who uses it shall die a beggar'. And why?

Because this buying and selling is the nursery of cheaters, it is the law of the conqueror and the righteousness of the scribes and Pharisees, which both killed Christ and hindered his resurrection, as much as darkness can to put out light.

And these cunning cheaters commonly become the rulers of the earth, and then the city mankind mourns, for not the wise poor man, but the cunning rich man, was always made an officer and ruler, such a one as by his stolen interest in the earth would be sure to hold others in bondage of poverty and servitude to him and his party.

And hence arise oppression and tyranny in the earth upon the backs of the weak younger brethren, who are made younger brothers indeed, as the proverb is, by their cunning elder brother; and as Daniel said, *The basest of men under kingly government were set to rule, who can command but not obey, who can take other men's labours to live at ease, but not work themselves.*

Therefore there shall be no buying and selling in a free commonwealth, neither shall any one hire his brother to work for him.

If the commonwealth might be governed without buying and selling, here is a platform of government for it, which is the ancientest law of righteousness to mankind in the use of the earth, and which is the very height of earthly freedoms. But if the minds of the people, through covetousness and proud ignorance, will have the earth governed by buying and selling still, this same platform, with a few things subtracted, declares an easy way of government of the earth for the quiet of people's minds and preserving of peace in the land.

For as, like a tradesman, I ask the highest price:
Yet I may fall (if you will rise) upon a good advice.

How must the earth be planted?

The earth is to be planted, and the fruits reaped and carried into barns and store-houses, by the assistance of every family. And if any man or family want corn or other provision they may go to the store-houses and fetch without money. If they want a horse to ride, go into the fields in summer, or to the common stables in winter, and receive one from the keepers; and when your journey is performed, bring him where you had him, without money. If any want food or victuals, they may either go to the butchers' shops, and receive what they want without money; or else go to the flocks of sheep or herds of cattle, and take and kill what meat is needful for their families, without buying and selling. And the reason why all the riches of the earth are a common stock is this, because the earth, and the labours thereupon, are managed by common assistance of every family, without buying and selling; as is shewn how more largely in the office of overseers for trades and the law for store-houses.

The laws for the right ordering thereof, and the officers to see the laws executed to preserve the peace of every family and the peace of every man, and to improve and promote every trade, is shewed in the work of officers and by the laws following.

None will be an enemy to this freedom, which indeed is to do to another as a man would have another do to him, but covetousness and pride, the spirit of the old grudging snapping Pharisees, who gives God abundance of good words in their sermons, in their prayers, in their fasts and in their thanksgivings, as though none should be more faithful servants to him than they: nay, they will shun the company, imprison and kill everyone that will not worship God, they are so zealous.

Well now, God and Christ hath enacted an everlasting law, which is love; not only one another of your own mind, but love your enemies too, such as are not of your mind: and, having food and raiment, therewith be content.

Now here is a trial for you, whether you will be faithful to God and Christ in obeying his laws; or whether you will destroy the man-child of true freedom, righteousness and peace in his resurrection.

And now thou wilt give us either the tricks of a soldier, face about and return to Egypt, and so declare thyself to be part of the serpent's seed, that must bruise the heel of Christ; or else to be one of the plain-hearted sons of promise, or members of Christ, who shall help to bruise the serpent's head, which is kingly oppression; and so bring in everlasting righteousness and peace into the earth. Well, the eye is now open.

Store-houses shall be built and appointed in all places, and be the common stock.

There shall be store-houses in all places, both in the country and in cities, to which all the fruits of the earth, and other works made by tradesmen, shall be brought, and from thence delivered out again to particular families, and to everyone as they want for their use; or else to be transported by ship to other lands, to exchange for those things which our land will not or does not afford.

For all the labours of husbandmen and tradesmen within the land, or by navigation to or from other lands, shall be all upon the common stock.

And as every one works to advance the common stock, so every one shall have a free use of any commodity in the store-house, for his pleasure and comfortable livelihood, without buying and selling or restraint from any.

And having food and raiment, lodging and the comfortable societies of his own kind, what can a man desire more in these days of his travel? *

Indeed, covetous, proud and beastly-minded men desire more, either to lie by them to look upon, or else to waste and spoil it upon their lusts; while other brethren live in straits for want of the use thereof.

But the laws and faithful officers of a free commonwealth do regulate the unrational practice of such men.

There are two sorts of store-houses, general and particular.

The general store-houses are such houses as receive in all commodities in the gross, as all barns and places to lay corn and the fruits of the earth at the first reaping: and these may be called store-houses for corn, flax, wool; for leather, for iron, for linen and woollen cloth or for any commodity that comes into our hand † by shipping; from whence [a] particular family or shop-keepers may fetch as they need, to furnish their lesser shops.

So likewise herds of cattle in the field, flocks of sheep and horses, are all common store-houses; so that from the herds and flocks every family may fetch what they want for food or pleasure, without buying and selling.

* Travail.   † Land?

So likewise all public dairies are store-houses for butter and cheese: yet every family may have cows for their own use, about their own house.

And these general store-houses shall be filled and preserved by the common labour and assistance of every family, as is mentioned in the office of overseer for trades.

And from these public houses, which are the general stock of the land, all particular tradesmen may fetch materials for their particular work as they need, or to furnish their particular dwellings with any commodities.

Secondly, there are particular store-houses or shops,

To which the tradesmen shall bring their particular works: as all instruments of iron to the iron-shops, hats to shops appointed for them; gloves, shoes, linen and woollen cloth in smaller parcels, to shops appointed for every one of them; and the like.

Even as now we have particular trade[rs?] in cities and towns, called shopkeepers, which shall remain still as they be, only altered in their receiving in and delivering out. For whereas by the law of kings or conquerors they do receive in and deliver out by buying and selling, and exchanging the conqueror's picture or stamp upon a piece of gold or silver for the fruits of the earth; now they shall (by the laws of the commonwealth) receive into their shops, and deliver out again freely, without buying and selling.

They shall receive in, as into a store-house, and deliver out again freely, as out of a common store-house, when particular persons or families come for anything they need, as now they do by buying and selling under kingly government.

For as particular families and tradesmen do make several works more than they can make use of: as hats, shoes, gloves, stockings, linen and woollen cloth and the like, and do carry their particular work to store-houses:

So it is all reason and equity that they should go to other store-houses, and fetch any other commodity which they want and cannot make; for as other men partakes of their labours, it is reason they should partake of other men's.

And all these store-houses and shops shall be orderly kept by such as shall be brought up to be waiters therein, as is mentioned in the office of overseers for trades.

For as there are some men more ingenious to work, so other men are more ingenious in keeping of store-houses and shops, to receive in and deliver out commodities. And all this easy work may be called waiting at such and such a store-house: as some may wait at corn houses, some at linen and woollen houses, some at leather, some at iron shops; and every general and particular commodity shall be known where they are by their houses and shops, as it is at this day. So that towns and cities, and every family almost, are but store-houses of one commodity or other, for the uses of the commonwealth or to transport to other lands.

Now this same free practice will kill covetousness, pride and oppression: for when men have a law to buy and sell, then, as I have said before, the cunning cheaters get great estates by other men's labours; and being rich thereby, become oppressing lords over their brethren; which occasions all our troubles and wars in all nations.

Come hither now, all you who challenge your brethren to deny Christ, as though you were the only men that love Christ and would be true to him.

Here is a trial of your love: can you be as ready to obey the law of liberty, which is the command of Christ, as you would have others to obey your kingly laws of bondage? It may be you will either storm, or go away sorrowful; does not Christ tell you, that if you have food and raiment, you should therewith be content? And in this common freedom, here will be food and raiment, ease and pleasure plentiful, both for you and your brethren; so that none shall beg or starve, or live in the straits of poverty; and this fulfils that righteous law of Christ, *Do as you would be done by*: for that law of Christ can never be performed till you establish commonwealth's freedom.

Therefore now let it appear, seeing the child is come to the birth, whether you will receive Christ who is the spreading spirit of freedom, righteousness and peace; or whether you will return to monarchy, to embrace that Egyptian bondage still. Well, here is life and death set before you, take whether you will; but know that unless your righteousness exceed the righteousness of the kingly and lordly scribes and Pharisees, you shall never enjoy true peace in your spirit.

CHAP. VI.

The Kings' old laws cannot govern a free Commonwealth.

They cannot govern in times of bondage and in times of freedom too: they have indeed served many masters, popish and protestant. They are like old soldiers, that will but change their name, and turn about, and as they were; and the reason is, because they are the prerogative will of those, under any religion, that count it no freedom to them unless they be lords over the minds, persons and labours of their brethren.

They are called the kings' laws because they are made by the kings. If any say they were made by the commoners, it is answered, They were not made by the commoners as the commoners of a free commonwealth are to make laws.

For in the days of the kings, none were to choose nor be chosen Parliament-men, or law-makers, but lords of manors and freeholders, such as held title to their enclosures of land or charters for their liberties in trades under the king, who called the land his as he was the conqueror, or his successor.

All inferior people were neither to choose, nor to be chosen; and the reason was because all freeholders of land, and such as held their liberties by charter, were all of the kings' interest; and the inferior people were successively of the rank of the conquered ones, and servants and slaves from the time of the conquest.

And further, when a Parliament was chosen in that manner, yet if any Parliament-man in the uprightness of his heart did endeavour to promote any freedom, contrary to the king's will or former customs from the conquest, he was either committed to prison by the king or by his House of Lords, who were his ancient Norman successive council of war; or else the Parliament was dissolved and broke up by the king.

So that the old laws were made in times under kingly slavery, not under the liberty of commonwealth's freedom, because Parliament-men must have regard to the king's prerogative interest, to hold his conquest, or else endanger themselves.

As sometimes it is in these days: some officers dare not speak against the minds of those men who are the chief in power, nor a private soldier against the mind of his officer, lest they be cashiered their places and livelihood.

And so long as the promoting of the kings' will and prerogative was to be in the eye of the law-makers, the oppressed commoners could never enjoy commonwealth's freedom thereby.

Yet by the wisdom, courage, faithfulness and industry of some Parliament-men, the commoners have received here a line and there a line of freedom inserted into their laws; as those good lines of freedom in Magna Charta were obtained by much hardship and industry.

Secondly, they were the kings' laws, because the kings' own creatures made the laws; or lords of manors, freeholders, etc., were successors of the Norman soldiers from the conquest, therefore they could do no other but maintain their own and their kings' interest.

And do we not see that all laws were made in the days of the kings to ease the rich landlord? But the poor labourers were left under bondage still; they were to have no freedom in the earth by those Pharisaical laws. For when laws were made and Parliaments broke up, the poor oppressed commoners had no relief; but the power of lords of manors, withholding the free use of the common land from them, remained still: for none durst make use of any common land but at the lord's leave according to the will and law of the conqueror; therefore the old laws were called the kings' laws.

And these old laws cannot govern a free commonwealth, because the land now is to be set free from the slavery of the Norman conquest; and the power of lords of manors and Norman freeholders is to be taken away, or else the commoners are but where they were, if not fallen lower into straits than they were: and the old laws cannot look with any other face than they did. Though they be washed with commonwealth's water, their countenance is still withered. Therefore it was not for nothing that the kings would have all their laws written in French and Latin and not in English, partly in honour to the Norman race, and partly to keep the common people ignorant of their creation-freedoms, lest they should rise to redeem themselves: and if those laws should be writ in English, yet if the same kingly principles remain in them, the English language would not advantage us anything, but rather increase our sorrow by our knowledge of our bondage.

What is law in general?

Law is a rule whereby man and other creatures are governed in their actions, for the preservation of the common peace. And this law is twofold:

First, it is the power of life (called the law of nature within the creatures) which does move both man and beast in their actions; or that causes grass, trees, corn and all plants to grow in their several seasons; and whatsoever any body does, he does it as he is moved by this inward law. And this law of nature moves twofold, viz. unrationally or rationally.

A man by this inward law is guided to actions of generation and present content, rashly, through a greedy self-love, without any consideration, like foolish children, or like the brute beasts; by reason whereof much hurt many times follows the body. And this is called the law in the members warring against the law of the mind.

Or when there is an inward watchful oversight of all motions to action, considering the end and effects of those actions, that there be no excess in diet, in speech or in action break forth to the prejudice of a man's self or others. And this is called the light in man, the reasonable power, or the law of the mind.

And this rises up in the heart, by an experimental observation of that peace and trouble which such and such words, thoughts and actions bring the man into. And this is called the record on high; for it is a record in a man's heart above the former unreasonable power. And it is called the witness or testimony of a man's own conscience.

And it is said, to the law and to the testimony etc., for this moderate watchfulness is still the law of nature in a higher resurrection than the former: it hath many terms which for brevity sake I let pass.

And this twofold work of the law within man strives to bring forth themselves in writing to beget numbers of bodies on their sides. And that power that begets the biggest number always rules as king and lord in the creature and in the creation, till the other part overtop him, even as light and darkness strive in day and night to succeed each other; or as it is said, *the strong man armed keeps the heart of man, till a stronger than he come, and cast him out.*

And this written law, proceeding either from reason or unreasonableness, is called the letter; whereby the creation of mankind, beasts and earth is governed according to the will of that power which rules. And it is called by his opposite, *the letter that kills*, and by those of the same nature with it, it is called *the word of life.*

As for example, if the experienced, wise and strong man bears rule, then he writes down his mind to curb the unreasonable law of covetousness and pride in unexperienced men, to preserve peace in the commonwealth. And this is called the historical or traditional law, because it is conveyed from one generation to another by writing; as the laws of Israel's commonwealth were writ in a book by Moses, and so conveyed to posterity.

And this outward law is a bridle to unreasonableness, or as Solomon writ, *it is a whip for the fool's back*, for whom only it was added.

Secondly, since Moses's time, the power of unreasonable covetousness and pride hath sometimes rise up and corrupted that traditional law.

For since the power of the sword rise up in nations to conquer, the written law hath not been to advance common freedom and to beat down the unreasonable self-will in mankind, but it hath been framed to uphold that self-will of the conqueror, right or wrong; not respecting the freedom of the commonwealth, but the freedom of the conqueror and his friends only. By reason whereof much slavery hath been laid upon the backs of the plain-dealing man; and men of public spirits, as Moses was, have been crushed, and their spirits damped thereby; which hath bred, first discontents, and then more wars in the nations.

And those who have been favourites about the conqueror, have by hypocrisy and flattery pleased their king, that they might get what they can of the earth into their possession; and thereby have increased the bondage of the painful labourer, if they could but catch him to act contrary to the conqueror's will, called law. And now the city mourns: and do we not see that the laws of kings have been always made against such actions as the common people were most inclinable to, on purpose to ensnare them into their sessions and courts, that the lawyers and clergy, who were the kings' supporters, might get money thereby, and live in fulness by other men's labours?

But hereby the true nature of a well-governed commonwealth hath been ruined, and the will of kings set up for a law, and the law of righteousness, law of liberty, trod under foot and killed.

This traditional law of kings is that letter at this day which kills true freedom, and it is the fomenter of wars and persecution.

This is the soldier who cut Christ's garment into pieces, which was to have remained uncut and without seam; this law moves the people to fight one against another for those pieces, viz. for the several enclosures of the earth, who shall possess the earth, and who shall be ruler over others.

But the true ancient law of God is a covenant of peace to whole mankind; this sets the earth free to all; this unites both Jew and Gentile into one brotherhood, and rejects none: this makes Christ's garment whole again, and makes the kingdoms of the world to become commonwealths again. It is the inward power of right understanding, which is the true law that teaches people, in action as well as in words, to do as they would be done unto.

But thus much in general, what law is: hereafter follows what those particular laws may be, whereby a commonwealth may be governed in peace and all burdens removed; which is a breaking forth of that law of liberty which will be the joy of all nations when he arises up and is established in his brightness.

Short and pithy laws are best to govern a commonwealth.

The laws of Israel's commonwealth were few, short and pithy; and the government thereof was established in peace, so long as officers and people were obedient thereunto.

But those many laws in the days of the kings of England, which were made, some in times of popery, and some in times of protestantism, and the proceedings of the law being in French and Latin, hath produced two great evils in England.

First, it hath occasioned much ignorance among the people, and much contention; and the people have mightily erred through want of knowledge, and thereby they have run into great expense of money by suits of law, or else many have been imprisoned, whipped, banished, lost their estates and lives by that law which they were ignorant of, till the scourge thereof was upon their backs. This is a sore evil among the people.

Secondly, the people's ignorance of the laws hath bred many sons of contention: for when any difference falls out between man and man, they neither of them know which offends the other; therefore both of them thinking their cause is good, they delight to make use of the law; and then they go and give a lawyer money to tell them which of them was the offender. The lawyer, being glad to maintain their own trade, sets them together by the ears, till all their monies be near spent; and then bids them refer the business to their neighbours, to make them friends; which might have been done at the first.

So that the course of the law and lawyers hath been a mere snare to entrap the people, and to pull their estates from them by craft; for the lawyers do uphold the conqueror's interest and the people's slavery: so that the king, seeing that, did put all the affairs of judicature into their hands. And all this must be called justice, but it is a sore evil.

But now if the laws were few and short, and often read, it would prevent those evils; and everyone, knowing when they did well and when ill, would be very cautious of their words and actions; and this would escape the lawyers' craft.

As Moses's laws in Israel's commonwealth: *The people did talk of them when they lay down and when they rose up, and as they walked by the way; and bound them as bracelets upon their hands*: so that they were an understanding people in the laws wherein their peace did depend.

But it is a sign that England is a blinded and a snared generation; their leaders through pride and covetousness have caused them to err, yea and perish too, for want of the knowledge of the laws, which hath the power of life and death, freedom and bondage, in its hand. But I hope better things hereafter.

What may be those particular laws, or such a method of laws, whereby a commonwealth may be governed.

1. The bare letter of the law established by act of Parliament shall be the rule for officer and people, and the chief judge of all actions.

2. He or they who add or diminish from the law, excepting in the court of Parliament, shall be cashiered his office, and never bear office more.

3. No man shall administer the law for money or reward; he that doth shall die as a traitor to the commonwealth: for when money must buy and sell justice and bear all the sway, there is nothing but oppression to be expected.

4. The laws shall be read by the minister to the people four times in the year, viz. every quarter, that everyone may know whereunto they are to yield obedience; then none may die for want of knowledge.

5. No accusation shall be taken against any man, unless it be proved by two or three witnesses or his own confession.

6. No man shall suffer any punishment but for matter of fact, or reviling words: but no man shall be troubled for his judgment or practice in the things of his God, so he live quiet in the land.

7. The accuser and accused shall always appear face to face before any officer, that both sides may be heard, and no wrong to either party.

8. If any judge or officer execute his own will contrary to the law, or which there is no law to warrant him in, he shall be cashiered, and never bear office more.

9. He who raises an accusation against any man, and cannot prove it, shall suffer the same punishment the other should, if proved. An accusation is when one man complains of another to an officer, all other accusations the law takes no notice of.

10. He who strikes his neighbour shall be struck himself by the executioner, blow for blow, and shall lose eye for eye, tooth for tooth, limb for limb, life for life; and the

reason is that men may be tender of one another's bodies, doing as they would be done by.

11. If any man strike an officer, he shall be made a servant under the task-master for a whole year.

12. He who endeavours to stir up contention among neighbours, by tale-bearing or false reports, shall the first time be reproved openly by the overseers among all the people; the second time shall be whipped; the third time shall be a servant under the task-master for three months; and if he continues, he shall be a servant for ever, and lose his freedom in the commonwealth.

13. If any give reviling and provoking words whereby his neighbour's spirit is burdened, if complaint be made to the overseers, they shall admonish the offender privately to forbear; if he continues to offend his neighbour, the next time he shall be openly reproved and admonished before the congregation, when met together; if he continue, the third time he shall be whipped; the fourth time, if proof be made by witnesses, he shall be a servant under the task-master for twelve months.

14. He who will rule as a lord over his brother, unless he be an officer commanding obedience to the law, he shall be admonished as aforesaid, and receive like punishment if he continue.

Laws for the planting of the earth, etc.

15. Every household shall keep all instruments and tools fit for the tillage of the earth, either for planting, reaping or threshing. Some households, which have many men in them, shall keep ploughs, carts, harrows and such like: other households shall keep spades, pick-axes, axes, pruning hooks and such like, according as every family is furnished with men to work therewith.

And if any master or father of a family be negligent herein, the overseer for that circuit shall admonish him between them two; if he continue negligent, the overseers shall reprove him before all the people: and if he utterly refuse, then the ordering of that family shall be given to another, and he shall be a servant under the task-master till he conform.

16. Every family shall come into the field, with sufficient assistance, at seed-time to plough, dig and plant, and at harvest-time to reap the fruits of the earth and carry them into the store-houses, as the overseers order the work and the number of workmen. And if any refuse to assist in this work, the overseers shall ask the reason; and if it be sickness or any distemper that hinders them, they are freed from such service; if mere idleness keep them back, they are to suffer punishment according to the laws against idleness.

Laws against idleness.

17. If any refuse to learn a trade, or refuse to work in seed-time or harvest, or refuse to be a waiter in store-houses, and yet will feed and clothe himself with other men's labours: the overseers shall first admonish him privately; if he continue idle, he shall be reproved openly before all the people by the overseers; and shall be forbore with a month after this reproof. If he still continues idle, he shall then be whipped, and be let go at liberty for a month longer; if still he continue idle, he shall be delivered into the task-master's hand, who shall set him to work for twelve months, or till he submit to right order. And the reason why every young man shall be trained up in some work or other is to prevent pride and contention; it is for the health of their bodies, it is a pleasure to the mind to be free in labours one with another; and it provides plenty of food and all necessaries for the commonwealth.

Laws for store-houses.

18. In every town and city shall be appointed store-houses for flax, wool, leather, cloth and for all such commodities as come from beyond seas, and these shall be called general store-houses; from whence every particular family may fetch such commodities as they want, either for their use

in their house, or for to work in their trades; or to carry into the country store-houses.

19. Every particular house and shop in a town or city shall be a particular store-house or shop, as now they be; and these shops shall either be furnished by the particular labour of that family according to the trade that family is of, or by the labour of other lesser families of the same trade, as all shops in every town are now furnished.

20. The waiters in store-houses shall deliver the goods under their charge, without receiving any money, as they shall receive in their goods without paying any money.

21. If any waiter in a store-house neglect his office, upon a just complaint the overseers shall acquaint the judge's court therewith, and from thence he shall receive his sentence to be discharged that house and office; and to be appointed some other labouring work under the task-master; and another shall have his place. For he who may live in freedom, and will not, is to taste of servitude.

Laws for overseers.

22. The only work of every overseer is to see the laws executed; for the law is the true magistracy of the land.

23. If any overseer favour any in their idleness, and neglect the execution of the laws, he shall be reproved the first time by the judge's court; the second time cashiered his office, and shall never bear office more, but fall back into the rank of young people and servants to be a worker.

24. New overseers shall at their first entrance into their office look back upon the actions of the old overseers of the last year, to see if they have been faithful in their places, and consented to no breach of law, whereby kingly bondage should any ways be brought in.

25. The overseers for trades shall see every family to lend assistance to plant and reap the fruits of the earth, to work in their trades and to furnish the store-houses; and to see that the waiters in store-houses be diligent to receive in and

deliver out any goods, without buying and selling, to any man whatsoever.

26. While any overseer is in the performance of his place, everyone shall assist him, upon pain of open reproof (or cashiered if he be another officer) or forfeiture of freedom, according to the nature of the business in hand in which he refused his assistance.

Laws against buying and selling.

27. If any man entice another to buy and sell, and he who is enticed doth not yield but makes it known to the overseer, the enticer shall lose his freedom for twelve months and the overseer shall give words [in] commendation of him that refused the enticement, before all the congregation, for his faithfulness to the commonwealth's peace.

28. If any do buy and sell the earth or fruits thereof, unless it be to or with strangers of another nation, according to the law of navigation, they shall be both put to death as traitors to the peace of the commonwealth, because it brings in kingly bondage again and is the occasion of all quarrels and oppressions.

29. He or she who calls the earth his and not his brother's shall be set upon a stool, with those words written in his forehead, before all the congregation; and afterwards be made a servant for twelve months under the task-master. If he quarrel, or seek by secret persuasion, or open rising in arms, to set up such a kingly property, he shall be put to death.

30. The store-houses shall be every man's substance, and not any one's.

31. No man shall either give hire or take hire for his work; for this brings in kingly bondage. If any freemen want help, there are young people, or such as are common servants, to do it, by the overseer's appointment. He that gives and he that takes hire for work, shall both lose their freedom, and become servants for twelve months under the task-master.

Laws for navigation.

32. Because other nations as yet own monarchy, and will buy and sell; therefore it is convenient, for the peace of our commonwealth, that our ships do transport our English goods and exchange for theirs, and conform to the customs of other nations in buying and selling: always provided that what goods our ships carry out, they shall be the commonwealth's goods; and all their trading with other nations shall be upon the common stock, to enrich the store-houses.

Laws for silver and gold.

33. As silver and gold is either found out in mines in our own land, or brought by shipping from beyond sea, it shall not be coined with a conqueror's stamp upon it, to set up buying and selling under his name or by his leave; for there shall be no other use of it in the commonwealth than to make dishes and other necessaries for the ornament of houses, as now there is use made of brass, pewter and iron, or any other metal in their use.

But if in case other nations, whose commodities we want, will not exchange with us unless we give them money, then pieces of silver and gold may be stamped with the commonwealth's arms upon it, for the same use, and no otherwise.

For where money bears all the sway, there is no regard of that golden rule, *Do as you would be done by*. Justice is bought and sold: nay, injustice is sometimes bought and sold for money: and it is the cause of all wars and oppressions. And certainly the righteous spirit of the whole creation did never enact such a law, that unless his weak and simple men did go from England to the East Indies, and fetch silver and gold to bring in their hands to their brethren, and give it them for their good-will to let them plant the earth, and live and enjoy their livelihood therein.*

Laws to choose officers.

34. All overseers and state officers shall be chosen new

* This sentence is incomplete.

every year, to prevent the rise of ambition and covetousness; for the nations have smarted sufficiently by suffering officers to continue long in an office, or to remain in an office by hereditary succession.

35. A man that is of a turbulent spirit, given to quarrelling and provoking words to his neighbour, shall not be chosen any officer while he so continues.

36. All men from twenty years of age upwards shall have freedom of voice to choose officers, unless they be such as lie under the sentence of the law.

37. Such shall be chosen officers as are rational men of moderate conversation, and who have experience in the laws of the commonwealth.

38. All men from forty years of age upwards shall be capable to be chosen state officers, and none younger, unless anyone by his industry and moderate conversation doth move the people to choose him.

39. If any man make suit to move the people to choose him an officer, that man shall not be chose[n] at all that time. If another man persuade the people to choose him who makes suit for himself, they shall both lose their freedom at that time, viz. they shall neither have a voice to choose another, nor be chosen themselves.

Laws against treachery.

40. He who professes the service of a righteous God by preaching and prayer, and makes a trade to get the possessions of the earth, shall be put to death for a witch and a cheater.

41. He who pretends one thing in words, and his actions declare his intent was another thing, shall never bear office in the commonwealth.

What is freedom?

Every freeman shall have a freedom in the earth, to plant or build, to fetch from the store-houses anything he wants, and shall enjoy the fruits of his labours without restraint

from any; he shall not pay rent to any landlord, and he shall
be capable to be chosen any officer, so he be above forty
years of age, and he shall have a voice to choose officers
though he be under forty years of age. If he want any young
men to be assistance to him in his trade or household employment, the overseers shall appoint him young men or
maids to be his servants in his family.

Laws for such as have lost their freedom.

42. All those who have lost their freedom shall be clothed
in white woollen cloth, that they may be distinguished from
others.

43. They shall be under the government of a task-master,
who shall appoint them to be porters or labourers, to do any
work that any freeman wants to be done.

44. They shall do all kind of labour without exception, but
their constant work shall be [that of] carriers or carters, to
carry corn or other provision from store-house to store-
house, from country to cities, and from thence to countries,
etc.

45. If any of these refuse to do such work, the task-master
shall see them whipped, and shall feed them with coarse
diet. And what hardship is this? For freemen work the
easiest work, and these shall work the hardest work. And to
what end is this, but to kill their pride and unreasonableness, that they may become useful men in the commonwealth?

46. The wife or children of such as have lost their freedom
shall not be as slaves till they have lost their freedom, as
their parents and husbands have done.

47. He who breaks any laws shall be the first time reproved
in words in private or in public, as is shewed before; the next
time whipped, the third time lose his freedom, either for a
for ever, and not to be any officer.

who hath lost his freedom shall be a common ser-
freeman who comes to the task-masters and re-
o any work for him; always provided, that

after one freeman hath by the consent of the task-master appointed him his work, another freeman shall not call him thence till that work be done.

49. If any of these offenders revile the laws by words, they shall be soundly whipped, and fed with coarse diet; if they raise weapons against the laws, they shall die as traitors.

Laws to restore slaves to freedom.

50. When any slaves give open testimony of their humility and diligence, and their care to observe the laws of the commonwealth, they are then capable to be restored to their freedom, when the time of servitude is expired according to the judge's sentence; but if they remain opposite to the laws, they shall continue slaves still another term of time.

51. None shall be restored to freedom till they have been a twelve month labouring servants to the commonwealth, for they shall winter and summer in that condition.

52. When any is restored to freedom, the judge at the senators' court shall pronounce his freedom, and give liberty to him to be clothed in what other coloured cloth he will.

53. If any persons be sick or wounded, the chirurgeons, who are trained up in the knowledge of herbs and minerals and know how to apply plasters or physic, shall go when they are sent for to any who need their help, but require no reward, because the common stock is the public pay for every man's labour.

54. When a dead person is to be buried, the officers of the parish and neighbours shall go along with the corpse to the grave, and see it laid therein, in a civil manner; but the public minister nor any other shall have any hand in reading or exhortation.

55. When a man hath learned his trade, and the time of his seven years' apprenticeship is expired, he shall have his freedom to become master of a family, and the overseers shall appoint him such young people to be his servants as they think fit, whether he marry or live a single life.

Laws for marriage.

56. Every man and woman shall have the free liberty to marry whom they love, if they can obtain the love and liking of that party whom they would marry; and neither birth nor portion shall hinder the match, for we are all of one blood, mankind; and for portion, the common store-houses are every man['s] and maid's portion, as free to one as to another.

57. If any man lie with a maid and beget a child, he shall marry her.

58. If a man lie with a woman forcibly, and she cry out and give no consent; if this be proved by two witnesses, or the man's confession, he shall be put to death, and the woman let go free; it is robbery of a woman['s] bodily freedom.

59. If any man by violence endeavour to take away another man's wife, the first time of such violent offer he shall be reproved before the congregation by the peace-maker; the second time he shall be made a servant under the task-master for twelve months; and if he forcibly lie with another man's wife, and she cry out, as in the case when a maid is forced, the man shall be put to death.

60. When any man or woman are consented to live together in marriage, they shall acquaint all the overseers in their circuit therewith, and some other neighbours; and being all met together, the man shall declare by his own mouth before them all that he takes that woman to be his wife, and the woman shall say the same, and desire the overseers to be witnesses.

61. No master of a family shall suffer more meat to be dressed at a dinner or supper than what will be spent and eaten by his household or company present, or within such a time after, before it be spoiled. If there be any spoil constantly made in a family of the food of man, the overseer shall reprove the master for it privately; if that abuse be continued in his family, through his neglect of family government, he shall be openly reproved by the peace-maker

before all the people, and ashamed for his folly; the third time he shall be made a servant for twelve months under the task-master, that he may know what it is to get food, and another shall have the oversight of his house for the time.

62. No man shall be suffered to keep house, and have servants under him, till he hath served seven years under command to a master himself; the reason is, that a man may be of age and of rational carriage before he be a governor of a family, that the peace of the commonwealth may be preserved.

Here is the righteous law; man, wilt thou it maintain?
It may be, is, as hath still, in the world been slain.
Truth appears in light, falsehood rules in power;
To see these things to be is cause of grief each hour.
Knowledge, why didst thou come, to wound and not to cure?
I sent not for thee, thou didst me inlure.
Where knowledge does increase, there sorrows multiply,
To see the great deceit which in the world doth lie:
Man saying one thing now, unsaying it anon,
Breaking all's engagements, when deeds for him are done.
O power where art thou, that must mend things amiss?
Come change the heart of man, and make him truth to kiss.
O death where art thou? Wilt thou not tidings send?
I fear thee not, thou art my loving friend.
Come take this body, and scatter it in the four, *
That I may dwell in one, and rest in peace once more.†

* The four elements.   † The Table of Contents is omitted.

Poems from other pamphlets

From *The Breaking of the Day of God* (p. 128)

Rev. 5.13.	Commander-in-Chief is God himself,
Rev. 19.6.	who rules the spirits of men;
John 14.27.	Wait then on him, uproars to quell,
Gen. 14.13.	and settle peace again.

Luk. 17.33.	Those that do rise for fleshy ends,
1 *Sam.* 23.	a kingdom for to trouble,
27.	Shall lose their pains, undo themselves
Isa. 2.22	and vanish like a bubble.

Eze. 38.19.	God's shaking nations, trying men,
Rev. 19.	and changing times and customs;
19,20.	Ruining the Beast and saving men,
Psal. 124.	amidst these great combustions.
1,2.	
John 5.22.	Cease striving then, ye sons of men,
Ro. 12.19.	destroy not one another:
Psal. 83.	God will avenge him that's oppressed,
2. &c.	by Christ our elder brother.

Dan. 2.44.	His turn is next, the realm to take,
Dan. 7.26,	and rule the sons of men,
27.	And Beast and devil, pope and sin,
Rev. 16.17.	shall never reign again.

Mat. 24.12.	But yet men's hearts unquiet are
Dan. 7.25.	and bitter, as we see;
Rom. 19.	Hot times have been, hot times yet are:
13, &c.	but hotter yet may be.

Revel. 13.   For now the image of the Beast
15, *&c.*   appears to act his part,
Dan. 8.25.   But he's a-falling, and saints shall sing,
Rev. 19.6.   Hallelujah with joy of heart.

Finis.

From *Truth Lifting up its Head above Scandals* (pp. 76–7)

Leave off your trade, ye proud priests then,
    and trouble not the spirit
By forcing sense from the saints' words,
    if ye would life inherit.
Let everyone speak what he knows,
    and utter what's received:
And let not any soul by you
    hereafter be deceived.
For you, as traitors to our God,
    have stood to justify
That your constructions are all truths,
    and other lights a lie.
Your fleshy learning ye have owned
    as sound, divine and good:
Though you by that in ages still
    have shed the children's blood.
But know ye now, the time is come
    for truth to spread all over:
And he will tread you down apace,
    and all your lies discover.
Leave off, therefore, I say, betimes,
    and stoop unto our God:
If ye would life and peace enjoy
    with them that know the Lord.

Postscript

If Reason, king, do rule in thee,
    There's truth and peace and clemency:
No rash distemper will there be,
    No filthy lusts, but chastity
In all thy actions to behold,
    Just dealing, love, as pure as gold.
When Reason rules in whole mankind,
    Nothing but peace will all men find:
Their hearts he makes both meek and kind,
    And troublesome thoughts he throws behind.
For he is truth and love and peace,
    Makes wars and lewdness for to cease.
He makes no prisons for the poor,
    He doth condemn and judge the whore:
He makes all men to sin nor more,
    As they have done in times before;
But restores all to what hath been,
    And heals the creature of his sin.
And why do men so clamour then,
    Against this powerful king in men?

From *Englands Spirit Unfoulded* (title page and p. 12)

Freedom is the mark at which all men should aim,
But what true freedom is, few men doth know by name;
But now a light is rise and ne'er shall fall
How every man by name shall freedom call.
Beware you women of the ranting crew,
And call not freedom those things that are vain.
For if a child you get by ranting deeds
The man is gone, and leaves the child your gain:
Then you and yours are left by such free men,
For other women are as free for them.

THE DIGGER'S SONG

You noble Diggers all, stand up now, stand up now,
   You noble Diggers all, stand up now,
The waste land to maintain, seeing Cavaliers by name
Your digging does disdain, and persons all defame.
        Stand up now, stand up now.

Your houses they pull down, stand up now, stand up now,
   Your houses they pull down, stand up now.
Your houses they pull down to fright poor men in town,
But the gentry must come down, and the poor shall wear the
                          crown.
        Stand up now, Diggers all.

With spades and hoes and ploughs, stand up now, stand up
                          now,
   With spades and hoes and ploughs, stand up now,
Your freedom to uphold, seeing Cavaliers are bold
To kill you if they could, and rights from you to hold.
        Stand up now, Diggers all.

Their self-will is their law, stand up now, stand up now,
   Their self-will is their law, stand up now.
Since tyranny came in they count it now no sin
To make a gaol a gin,* to starve poor men therein.
        Stand up now, stand up now.

The gentry are all round, stand up now, stand up now,
   The gentry are all round, stand up now.
The gentry are all round, on each side they are found,
This wisdom's so profound, to cheat us of our ground.
        Stand up now, stand up now.
           * Trap.

The Diggers' Song

The lawyers they conjoin, stand up now, stand up now,
   The lawyers they conjoin, stand up now.
To arrest you they advise, such fury they devise,
The devil in them lies and hath blinded both their eyes.
          Stand up now, stand up now.

The clergy they come in, stand up now, stand up now,
   The clergy they come in, stand up now.
Thel clergy they come in, and say it is a sin
That we should now begin, our freedom for to win.
          Stand up now, Diggers all.

The tithes they yet will have, stand up now, stand up now,
   The tithes they yet will have, stand up now.
The tithes they yet will have, and lawyers their fees crave,
And this they say is brave, to make the poor their slave.
          Stand up now, Diggers all.

'Gainst lawyers and 'gainst priests, stand up now, stand up
                       now,
   'Gainst lawyers and 'gainst priests, stand up now.
For tyrants they are both even flat against their oath,
To grant us they are loath, free meat and drink and cloth.
          Stand up now, Diggers all.

The club is all their law, stand up now, stand up now,
   The club is all their law, stand up now.
The club is all their law to keep [poor] men in awe,
But they no vision saw to maintain such a law.
          Stand up now, Diggers all.

The Cavaliers are foes, stand up now, stand up now,
   The Cavaliers are foes, stand up now.
The Cavaliers are foes, themselves they do disclose
By verses not in prose to please the singing boys.
          Stand up now, Diggers all.

The Diggers' Song

To conquer them by love, come in now, come in now,
   To conquer them by love, come in now,
To conquer them by love, as it does you behove,
For he is King above, no power is like to love.
        Glory here, Diggers all.

MORE ABOUT PENGUINS
AND PELICANS

Penguinews, which appears every month, contains details of all the new books issued by Penguins as they are published. From time to time it is supplemented by *Penguins in Print*, which is a complete list of all available books published by Penguins. (There are well over four thousand of these.)

A specimen copy of *Penguinews* will be sent to you free on request. For a year's issues (including the complete lists) please send 30p if you live in the United Kingdom, or 60p if you live elsewhere. Just write to Dept EP Penguin Books Ltd, Harmondsworth, Middlesex, enclosing a cheque or postal order, and your name will be added to the mailing list.

Note: *Penguinews* and *Penguins in Print* are not available in the U.S.A. or Canada

Pelican Classics

LEVIATHAN

HOBBES

Edited by C. B. Macpherson

From the turmoil of the English Civil War, when life was truly 'nasty, brutish, and short', Hobbes's *Leviathan* (1651) speaks directly to the twentieth century. In its over-riding concern for peace, its systematic analysis of power, and its elevation of politics to the status of a science, it mirrors much modern thinking. And despite its contemporary notoriety – Pepys called it 'a book the Bishops will not let be printed again' – it was also, as Dr Macpherson shows, a convincing apologia for the emergent seventeenth-century market society.

THE PELICAN CLASSICS

'A boon to students young and perennial ... The admirable introductions by reputable scholars are required
reading' – *The Times Literary Supplement*

Some volumes in this series